WITCHCRAFT

Its Power in the World Today

WITCHCRAFT

Its Power in the World Today

BY WILLIAM SEABROOK

HARCOURT, BRACE AND COMPANY, NEW YORK

BF
1571
.S4
1940

Designed by Robert Josephy
PRINTED IN THE UNITED STATES OF AMERICA
BY QUINN & BODEN COMPANY, INC., RAHWAY, N. J.

AUTHOR'S NOTE

This book is factual. Nearly all the names of people and places are obviously and recognizably real. In a few rare instances it has been necessary, however, to change names and locales in order to protect certain people in high places who are still alive.

Contents

vii

CONTENTS

Part Three

WHITE MAGIC, PROFESSOR RHINE, THE SUPERNORMAL, AND JUSTINE

Part Four

APPENDIX: SUPPLEMENTARY NOTES, ANECDOTES AND ILLUSTRATIONS

CONTENTS

Foreword

Foreword: Exploding a Non Sequitur Perched on the Horns of a Dilemma

ALTHOUGH this book may boil and bubble with the dirty doings of modern witches, white and black; with current sorcerers, incantations, human vampires on the Riviera; panther men in Africa and Satanists in Paris; Devil Worshipers in New York; werewolves in Washington Square; witchcraft cures and killings dated 1940 here in the United States —it is going to be a disappointment to all who believe in the supernatural.

I am addressing it to rational people only. It is going to show them, if I can, that while witchcraft is not demoniac, it is a specific, real, and dangerous force, evil when used for evil, mysterious in some of its manifestations, but always analyzable, always understandable *within* the bounds of reason, and combatable in consequence, like crime, snake bite, insanity, and yellow fever.

A thousand books, histories, and treatises were written in the age of superstition, to prove that this deadly snake was a basilisk. Another thousand volumes have been written in our age of so-called reason to prove that since the snake is not a basilisk, it consequently cannot bite you. I am a firm disbeliever in basilisks, but also a disbeliever in non sequiturs.

3

I have outgrown the puzzlement, and outgrown, too, the attitude of willing and romantic wonder which characterized some of my earlier books. It was never an attitude of superstitious credulity, and I tried never to let it interfere with honest and objective—if sometimes too sensational—reporting. My puzzlement was completely sincere. I left many questions concerning the limitations of magic wide open, because I did not know the answers, and suppressed many episodes because their treatment would have seemed out of place in books of travel and adventure. Travel and adventure is a surface subject, and they were surface books. For a long time, I didn't know what to do with the under-the-surface material. Conversations with Dr. Alexis Carrel after I'd returned twice from Africa did not help any. He believes that white magic (Lourdes), and black too, can wield a power over the organic—including the inflicting and healing of gaping wounds—which by ordinary definition comes pretty close to the edge of the supernatural. I have never seen anything to confirm that great biologist's credulity. I learned, ten years after the event, that my "little black girls pierced with swords" had been either phony or the victims of a particularly ugly ritual murder.

When you see phenomena of that sort, criminal or harmless, whether in Africa or India, in a spiritualist séance or at a Coney Island side show, it is always either crime, trickery, or innocent illusion. The lady sawed in two at Coney Island and the rope trick in India are out of the same rabbit hat—and I hope my little girls were.

Despite all that, I was hooked for years on the horns of a dilemma which I am now trying to solve in this book. It was the only pair of horns I brought back from Africa, and many a time I've wished I'd left them there. They are not nice to live with.

Here was the dilemma, from which this work has slowly grown:

A confirmed disbeliever in the supernatural, refusing to believe in demons, jungle gods, and devils, refusing for that matter even to believe in spiritualism, telepathy, clairvoyance, or ghosts, I yet became convinced after years in the jungle that the witch-doctors wield a seemingly "occult" power, deadly, dangerous, and real. Taking the commonest manifestation for an example, I became convinced they can kill by the use of witchcraft solely, that is, by pure sorcery, without recourse to poison, pseudo-accident, violence, or any chemical-physical-material contributory causes whatsoever.

I lived hand in glove with sorcerers who possessed and used this power, and who finally gave me, I believe, as full a measure of their confidence as any native ever had, but while they exposed their sometimes hideous technique, they were totally unable to throw any light on what for me was the crucial problem, because they themselves *believe profoundly in the supernatural sources of the power they wield, believe with deep conviction in their old jungle demon-gods.*

There are charlatans, crooks, and fakers among African witch-doctors, just as among "doctors" in New York and London. I am writing here about the sincere and real ones.

I was sure they were completely wrong in their belief, but equally sure they possessed a power of some sort. They possessed also the pragmatic knowledge of how to aim, focus, and wield it with an appalling efficiency. It was not easy for me to reconcile the two elements:

1. Delusion in the operator concerning the nature of his tool or weapon.

2. Pragmatic efficiency in the use of it.

To clarify that preliminary point for myself, I devised an analogy which I am willing to stand on. I call it the "gun analogy," and here it is:

I ask you to imagine a hypothetical man, a savage if you like, who has a keen natural intelligence, but is totally ignorant of gunpowder, explosives, ballistics, firearms. He sees in action a heavy, modern automatic pistol. He sees it used. He sees it close up. He studies it with ignorance of its essential nature, but with keen, not stupid eyes. He subsequently obtains possession of it, loaded. He doesn't know what it's loaded with. But he knows pragmatically that if you release the safety catch, point it at your intended victim, and pull the trigger, you get a loud noise, a flash of fire, a whiff of smoke, while the victim lies blasted with the top of his head blown off or a hole in his belly. Now this hypothetical gunman has invented a false theory. He believes with a profound conviction that what has killed his victim is the loud noise, the flash of fire, the whiff of smoke. He is superstitiously wrong about the nature of the power he wields, but he has learned to wield it with deadly efficiency. Here, I believe, is a parallel with the psychology of the true witch-doctor, the true sorcerer, the true witch. If you grant the parallel, I'm sure you will carry the analogy a step further. I suggest to you, in the cases of both my hypothetical gunman and the witch-doctor, that the victim is just as dead and the operator just as guilty as if no ignorance or superstition had been connected with the death. Delusion as to the nature of power doesn't necessarily render the power nil or harmless nor make of the sorcerer or witch a poor, misguided soul to be smiled at, pitied, and acquitted because he or she has merely stuck pins in a doll instead of sticking a knife in the neighbor's gizzard. The true witch in history, like the witch today, is not and never was the pitiful, deluded victim of an empty superstition. The fact that many innocent old women and occasional young ones were wrongly convicted and burned at the stake is the tragic side-truth most emphasized in history, but it isn't the whole truth about witchcraft.

All primitives and more than half the literate white population in the world today believe in witchcraft, and no amount of false rationalization, no spread of higher education can ever shake that belief, because witches still live, operate, help, harm, cure, and kill without recourse to scientifically accredited means of curing and killing. This believing majority is right in the belief that witches wield real power, but wrong in supposing it to be supernatural.

I am proposing to prove that witchcraft is simply the dark, reverse image of a familiar coin which has become common currency in the everyday fields of psychology and education, and particularly in the now almost equally familiar specialized fields of medical psychology, psychiatry, and mental therapy.[1] I intend to prove that "suggestion" pure and simple is the elemental key to witchcraft's power, and believe I can give its complete definition in two simple words:

INDUCED AUTOSUGGESTION

I am using these words in their simplest and not too technical connotation. By "suggestion," I mean no more than

[1] See Appendix, p. 291.

that if people keep telling you you are nervous, you are likely to become so, even though you had no inherent tendency in that direction. By "induced," I mean no more than that the germs of the suggestion have been deliberately implanted in you from outside sources. By "auto," I mean that the suggestion has taken root and that you begin to generate your own worries and fears—that the suggestion implanted from the outside begins to "eat in on you." I don't mean anything subtle, hypnotic, or esoteric. I mean that you can take any mentally and physically normal, balanced person—child, adolescent, or adult—in your own home, or in your neighbor's home. Keep telling him he is awkward, keep harping on it. He will presently knock over something by sheer accident, as we all occasionally do. Now take advantage of the accident. Keep harping, and you'll keep him awkward all his life. Keep asking what's the matter with his feet, keep harping on it—and he'll presently begin to stumble. Keep telling him he's sick, keep harping on it—and he'll presently begin to feel awful, go to bed, call in the doctor. Here, shorn of labels, technique, and paraphernalia, is the essence of "black magic." It is the dirty side and reverse image of all mental therapy, whether in hospital clinics or Christian Science churches.

Now, dress up induced autosuggestion with the superstition technique and paraphernalia of the jungle, or of medieval diabolist tradition. Pierce the doll with needles. Bury the lock of hair. Howl and chant the incantations. Beat the drums. Tom-toms and incantations have a terrific emotion impact. The drums are as elemental as your own pulse and heartbeat. The incantations, analyzed, have the repetitive simplicity, the direct emotional appeal of Edith Sitwell, Gertrude

Stein, and Mother Goose. Nursery rhymes from hell. When you add superstition, fear, and horrid paraphernalia—you have explained the curse that came upon the Lady of Shalott. You have explained why the Pennsylvania hex "murders" of witches by the intended victims may have been legitimate homicide in self-defense. In Africa you have explained the jungle Death Curse, the Great Ouanga.

If this theory of mine is true, that witchcraft lodges solely in the mind and emotions, we can begin immediately to limit witchcraft's powers, and to consider a number of forced corollaries which I propose to present and examine:

1. The intended victim must *know*, i.e., must literally have been informed of what is being done against him.

2. He must fear it. He must become at some time afraid of it, either consciously or subconsciously. I believed for a while that, if my theory stood up, he must have a *conscious* fear. I have since learned, not from the witch-doctors but from Doctors A. A. Brill, Smith Ely Jelliffe, and the consensus of their colleagues, that conscious and rationalized absence of fear doesn't necessarily create immunity. The intended victim may be armed with complete intellectual disbelief, defiance, scorn, against the witch-doctor's mumbo jumbo, but if a residue of unconscious or subconscious fear is there, he may succumb *even more quickly* than the victim whose fear is on the surface. This is an unpleasant thought, and I was sorry when I learned it. I have never been able to authenticate a case in which knowledge on the part of the victim was absent, but have known a number of cases in which the victim seemed unsuperstitious, and seemed to have no conscious fear—yet succumbed to the witch-doctors.

3. A third obvious corollary is that if true witchcraft oper-

9

ates through the mind and the emotions, it can operate only functionally, and can operate only on animate, sentient beings. I am convinced that this is true. I am convinced that not all the witchcraft in Africa or that ever existed in Egypt or medieval Europe can move the tiniest pebble or break the thinnest glass—without resort to "stage magic," to trickery, legerdemain, stage props, illusion. It can't break an egg or the most fragile wineglass—much less knock down stone walls or open locks—and it can't mend a broken egg either. It can't knock Humpty Dumpty off the wall, and it can't put him together again. If Humpty Dumpty's an egg, witchcraft cannot even make him wobble. If Humpty Dumpty's sentient, witchcraft can make him *fall off the wall* and perhaps break his neck—but that's a different field of force entirely. In the physical field of "stage magic" I don't believe there has ever been or ever will be a jungle sorcerer or Hindu fakir capable of doing anything that the late Houdini or the current John Mulholland could not duplicate. As for table-tippings, tambourines, and other physical-mechanical phenomena that occur in spiritualist séances, I believe, as Houdini did and Mulholland does, that they all have a physical-mechanical origin.

In stripping witchcraft of its supernatural aura, attempting its analysis, and attempting to define its limitations, I am aware that one of these limitations on which I propose to stand throughout this book will have to be modified, if and when Professor J. B. Rhine at Duke University (who followed the late William McDougall of Oxford, Harvard, and Duke) and Gardner Murphy at Columbia succeed in proving the existence of extra-sensory perception, telepathy, clairvoyance. Their laboratory work, as yet inconclusive to the majority of their fellow-psychologists, has lifted into the field of science, out of the old field of superstition and fortune-tellers' booths at country fairs, the possibility that perception may enter through some means other than any of the five senses. If this be true, it would open a new, epoch-making vista for honest folk, but would open at the same time the hideous possibility that the witch possesses, and may have always possessed, the power to send out effectively his evil spells, even from a great distance, *without the conscious knowledge* of the intended victim. If there is anything deeper, more dangerous, more mysterious in witchcraft than I am prepared to admit, it derives from extra-sensory perception rather than from devils, spirits, ghosts, and demons. To contend that it derives from the supernatural is simply going back to the nursery-child mind, the jungle primitive mind, the superstition-ridden European mind of the Dark Ages. If there is anything deeper than I contend, it lies in the yet unproven field which Rhine is exploring.

If extra-sensory power does exist and anyone possesses it, it is certain that those who have proclaimed themselves special possessors of it and frequently made lasting spots in the world's history for good and evil for close to ten thousand years, including spiritualists, *illuminés,* and faith healers, but also including Satanists and "faith killers," have been using it since the dawn of time, and must know more about it intuitively and pragmatically than has yet been learned by honest scientists in laboratories.

I visited the laboratories of Profesor Rhine at Duke University, and discussed this disturbing corollary of *their* main thesis with him and his associates. We agreed that if supernormal forces do exist they can obviously be used—in the same way as normal forces such as superior executive ability, high explosives, electricity, and the radio—for both good and evil. It is an exciting but unpleasant certainty that if Professor Rhine's cold cards marked with stars and circles can send out any emanations whatsoever that can be picked up by any means whatsoever other than the five normal senses— then a doll pierced with needles can send out emanations too. This side angle, this side issue, is a wide open one—whether it touches faith curing and witchcraft killing, the blind reading of marked cards in laboratory tests, or your Uncle Charlie's premonition that his wife would be run over by a truck. I have seen things happen among witches and witch-doctors which are more startling and superficially convincing than anything your Uncle Charlie ever saw by premonition, or than any positive result obtained in any laboratory. Yet I remain on the negative side. I just don't believe in them. However, I'm going to be as fair about it as a man with a set thesis can, in chronicling events which have occurred outside all laboratory control—outside the possibility of scientific checking.

W. S.

Rhinebeck, 1940

Part One

THE WITCH AND HER DOLL

I. Concerning Dolls in General

DOLLS—soulless and intrinsically inanimate reproductions of animate human beings, and also of gods, hobgoblins, and animals—have held a peculiar and not always wholesome fascination for human beings young and old, from the cradle to the grave.

In babyhood they are generally rag dolls, china-headed, or dolls stuffed with sawdust. In the nursery, they become more elaborate and now include dolls which squeak "mamma" or "papa"—and wet their diapers. They also include kewpies, Punches, Judys, gnomes, shepherds with their sheep beneath the Christmas tree, and all the little wooden animals that come out of Noah's Ark. Tony Sarg's puppets are the child's first and greatest joy in the make-believe world of the theater. All these childhood dolls are toys. They are manufactured and sold—as toys. As children, we *play* with them.

But after we've grown up and reached the supposed age of reason, we so-called civilized whites as well as jungle savages fabricate a whole new category of dolls, and what do we do with them? We habitually worship them, kiss their brass toes, burn them as effigies, adorn them with glittering jewels, and travel thousands of miles to kneel before them, ride them on rails, beat them with clubs, shoot them,[1] hang them—bless them and enshrine them in cathedrals if their cult is currently popular—lynch them if their "cult" is currently feared or hated—spend millions of dollars for them and enshrine them in museums if their cult is dead.

The emotional reaction of adults toward dolls is by no means always limited to worship and violence. Store windows on Fifth Avenue contain as many dolls, manikins, and life-sized plaster images as St. Thomas's Church or St. Patrick's Cathedral—and arouse emotions of admiration, envy, jealousy, and whatnot in the ladies. Charlie McCarthy is heard weekly by audiences as vast as those which listen when His Holiness the Pope broadcasts from Vatican City. Dolls that maintain a steadfast silence, as Saint Peter does when throngs kiss his toe in Rome, or Our Lady of the Immaculate Conception when throngs visit her grotto at Lourdes, already exercise an immense power over a large, intelligent cross section of superior humanity. But when you persuade a doll to speak, whether in a broadcasting studio or in a temple, then, indeed, professor, you've got something! Whether you're Edgar Bergen in Hollywood, or that old Egyptian priest of Memnon who used to make his statue hoot at sunrise, you're going to reach more listeners and be longer remembered than if you'd said it with your own simple tongue—or with flowers.

Dolls of every sort and size have always intrigued humanity—rag dolls, plaster saints, and brazen idols, images in bronze, wood, and marble; kewpies, Teddy bears, Madonnas, and Saint Josephs; Jupiter and Venus, Mammon, Memnon, Vishnu, Baal, and Buddha; fashion-decked dummies in windows and blood-spattered Juggernauts on wheels; sacred,

[1] See Appendix, p. 300.

satanic, or silly, from Donatello's wooden Christ on the cross to Bergen's wooden ventriloquist dummy on its owner's knee.

I have been a "collector" and connoisseur of a peculiar type of doll for many years—the kind that are made in secret, then pierced with needles; or wound round with scarlet death thread; or made of wax to melt before a fire. And I propose to tell all about them in this book.

If I have "collected" more of them than seems credible, or know more about them than seems respectable, it is because they tie up with the far-from-respectable subject that has been my major interest and obsession all my life.

If I attribute to these evil dolls a greater power for evil than you are at first willing to believe, I ask you to remember that I shall never contend they are anything more than symbols. And I ask you also to remember the incalculable power wielded by sacred doll-symbols in the field of religion. I intend no blasphemy by this analogy, nor even any shadow of disparagement toward religion. I regard religion, with profound respect, as the bright and shining face of the coin whose reverse evil image I propose to expose and examine.

II. The Witch's Doll and Its Equivalent

IN most cases where witchcraft plans to blast a human life, and to do it by real witchcraft, i.e., without recourse to knife, gun, poison, or any normal murder methods, a doll or doll's equivalent is used. It can begin by being any ordinary doll such as children still play with the wide world over as they have since Egypt's early dawn. While an ancient childish symbol, it can become saturated with an equally ancient evil. These dolls, generally pierced with nails or needles, or made of wax to melt before a fire, or wound round with scarlet woolen thread, occur continually in the records and literature of sorcery in classic times and through the Middle Ages.

They, or their equivalent, occur today in nearly all cases of so-called "primitive" sorcery, whether in Africa or the South Sea Islands. They occur also with a steady frequency here in our own United States[1] and in all other civilized countries.

Last summer, in its issue of June 19, 1939, *Life* published a series of Ozark Mountain pictures taken by D. F. Fox and captioned by Vance Randolph, of Galena, Missouri. The first one shows an Ozark "witch-woman" with a doll of dirt and

[1] See Appendix, p. 301.

beeswax which she had made and named after an enemy. Nails are shown driven in the doll to "hurt" corresponding parts of the enemy's body. It is not a pretty picture, and the fact that nonsuperstitious Missourians mildly protested its publication on the ground that they had lived there all their lives and never seen such a doll, doesn't wipe out the picture, which is followed in the same issue of *Life* by the sinister photograph of two rag dolls, one dressed as a man and one as a woman, laid prone on an altar before a Bible surmounted by a skull. Near St. Rémy, in Southern France, in 1932, I helped smash a similar setup in which the Bible was surmounted by an inverted crucifix on which hung a toad crucified head downward. In that case, a doll lay pierced through and through with needles, smeared with the toad's blood, and murder had been intended. In the Ozark picture, the female of the two dolls has had nails driven into its back. The caption, written with caution, reads, ". . . muttering secret spells, a jealous wife hopes to *separate* her husband from another woman. The dolls represent the adulterous pair." The italics are mine. In the caption under the first Ozark picture, the nails are described as being driven to " '*hurt*' corresponding parts of the enemy's body." I don't know what Messrs. Fox and Randolph thought they were playing with. They may have merely persuaded some old woman to show them how such things are set up, but the pictures intrinsically stink of murder.

In August, 1939, from Cairo, Illinois, Ben Lucien Burman, who had been studying folklore with the roustabouts of the Mississippi River steamboat *Golden Eagle*, wrote a syndicated article, in the course of which he recounted a technique by which a photograph of the intended victim is used as a substitute for the doll:

"A sure way to kill a man is to place his picture under the eaves at the corner of your house during rainy weather and let the water pour upon it."

In August and September, 1939, the *Omaha Evening World-Herald* devoted columns and pictures to a witchcraft case in which the alleged doll substitute had been "a big piece of bone with meat on it, buried under the intended victim's window." This is a variant I have also seen in Africa, but rarely. The Omaha case had some curious aspects, including a solemn session in Catholic Sokol Hall, with the press present, the police also unofficially present, in which Alfio Laferla, president of the Italian-American *Società Risveglio,* accused a woman of practicing witchcraft against his mother-in-law, Mrs. Grazia Trino, and of having buried the bone with ancient *maiaria* incantations so that "just as the worms would eat the meat off the bone, so would Mrs. Trino waste away and die." Mrs. Trino meanwhile knew all about it—of course —believed it effective—was desperately afraid—became very ill, "felt her flesh melting away." If my main thesis is true, she might well have died, murdered as surely by induced autosuggestion as if it had been by arsenic, and may only have survived through the exposure of the alleged witch and exorcism of the evil spells. At any rate the *Risveglio* sat in its full regalia, heard the accusations and evidence, during which the accused woman rose and screamed denials. They found her guilty, and expelled her from the society. She has sued the society for damages and reinstatement. She may be completely innocent.

In the York, Pennsylvania, hex powwow murder, November, 1928, which became a nationwide newspaper sensation,[2] and was revived last year by the release from prison of the two younger men convicted of participation in the "witch-craft killing," the doll's substitute was to be the lock of hair which the witch-doctor, John Blymyer, was trying to snatch from the head of the rival witch-doctor, Nelson Rehmeyer. They fought, you will recall, and Rehmeyer was killed not by witchcraft but by being clubbed and strangled. If Blymyer, however, had been able to obtain the lock of hair, he would have done no further violence. He had planned another way—to bury the hair eight feet under ground, with the old incantations. If Rehmeyer had known about it and believed it and feared it—he could be just as dead as he is from being clubbed. Blymyer was accused of having caused the death by "pure witchcraft" of other victims. The lock of hair, the doll's substitute, was the central object, central motivation. It is the common history of witch-craft today, as in the past, that in addition to "pure witch-craft," there occur also continually these "by-product" murders by ax, club, gun, knife, or arsenic. Murders of this latter sort, by a poison ring out to collect insurance, supplied head-lines during 1939 for columns of Associated Press reports on the Philadelphia "Mass Witchcraft Murders." Interwoven continually with the crime fabric of that drama has appeared a warp or background of vicious and authentic witchcraft, used here not to kill—they used arsenic for that—but to intimidate and terrorize tools, victims, relatives, neighbor-hoods. The dupes of the arsenic ring who are still alive have amply testified to this. There is a large Italian population in

[2] See Appendix, p. 309.

Philadelphia, and Italians figured largely in this picture, among the dupes and the conspirators.

Sometimes the doll's substitute among Italians is the "Hand of Glory" or the "Hand of Power," which may be an actual human hand severed and mummified, or a tiny hand of ivory or bone with the thumb and two middle fingers closed, while the index and little fingers point outward to make a pair of horns. Often it is a piece of metal known as "the knife," but knife is here a misleading term since it is never used to cut, or as a weapon. Morris Bolber of Philadelphia, who admitted that he practiced witchcraft and claimed (to evade the electric chair) that he did it as a healer and not a destroyer, possessed such a knife. Its metal was no different from that of any tiny knife you buy in any ten cent store. Neither is the plaster in a sacred image or the metal in an icon any different from the plaster in a wall or the metal in a nail. It had been made "different" in its emotional field, as plaster saint and icon are made "different" in their emotional fields, by a method similar to, but the reverse of, consecration.

First [Bolber disclosed], it was buried for three days and three nights in the earth, the open blade buried downward so that the spirits might penetrate its steel point and surface. Then it was taken from the ground and put under the pillow and slept on for three nights. On the seventh day it was put in my pocket infused with the spirit that will dominate devils, and was ready as the assistant to the witch doctor.

We don't need to believe with Bolber, as he claimed, that by waving it he could stop an engine or derail a trolley car, any more than we need to believe that a sacred image will stop the flow of lava from Vesuvius, but if I am right about anything, and if the body of medical psychology is right in its present-day certainty concerning the relation of nervous and mental conditions, then Bolber could start, stop, or derail, that is, help, hurt, make ill, any dupe who *believed in the power* of this doll's substitute.

During the past ten years, in the decade between the York hex murder and the Philadelphia witchcraft murders, there were many other American witchcraft cases and witchcraft killings. These practices, beliefs, and their attendant dangers persist today. Not the least of the attendant dangers (though this book will not be directly concerned with them) is that the terrors and hatreds engendered by witchcraft frequently lead to plain, brute-mechanical ax, arsenic, strangling, and gun murders, as a police-court by-product of the subtler crimes and attempted crimes which seldom reach newspapers, because they seldom result in arrests.

I intend presently to take you behind the scenes, in Africa and America, in New York, London, Paris, Southern France, in my own back yard too, and show you, step by step, how those dolls or their equivalent, though endowed intrinsically with no supernatural quality and no supernormal power, yet work potently for evil. If presently, in getting down to brass tacks driven into dolls for murder, I seem to know more about these things than any decent white adventurer or author should, and seem to have intimate knowledge of so many horrors over a period of so many years in so many lands as to transgress the bounds of credibility, I beg you to remember that black magic has been my lifelong obsession and chimera. If there is anything in heredity, I must have been tainted from birth. There was bad blood in me, from

23

the angle of magic, and it came, mandragora-like, from the best roots of my family tree. My only distinguished ancestor was a great-great-grandfather on the maternal side, a Bishop Peter Boehler, of the Moravian Church, who had been a friend of Wesley's. He was born at Frankfurt, ordained to the Moravian ministry by Count Zinzendorf, and sent to the United States as a missionary. He worked among the Indians, the Negroes in Georgia, and among the Germans in South Carolina, some of whom he ultimately transferred to Bethlehem, Pennsylvania, where he helped found the Moravian Seminary and College for Women. A portrait of him hangs in the vestry of Central Church, at Bethlehem. So much for his distinguished importance. The *New International Encyclopaedia* says, in addition to the above facts, that he was instrumental in aiding the spiritual development of the Wesleys. What our family tradition adds, and what is not in any encyclopedia, is that my distinguished great-great-grandfather was up to his ears in black magic. Shortly after he had been consecrated "Bishop of the Moravian Churches in America, England, Ireland and Wales," leaders in the Welsh Diocese nearly succeeded in having him deposed. The old gentleman ably defended himself by admitting that he dabbled in magic, but asserted he had been doing it all for the glory of God, seeking to "fight the Devil with his own fire."

Hair-raising tales of him were told in my nursery, at Gettysburg, and whether you choose to attribute it to heredity, or to John Watson's behavioristic early childhood conditioning, I cannot remember when I didn't have an obsessed curiosity about these forbidden things. It sent me finally to the voodoo altars of Haiti, where the priests accepted me as one of them and traced their cross in blood on my forehead. It sent me later to Africa, and has ridden me all my life.

I shall be showing in successive chapters an intimate, sometimes dangerous, knowledge of witch dolls in actual operation. Where to begin has been a problem. I have decided to begin with a witchcraft killing which contained all the elements in their controlled completeness.

III. Monstrous Doll in Africa

DURING one of my stays in Africa, I had been living alone for several months with a native household in a large Malinké tribal town, in jungle-mountain country, northeast of Bassam. I was studying fetish ritual, religious ceremonials and beliefs, and saw little or nothing of the few whites scattered in the region. The French *fonctionnaires,* most tolerant of all colonial administrators, had let me consort with the witch-doctors to my heart's content. One night my black friends said to me:

"We have taught you all we can. We are going to send you back in the higher mountains where you may learn more. There is a great Ogoun . . . Nahaou-don-ba is one of his names . . . and he is sometimes called Wôrôn. He is a man of power, a mighty drinker of banghi like yourself, and if you become friends he can disclose further mysteries." They gave me additional names, maps, guides, porters, letters.[1]

Before leaving my Malinké friends, I went up to the ad-

[1] Letters are no longer rare among African witch-doctors. They write usually in Malinké or Bambara, using phonetic Arabic script, and sometimes phonetic French transliteration. I knew a witch-doctor with panther teeth braided in his hair who possessed a fountain pen, and used it. An-

ministration compound, found Monsieur Lauriac at home, thanked him for his kindnesses, not the least of which had been to let me consort unspied-on with the local *féticheurs*, and told him I was headed, with his further kind permission, a hundred miles or so up into the jungle. He asked me to stay to dinner, and during the evening, as we talked about the region I planned to visit, he said:

"We've had some recent trouble from there, made by a white man who'd have been in jail long ago, back where he came from . . . that damned commercial hunter, Albrecht Tellier. He has a Belgian passport, and I've been in a quandary more than once what to do about him."

"I know," I said. "I've met him a couple of times. What happened?"

"The same old thing," Lauriac replied. "Apparently he hired a couple of hundred Yafouba, the whole male population of three villages, to go with him for ivory and skins, and failed at the end of the hunt to pay them off. His licenses are all in order, and he's got some traders down on the coast backing him, but if it weren't bad policy to put a white man on public trial with a lot of howling savages as the only witnesses for the prosecution, I'd have had him in the jug long ago. He's back here, I'm told, saying it's the other way around . . . that the Yafouba broke their contract . . . deserted him."

"Who's telling the truth?"

"We know who's telling the truth! It's happened four or

other had a safety razor, and sent three hundred miles to buy new blades. Another manufactured his own gunpowder, and still another took delight in an old German phonograph with a green tin horn. He liked best an old record of "Johnny" made by Marlene Dietrich.

five times. He's failed to pay off more than one expedition, and some of the men have never come home to their families."

"I'm surprised they haven't shot him by 'accident' with one of his own guns," I said.

"Not any more," said Lauriac. "Unofficially I wouldn't blame 'em, but officially I'd have to hang some of the headmen, probably the wrong ones, and they know it. It's tough on the natives when a crooked white exploits them, because legal recourse or private retaliation are both pretty difficult."

I went away and soon forgot about Albrecht Tellier, whom I'd known only slightly, and whose mistreatment of the natives was an old story in the region.

The Ogoun Nahaou-don-ba whose other name was Wôrôn, informed of my coming, had prepared a wing of the guesthouse in his own compound. It was mud-thatched, earthenfloored, clean, comfortable, and had a spacious veranda which I could use as a sleeping porch. Two handsome wenches and an old woman, all apprentice sorceresses, were to keep house and cook for me. Probably also to spy on me until they decided it was all right. The Ogoun, in robes of soft, brilliantly dyed leather, red, peacock blue, and yellow, was corpulent, powerful, impressive. His first name meant "Learned Scholar" and his other name meant "The Big Gorilla." He was a little of both, and was head of what amounted to a Witch-Doctors' Theological Seminary, whither I'd been sent by my Ivory Coast friends for a sort of postgraduate course. After some weeks of hard study, I felt I had come to the right place. The work—ritual, instruction, ceremonials, incantations—was broken once a week by all-night drunken parties, when the Ogoun and I got roaring tight as anybody. A considerable time passed. On the final night, before I was to depart, he invited me into his own house for a private conference.

Said he, "You know as much theory now as you ever could, without being born into it. You're a black man in a white skin. Before you go away, we'd like to show you some practice . . . work in progress . . . a big enchantment . . . a great ouanga."

Ouanga meant a death-sending, and the Ogoun had me in a spot. He was a tough-minded, intelligent, practical man, and I said after considerable reflection,

"We are on the edge of French territory. The administration has been kind to me and trusts me. They have lent me motor trucks more than once, permit me to wander freely, and do not spy on me. Monsieur Lauriac, down yonder where I came from, trusts me as you do. If it is anything to the hurt of the French, or to the hurt of anybody connected with them, I must not see it."

"It is nothing like that," said the Ogoun. "It concerns us only. It is a matter of private justice."

They took me next afternoon in broad daylight, in ritual procession with drums, the witch-doctors ceremonially garbed, and with singers, to a ledge in a dark ravine where they had set up a monstrous "doll" which was more than an effigy.

It was the guarded corpse of a black man which had been requisitioned on his natural death in a neighboring village. As in the case of inanimate dolls, what he had once been was of no consequence, for they had solemnly rebaptized the corpse by their jungle rites with a new name—with the name of Albrecht Tellier—and were using it as the ritual symbol

29

for their concentrated, focused mumbo jumbo. It had been lashed upright against a tree with vine ropes, tarred so that it would disintegrate slowly in the jungle sun, rain, mists, and night miasmas. Twisted into its black hair were combings of Tellier's own, filched by servants from his comb and brush. Fastened to its finger tips were his own filched nail parings. They had dressed the body in one of Tellier's hunting shirts, "soaked," as they said, "in his vital juices." In plain English, an unwashed shirt in which he had perspired.

Their technique was classic and old as Africa. In construction of the "doll," they had combined the two methods which Frazer and most anthropologists differentiate under the terms of "imitative magic" and "sympathetic magic." If you buy or make a doll, simply dress it up to resemble the intended victim and "baptize" it with his name, the magic is purely "imitative." It remains purely imitative if you use a picture such as the one described under the eaves in Cairo, Illinois, or even a corpse such as this one in Africa, merely "rebaptized" in the intended victim's name. It is purely "sympathetic" if you use as a substitute for the "doll" some object which has been an actual part of, or has been in physical contact with, the intended victim. The lock of Rehmeyer's hair in the Pennsylvania case was in this "sympathetic" category. Similarly in this category are fingernail parings, combings, a shirt or dress previously worn by the intended victim, stolen to rot slowly. When you buy or make a doll, and instead of dressing it with something to merely resemble the victim, dress it in something actually previously worn by the victim, or fasten upon it the victim's own hair, you have then, as in the case of this monstrous human effigy here in the jungle, a combination of the two techniques. Incidentally, any learned discussion of their relative intrinsic importance or efficacy, is jargon, nonsense. The importance is precisely the same as whether you make a sacred statue out of plaster or carve it out of wood. If you feel that such things can have a mysterious intrinsic importance, an analogy would lie in the question of whether the bones of some saint—some sacred relic which had once been part of his anatomy—can be more efficacious than a mere statue of him. If you think the saint's bones or bloodstained handkerchief might cure your boils, or stop an eruption of Vesuvius, where the saint's mere statue wouldn't, you are at liberty to suspect that sympathetic magic can be more deadly than imitative. To me they're all intrinsically zero, potent only as symbols on which to focus love or hatred, fear or faith.

Now here in the jungle, as tom-toms began to throb, was focused malignant hatred—and far away down yonder in Albrecht Tellier's house, as I shall presently show, was focused fear.

Invoking all their jungle gods and demons, and invoking them with frenzied faith, the witch-doctors first roared and howled their unholy hymns, deep bass and screeching treble, until they judged the demon-gods had heard. Then to a different and simpler steady drum throb they began their magic chants, their incantations. Repetition and simplicity. Like London Bridge Is Falling Down and Ring-around-a-Rosy. A rose is a rose is a rose is a rose. This is the way we wash our clothes so early in the morning. Three blind mice, up and down the clock, Mother Goose, Edith Sitwell, echolalia, Gertrude Stein.[2] Black Mrs. Behemoth, in long steel grass, and pigeons on the grass alas. Cut off their tails with a carv-

[2] See Appendix, p. 310.

31

ing knife, and *sonnez la matine*. They were like Frère
Jacques and Wee Willie Winkie. Also they were horrible.
They sang in a sort of simplified, bastardized Malinké and
Bambara:

> *Gneni dimi dogomani*
> *Gneni dimi kounba ba*
> *Gneni dimi yan dakoro*
> *Gneni di yoradian!*
> *Farikolo balolé*
> *A-dama-den sa!*

The words are as simple as any nursery rhyme, and as easy
to translate. What's difficult to translate—just as it would
be difficult to translate the charming but contagious nonsense-
emotional impact of "A tisket, a tasket, a green and yellow
basket"—is the ugly emotional impact of this doggerel, accompanied by the rhythmic patter of the drums. The nearest I can come to it, with no talent for nursery rhymes, and
sticking to the literal meaning of the words, is:

> A big pain, a little pain,
> A small pain, a great pain,
> Growing here and growing there,
> Growing slowly everywhere,
> While a dead man lives
> And a living man dies!

When this endlessly repeated doggerel had ceased, a little
woman, monkey-thin, with shriveled breasts, danced forward
and did a thin-voiced, cackling solo, while the drummers
tapped a light treble beat with their fingers, on the drum
rims. It was nursery rhyme again. It was the incantation for
"clogging the throat." As the body disintegrated here, they
told me, and its throat began to clog and swell, so the man
down yonder would begin to suffer difficulty in breathing,

speaking, swallowing. The little monkey-woman sang, smiling and grinning, as if chattering singsong nonsense to a baby:

Lafa lafa lafa!
Boli an-ou kli!
Mina mina mina
Seguén tji kari ki
Kési kási kési
Baribo sienta
Banabato Sa-a-a!

It meant, still translating as literally as I can:

Choke, choke, choke!
Devils we evoke!
Thirst, thirst, thirst,
Suffer till you burst.
Cry, cry, cry,
Try, try, try.
Die, die, die! [3]

"What would happen," I asked, "if you stopped all this?"

"He is very sick, but he would get well," said the Ogoun. "We could stop it by twisting the magic backward, and he would not die. But we are not going to do it, and no other witch-doctors are going to do it either, for this man has been condemned, and justly so, by the forest."

"Could you teach me how magic is twisted backward?"

"I thought you knew it already," said the Ogoun. "Since you know forward magic, you could teach yourself."

[3] Readers who have lived in French West Africa and probably have a knowledge of Malinké or Bambara, will understand the difficulty, arising from the almost childish simplicity of the words, of putting them into an English equivalent. No English-Bambara dictionary exists, so far as I know, but in 1913 the Librairie Paul Geuthner, 13 Rue Jacob, Paris, published a pretty good French-Bambara one.

"I might need it some day," I said.

"If it's a doll," he said, "you unbaptize it, remove the nails or needles, and burn it in purifying fire. If it's a lock of hair, you dig it up and burn it. If we unbaptized this body here, removed and burned the hunter's own hair and nail parings, removed and either washed or burned the shirt, and then laid the body back in its own name and in its own grave, it would lie there in peace and the man down yonder would get well."

"Don't you think the man would have to know all this?" I asked.

And the Ogoun replied cryptically,

"They always know it."

Presently he added, "There was an older magic by which time is twisted backward, so that the forward magic becomes as if it never had been, and the man as if he had never been sick—as if it had all been a dream, or a thing done by shadows, which are as if they never had been, and leave no trace when light appears. But it is something nobody can teach you, because it has been lost."

"Another thing," I asked, "and since you tell me this man has been justly condemned to die by your forest code, you will perhaps not mind giving me a true answer. If by any chance the magic didn't work, you'd poison him?"

"When the magic is real," said the Ogoun, "poison is never necessary. And besides," he added practically, "his servants or somebody would be caught and hanged. White doctors and the white police have a different kind of magic with liquids that change color."

My conscience was none too clear, nor was it entirely clear

34

just what I might have accomplished if I'd gone and reported the whole tale to the administration. They'd have probably said, "Well, *we're* not rival witch-doctors. We're the police. If a man's shot or poisoned, or going to be, we know what to do. But demons, jinxes, and Mother Goose rhymes are not exactly in our line."

I washed my hands of the whole business, like a little Pontius Pilate, borrowed an old Renault, and went clean out of the forest, over toward Bobo Dioulasso. Returning two weeks later, rolling down toward Bassam again, I got into the edge of my own forest, and presently fell in with an old acquaintance, a Baouli truckman named Yo-Ouro, nicknamed "Joe," who was trucking kola nuts north, to return with salt, and who had all the latest gossip. Over a couple of bottles of beer and a game of *belotte*, Joe said,

"There's one piece of news from your town. That Belgian *saligaud* of an Albrecht's on his deathbed, and nobody's sorry."

"What's he dying of?"

"*Shortness of breath*," said Joe with a malicious grin. "He can't draw his breath any longer. That's what most of us die of, isn't it?"

"But what's really the matter with him?"

"He thinks he's been poisoned," said Joe, "and he's had doctors and the *gendarmerie* and all that, but you're one white man I can tell the truth to. He's dying because they put the great ouanga on him—the death ouanga."

"How?"

"I wouldn't know," said Joe. "I had a Malinké grandmother who knew plenty, but I went to mission school, and now I work in a garage. All I know is that when it's put on you, whether you're white or black, you get sick, and die."

When I finally got down there, a couple of weeks later, Albrecht Tellier had been dead for a fortnight. Since he'd accused the blacks of poisoning him (though Lauriac told me there had never been any poison symptoms), a complete autopsy had followed, and the result had been—zero. Ever since the Dakar yellow fever clean-up, West Africa has had as good medical laboratories as exist anywhere, and it is not true that mysterious poisons exist which leave no trace and are unknown to the materia medica.

"If you ask me," said Lauriac, "he cracked up under his own fears and a guilty conscience, but I'd like very much to know more about it. The natives say it was magic, and I think he thought so at the last. But since he was not murdered, if he was murdered at all, in any sense that we define as murder in court, I'm not going to undertake punishing anybody for it. I'd just like to know. . . ."

"So would I," I said, and I didn't mean it hypocritically. I felt it would serve no good purpose to inflict my private knowledge on Lauriac's official conscience. And I wanted to learn, if I could, what had happened down here, in Albrecht Tellier's own household.

It was Lauriac's superb, black mistress-housekeeper, with one ear in the jungle and another close to the administrator's own, who turned up the complete, unequivocal inside story of how Tellier's black entourage, as ignorant of Freud-Jung-Adler-and-our-learned-psychology-psychiatry-jargon as we would be of language spoken on another planet—and on top of that believing in the supernatural power of their witch-doctors and demons—had nevertheless destroyed Albrecht Tellier by *induced autosuggestion*, applied as expertly for their sinister ends as it ever is for good in any of our advanced medical and psychiatric clinics.

It had begun when one of Tellier's native hunters, permanently employed, and pretending deep sympathy for his master, had come to him, and said, "I've just had dreadful news. A ouanga has been put on you. Perhaps you have already felt it. In a month you will be dead."

Tellier scoffed, grew angry, raged, beat the old man, and went around saying nobody could play on him with silly superstitions. It was either, he said, a scheme to frighten him out of the country, or a threat to poison him. He went to natives he thought he could trust, and they promised to find out what they could. They soon returned saying that, alas, the great ouanga was indeed in operation, and *described it to him in all its ugly detail*. He checked on his hunting shirts and found one missing, as described. The women said it had been "stolen." Where was the ouanga? It was hidden far away, beyond the mountains. Who were the witch-doctors? Nobody knew. They were "far away," of "another tribe." Natives began false-condoling with him, saying he looked sick, assuring him that he would surely die, telling him more and more about the rotting effigy. Pretended-pitying old women kept supplying him with further details, other "cases." He began to feel sick, and was sure he had been poisoned. The doctors who tended him were sure he had not been poisoned, could find nothing the matter with him—and told him so. He had sent for Lauriac, demanded protection, arrests.

"What can I protect you against?" had asked Lauriac. "If they have dug up a corpse somewhere and put your shirt on it, and you believe in that stuff, I might arrest them—for stealing your shirt. But who are they and where is it?"

"I don't believe in it!" Tellier had protested.

But he was sick, and getting sicker, and how much he believed by that time is a point on which there can be no control, and a point on which not even he himself could have been sure.

One day after he had become quite ill, the old Yafouba nurse who had come to his cot with a glass of water said,

"Poor Monsieur Tellier. Does your throat hurt yet?"

"No! Why?" he had demanded. "And what do you mean by yet?"

"Oh, it will, soon now," she had pityingly replied, "because they are now doing this in the mountain." And she had begun the "throat clog" chant, tapping out the rhythm with her fingers on the edge of his cot. It was a simple nursery doggerel, sung to a simple drum rhythm, tapped out by the old black woman's horny-nailed, black, wrinkled hands in that nursery of death:

> Ta-da-da-da-doom . . . . Doom
> Ta-da-da-da-doom . . . . Doom
> Ta-da-da-da-doom . . . . Doom

He was already a sick and frightened man. He had listened to and understood the horrid words, then automatically clutched at his throat as if in some new pain, then screamed,

"Get out! You're either crazy, or you've poisoned me! Or am I crazy?"

And he soon was crazy, crazed with fear, and crazed by

new fear-induced difficulty with his throat muscles, difficulty in speaking and in swallowing. For, from the morning the old woman had come in, by day and night from then on to the end, his ears were never free from that little tapping rhythm whose words he knew. It hadn't been kept up by an occult, astral "sending." And it hadn't been hallucinated ghost tapping inside his own terrified brain. It had been impacting relentlessly on his physical eardrums, as the old woman and her accomplices, including children, had tapped it out with sticks on the bamboo fence toward the forest, on porch railings of the rambling house in which he lay; faint, far away, then close, receding and returning, day and night. He had died of a nervous and functional crack-up, caught in the autosuggested clutches of his own crazed and paralyzing fear.

I have told this as dramatically as I could, not for the sake of dramatizing horror, but because it contains all the paraphernalia, elements, and controls necessary to my thesis.

If I am right, the corpse effigy and stolen shirt were empty symbols. I believe them always to be intrinsically empty. They serve two symbol purposes:

1. A focusing point on which to concentrate the rituals;
2. An objective means of arousing dread in the informed victim.

Could the witch-doctors have obtained an identical result without ever setting up the effigy at all? I believe they could, *if they had believed they could.* Can a priest pray and perform his good works as efficaciously without his rosary? Without his holy water? Without his altar? Without the sacred image in the consecrated shrine? Of course, he can, and does, when he believes he can.

Witchcraft instead of being superstitious nonsense, is mental therapy reversed, with mystery, horror, and superstition added.

IV. Ten Cent Store Doll in France

I HAVE a friend, a certain celebrated Paris journalist, who has made a deep study of sorcery and witchcraft all his life. Like my maternal great-great-grandfather, he sometimes "fights the devil with fire," and has been called into consultation more than once by the French police and by the Roman Catholic exorcists of St. Sulpice. Fighting evil with its own weapons is a dangerous warfare, and my friend has been in foul danger more than once. An attempt was made some years ago by Satanists from Lyons to murder his little daughter, a case which never went to the police because he took the vengeance into his own hands.

It was through my friend Orlet, as we shall call him, that I became a partial participant in the episode of the pianist and the doll, which ended less disastrously than murder, but cost the young victim his career. In this case, what I have to tell is partly reconstruction, because the harm had already been done on the night when Orlet invited me to drive with him out to Le Touquet (Paris Plage), the seaside resort on the channel, and help him burglarize, if he could, a certain beach bungalow, remote from the town, which contained something that ought to be destroyed. It was an isolated shack, with apparently nobody at home, and we crept toward it from the back, a little after dark. While I kept watch, he smashed the fastening of a heavy shutter and pried it open. We climbed inside, closed the shutter, and began looking around with our flashlights. The shack was roughly furnished like a camp, or hide-out . . . a couple of cots which had been recently slept in . . . dirty dishes on a table . . . an oil stove recently used . . . over in a corner, an old rocking chair. In a closet behind a locked door which he had some difficulty in forcing, we found a wooden carpenter's vise screwed to the wall, and from the vise, with its hands caught and crushed in the vise, dangled a little doll—a cheap modern novelty doll, a tawdry manikin in Lilliputian garb, like a puppet in full-dress evening clothes.

"I'd like to ram it down their dirty throats," said Orlet. "If I believed, as they do, in an actual Satan, we'd burn it here and now. What we'd better do is take it along as evidence."

On the way back to Paris we stopped at a roadside restaurant, and he showed me a longish press clipping, a week or two old—one of those mixed news-and-gossip stories that imply between the lines more than is said in them. What it boiled down to was that Jean Dupuis, a brilliant and promising young concert pianist, had unaccountably made a sensational botch of his first important public appearance, in a small but crowded concert hall. He had begun well enough the rendition of Beethoven's "Appassionata" . . . when suddenly a false note, then a succession of jangling chords, followed by worse fumbling, had brought whispers and hisses from the outraged audience. The young man had stopped playing, half turned to the audience, resumed desperately, and, after a ghastly parody of the next few bars, had fled from the stage in shame and confusion.

And then came the gossip and comment, as recounted in the clipping. "Neuritis . . . a cramp in the fingers," had said his friends, his manager, and the kindlier critics next day. "Bah, he was drunk," had said others. Or, "He was a bad pianist anyway, and succumbed to stage fright in the crucial test." His budding reputation and career were ruined, said the clipping, and suggested, indirectly, that there was some sort of unsolved mystery. It ended by adroitly hinting that, as in the case of more than one brilliant young French artist who had gone to pieces in other fields, the mystery might be an addiction to cocaine, if he had absorbed too little, or too much, before he sat down at the piano.

The clipping dropped the mystery there, and it was Orlet who supplied the rest of the story. Dupuis's own privately given explanation of what had happened had been so fantastic as to cast doubts on his sanity, but his devoutly Catholic mother had believed him, and as devout Catholics have been doing for centuries, told his story to her priest. The priest, with her permission, had called Orlet into conference, and Orlet, after obtaining a complete confession from the young pianist, who now mentioned certain names and facts he had withheld, had been busy day and night, aided unofficially by the police and by friends in the Paris underworld in which occultism, fortune-telling, fake mysticism in all its racketeering forms, are rampant.

The pianist had confessed to Orlet that he had been secretly dabbling in the esoteric, including black magic, and had joined some months before a dubious sect of so-called

"Rosicrucians" who had no honest connection with the true followers of Christian Rosenkreuz.

With these facts and actual names to go on, Orlet had succeeded in smoking out the dirty plot. The pianist had made enemies who wanted to ruin him, and since they knew of his occult interests, had hired Satanists instead of ordinary thugs. As a matter of cold, criminal fact, no matter how strongly the Satanists may have believed in their own evil and diseased minds that the Devil helped them, they had been paid to ruin the musician. They had "done their stuff," and earned their money.

A certain Mère Levin who lived in Vincennes and frequented the Rue de Lappe, had bought and dressed the doll and taken it to Le Touquet, which had become the center in the north for the black mass celebrants after Monsieur Chiappe, then Prefect of Police, had driven them from Paris. She and her associates had performed their unholy baptismal rites over the doll, clamped it in the vise where we later found it, and where she had returned from time to time to perform her incantations. One might doubt that such witches themselves have any real belief in the supernatural, in demoniac emanations of evil from the actual doll, since they seem always to see to it that the victim is made to *know* and *fear* it. Yet I am convinced that, precisely as witch-doctors in the jungle, they often do illogically believe it.[1]

Whether Mère Levin and her associates believed it or not, I cannot tell. But whatever she may have believed, the cumulative job they did by direct, if devious approach, would have

---

[1] ". . . our witches are justly hanged, because they think themselves to be such; and suffer deservedly for believing they did the devil's mischief."
—DRYDEN.

more than sufficed in its purpose, even if they and the victim too had been devoid of superstition. What put Orlet on the track was the pianist's confession of a series of "coincidences" that had worried him. The undermining of his confidence had been a slow process. It had taken time. It had cost money. And it had proven at the last that some of his own supposed friends were Judases. Here are some of the successive steps they'd used:

A musician who visited his study on casual pretext, had heard him practicing, had praised his playing, but had added that his finger dexterity seemed slipping a little, and advised him to rest for a few days. "Nonsense," he'd replied. He knew that his dexterity hadn't slipped, and forgot the episode.

But not long afterward, one night after he had been playing, a young woman said, "Have you sprained your hand?" "Why?" he had asked in astonishment. "Do you think I played so badly?" "Oh, no," she had evaded, "I was thoughtless. You played beautifully. It was nothing."

A while later a false friend had come to him and said,

"Whether you will admit it to yourself or not, there is something the matter with your mechanical technique. If you've a touch of neuritis or something of the sort, you ought to face it, for your own good, and see a doctor."

By this time he had begun worrying and wondering, concentrating on the nerves and muscles of his fingers, flexing and moving and testing them when not at the keyboard, becoming cerebrally conscious of his fingers, which meant self-conscious about movements which should be pure automatic reflexes. So that naturally his fingers began occasionally to "tangle," or fail to respond automatically in difficult passages.

He went to a doctor, and then to specialists, who told him there was nothing the matter with his hands. From their point of view, they were right. He began brooding, certain now that there was something mysteriously wrong with his hands which the doctors couldn't diagnose.

What had been done to him by open and direct suggestion up to now had been merely the groundwork.

When they thought he was ripe for it, a little before the concert, an anonymous letter was sent him:

"I can tell you what is wrong with your hands, but it is so frightful that I am almost afraid to tell you." The letter then played on "emanation," "vibrations," so-called Rosicrucian mysteries which they knew the young man had read and studied. It ended by telling him about the doll with its hands squeezed in the vise. It was cruelly and cunningly signed, as if coming from some fellow-esoteric afraid to divulge his name, "A Sympathetic Friend."

On the night of the concert, he had found pinned in his dressing-room a shorter note, in different handwriting, which said:

"The handle of the vise will be slowly turned tonight, until your hands are crushed."

If you think the victim of a plot like that had to be temperamental, credulous, and neurasthenic to begin with, or that such ugly influences as I describe are too far removed from the everyday life of normal people to be of anything but clinical interest, there are unpleasant ways by which it can be proved and has been proved, that such influences, though often unco-ordinated, often unconscious, and happily seldom organized or directed, are at work and affect people in every walk of life and every grade of society. Take the healthiest, most hard-boiled, nonimaginative adult you know. Let several people, separately and at intervals, tell him he seems nervous and ought to take a rest. Let somebody say to him, "Aren't you feeling well?" Let another say casually some day, "Have you been sick?" By the time it's gone that far, he will be feeling "awful," having symptoms of functional or nervous disorders, and will be consulting the specialists. You can't "wish" cancer, a broken leg, anthrax, influenza, or malaria on him, but you can "wish" him into his bed, and sometimes into his grave, if you're vicious and patient enough. Without ever having studied the so-called "Black Art," you will have been practicing it, as truly as any coven witch in Hungary, hex-doctor in Pennsylvania, or witch-doctor in Africa. These are the crude elemental principles of witchcraft at its wickedest.

And that sort of unconscious "witchcraft," alas, instead of being rare, is as common as the air we breathe. It seldom produces fatal illness or death, but too frequently in a thousand homes or groups, some of which you doubtless know, it produces depression, inefficiency, brooding, and unhappiness. Take a healthy, charming, well-co-ordinated child, a completely normal, bright, but sensitive little girl, for instance. Start telling her she's stupid. Keep telling her on every possible occasion that she's stupid. Keep drilling it into her . . . you'd deserve to rot in hell for it if you did, as much as if you'd put disease germs in her morning oatmeal . . . and if you keep at it patiently, at the end of six months or a year, you'll have a stupid and unhappy child.

It's just as much a moral crime to put "poison" in the mind, as it is to put it in the soup. It works more slowly, but it works. "Give a dog a bad name," and no matter how well-bred he is, he'll soon be feeling, and consequently acting, like a slinking cur. I am intimate and friendly with a family of former city people always kind to dogs, to children, to their friends, who have a farm here in the country, and who have been puzzled for years because they can't get loyal, honest, and trustworthy farm help in a countryside which has a tradition of honesty. The reason is simple. From the start, no matter whom they employ, they have always suspected that he was going to let them down. They have always suspected that he would cheat them on the apples, eggs, or fertilizer bill, or that he would be "loafing on the job." Now, no matter how polite and smiling employers may be, or how careful they think they are in concealing their misgivings, the employee always knows it. No extra-sensory perception or nonsense of telepathy is required to explain his knowledge. He might say he "feels" it, or "senses" it, instead of that he knows it. He might say it was "intuition." But it has all come in through his five senses, so that saying he "sensed" it is the simple truth. He "feels" what they "feel," and since they feel that way and since he's no miracle of incorruptible integrity (are any of us?) but simply a decent, ordinarily honest fellow, inclined to be decent and honest under decent circumstances, he says to himself sooner or later, "What the heck, if that's how they feel about me anyway . . ." and starts gypping them.

"Since that's how they feel, since that's what they think of me anyway, why disappoint them?"

If their psychology had been the opposite, if they had trusted him (and they should never have hired him unless they intended to trust him), he might not have disappointed them in that case either.

Carl Sandburg tells about an early sodbuster settled in Kansas. The sodbuster leaned at his gate. Drove up a newcomer in a covered wagon: "What kind of folks lives around here?" "Well, stranger, what kind of folks was there in the country you come from?" "Well, they was mostly a lowdown, lying, thieving, gossiping, backbiting lot of people." "Well, I guess, stranger, that's about the kind of folks you'll find around here." And the dusty gray stranger had just about blended into the dusty gray cottonwoods in a clump on the horizon when another newcomer drove up: "What kind of folks lives around here?" "Well, stranger, what kind of folks was there in the country you come from?" "Well, they was mostly a decent, hard-working, law-abiding, friendly lot of people." "Well, I guess, stranger, that's the kind of folks you'll find around here."

If the stranger is strong enough on the side of the angels, he can work miracles for good. One did once, though he was born a carpenter's son, native peasant in the local village, and turned "strange" inside himself without the exterior aura of remote origin. But most of us are more facile agents for contagious evil than contagious good. Magic is contagious, particularly when unconscious and unfocused. When *one* suspicious man or family moves into an honest community, expecting to be cheated, the community will remain generally honest, and confine its cheating to the strangers *who asked for it*. But if enough people of his sort move in, the whole community will become corrupt, including the oldest inhabitants, and start cheating each other.

Bad people are almost as rare as bad dogs. It isn't often,

not once in a thousand or a million mongrel births, that dog or man loves evil. But dogs and men are sensitive. They vibrate. If you feel strongly that the dog will bite you, or that the man will cheat you or do you in the eye, the dog or man is pretty likely to vibrate in harmony with your emotion-expectations, and do it to you—and it serves you damned well right.

Rhinebeck, my village, your village, your family, is always the Lion of Androcles. It will almost never attack you wantonly, unless it is terribly hungry—and in that case you can forgive it. Any village, city, or family group is the magical equivalent of the lion. Be friendly and trustful toward the animal (your own family, the grocer, your wretched sister, your difficult mother, your sexful or long-lost-to-sex wife) and they will be friendly toward you. Beware however of hypocrisy. If you pretend to do it without feeling it, the grocer, your mother, your sister, your wife, will outdo you in devilish hypocrisy and nail your worse-stripped skin to the nearest barn door.

My friends think I lean too far toward the side of the angels. My gardener has all my keys, except the one to my cash drawer, and the reason he hasn't that is that it's never locked. He goes to it frequently, to buy this and that for cash. I don't keep count, but my gardener John, I'm sure, has never even had the "concept" of gypping me. It would be as absurd as gypping himself. Yet perhaps he's no more basically incorruptible than any of the rest of us. Remember Judith Anderson in Pirandello's *As You Desire Me?* Perhaps I have been applying "white magic" to my gardener. At any rate, it works.

My friends, I am sure, have never dreamed that their

own psychological distillation of a mild elemental form of "black magic" has ruined their successive farmers, made them disloyal and dishonest, as truly as "black magic" ruined the Paris pianist. There's nothing diabolic about any of it in a supernatural sense, but "black" is the right adjective for it.

V. Wooden Doll in a Cave

IN the cases of Albrecht Tellier, cynical Belgian globe-trotting scoundrel, soldier of fortune and big game hunter, and of Jean Dupuis, cultured but esoterically inclined Parisian, it is by no means certain that Tellier believed at all, or that Dupuis believed completely, in any diabolic, superhuman, supernatural power behind the doll. In the case I propose next to relate, the intended victim believed as implicitly and unquestioningly in the deadly supernatural power behind the doll as you believe in poison gas or cholera germs. When the intended victim believes the force attacking him is superhuman, the doll, for him, becomes a fatal image of certain doom, and he tends more easily to crack up emotionally and functionally. All savages and primitives believe in this supernatural element, and so do millions of otherwise civilized whites in Europe and here in America. Rehmeyer fought to the death, and John Blymyer killed him by violence because they both believed that the "hexing" of a lock of hair would have been just as murderous and deadly. In Africa, in the case of the wooden doll in a cave, my savage friends wiped out, by similar physical violence, and with clean consciences according to their standards, a rival witch who was slowly

52

murdering one of them—with no other weapon than that wooden doll.

I was living up in the Ivory Coast, near Dananae, and the young black witch and priestess Wamba came to my house one day to ask a favor. She had done me many, and knew that I could scarcely refuse. It seemed an "uncle" of hers was sick in the hospital at Huan, three hundred miles away, and she wanted to pay him a visit. His name was Bénké Kono (Uncle Bird), and she hadn't seen him since she was a little girl. He had sent word that he was afraid he was going to die, and hoped he could see her. *"Bénké,"* the Bambara word for uncle, is loosely used, as is its equivalent in all languages, as an affectionate term for any old man one is fond of. Wamba consequently felt it necessary to add that this old gentleman was blood kin, and that she felt it her duty to go. Wamba was a wayward, usually selfish wench, and I was surprised at this display of family affection toward a distant relative she hadn't seen in years. She was deliberately piling it on so that I could scarcely refuse. She had come dressed in all her finery; scarlet leather hat surmounted by red, white, and yellow ostrich plumes; bracelets, bangles, grigris, anklets, tinkling bells . . . and indeed I was not going to refuse . . . though I couldn't help reflecting that unless she went home and changed her clothes before we started, she'd be a startling apparition seated beside a white man in the front seat of an open Renault truck that had a government official license! For the truck was what she'd come for. It would take three weeks for her to make the trip to Huan with carriers in the hammock swung on poles in which she usually traveled, and it could be done in three days or less

53

in a motor car. Poor old Uncle Bird, she said, might be dead when she got there, unless I helped her.

"Why do you really want to go to Huan?" I asked her.

"My uncle is sick. I've told you the truth."

"I doubt it," said I, "and if you have told me the truth, I don't believe you've told me all of it, but I'll find out whether the roads are passable, and if they are, we'll start tonight."

"The roads are passable. The kola-nut trucks have been going through," she said—and added, "We'll have to take Diisi. He can sit on the bags in the rear."

"Why do we have to take Diisi? What are you planning to do at Huan?" I asked.

She replied impatiently, "I tell you, my uncle is sick! Do I need to keep telling you I want to comfort him? Wouldn't you want to, if you had a sick uncle?"

"And I suppose you need Diisi to help comfort him?"

"Fate," said Wamba, who was a real jungle priestess, despite her handsome impudence, "is always fan-shaped. Perhaps I will need Diisi."

This Diisi, whom I'd known for a long time, was Wamba's "brain trust." She seldom went far afield, or undertook anything serious, without him. He was an elderly, skinny, little fetish-temple soothsayer, with keen eyes, a seamy smile, and grizzled beard. His grandfather had been a great witchdoctor, and he was the custodian of the "sacred relic"—his grandfather's mummified arm, which they used as a sort of jungle ouija board. It was a shriveled human forearm with the clenched hand attached . . . dry and hard as wood . . . almost like petrified wood. I had seen it "consulted" on more than one occasion. You suspend it by the middle, on a single, long, slender thread, from the ceiling of the temple, or if it's outdoors from the branch of a tree, so that it dangles, balanced horizontally. Then you build a tiny altar of pebbles under it, on which you place offerings of food . . . a fine, ripe mango, a chicken liver . . . anything small and tasty that comes handy. Sometimes you lay a little bouquet of flowers against the side of the altar. Sometimes, if the arm is slow in answering, you build a little fire under it—as good Catholics among the peasants of the Roman Campagna stand the little image of Saint Joseph on his head in a basin of water, to "persuade" him to answer their prayers. Then you invoke the spirit of the long-dead witch-doctor, and presently the arm begins to gyrate slowly. It does too—nearly always— and without needing to be jiggled or tricked. The temple ceilings are bamboo-latticed, thatched, thick, but not very solid or stable, and any slight vibration does it. Sometimes there's a slight breeze, nearly always the vibration of the drums. Sometimes in complete silence, with no drums and apparently no breath of air, the "hand of power" revolves slowly on its axis-arm, or dips upward or downward, as if it wants to say or point out something. No spirit speaks through it, and no spirit ever has or ever will speak through any medium, animate or inanimate, in my opinion, but it's eerie, there in its own setting, and it's easy to understand how they believe a spirit moves it.

I knew that if we were going to take Diisi along, we would also be transporting what was left of Diisi's grandfather. So that when they turned up that night, with Wamba, thank God, divested of her scarlet ostrich plumes and bangles, swathed now in a dark-blue *pagne* suitable for inconspicuous travel, I was not surprised to see in Diisi's luggage the little mahogany casket bound in leopard skin, in which reposed the long-dead sorcerer's black hand.

We got there in less than three days, and the hospital turned out to be a Catholic medical mission of the Pères Blancs. To the kindly monks and doctor who received us, I was simply a white colonial who had brought a couple of natives to visit a sick relative. Diisi, and Wamba too, were circumspect and humble. The hospital had many patients, all black, and they weren't sure whether a Bénké Kono was among them or not. If the records didn't show anything, we were welcome to have a look at all the men patients, and would doubtless recognize him, if he was there. Native names were sometimes difficult to get straight, they explained to me. But presently they found Bénké Kono's name, and then remembered him perfectly, since he had been there for several weeks and had been an "interesting case." He had gone home, probably to die, they said, a few days before. He had been "an interesting case," the doctor repeated.

"Why had the case been interesting?"

"Well, to be frank," said the doctor, "we are equipped with laboratories and technicians, and I have had a lifetime's experience with native diseases . . . but we couldn't find out what was the matter with the old Malinké." He had seemed to be wasting away from pernicious anemia or something of the sort, the doctor continued, but the blood tests, and all the other tests and attempted diagnoses, had failed to show anything whatsoever.

I thanked them, got permission to leave the truck for a few days.

From then on it was up to Wamba. Since I had come that

far to visit her sick uncle, I was willing to tag along a little further, and let her find him if she could. It proved to be simple enough. Uncle Bird's village was distant only fifteen kilometers, and we got there, with porters, late that night. Uncle Bird was one of the village headmen, had a sizable compound, several houses, several wives, a flock of chickens, and a herd of goats. The village helped install me in the thatch-roofed guesthouse—nearly every forest village has one—while Wamba and Diisi were looked after by Uncle Bird's wives. Next morning she sent for me to come over and meet Uncle Bird. He was a pleasant, sad, old savage who must once have had a powerful physique and commanding presence . . . elderly rather than really old . . . and not precisely a savage either, since I soon discovered he could speak good pidgin French, and saw hanging from pegs in the wall two suits of store-bought clothes. Like many native headmen in that part of Africa, he had worked a good part of his life for the administration, had been a sort of tax overseer. Now he was wasted, emaciated, melancholy, and depressed. He had been lying in a bamboo wall bunk on a straw mat, with a pillow, but sat up to talk with us. It was the administration, he said, who had persuaded him to go to the hospital, and he had consented to go, not because of the medical doctors but because the Pères Blancs were *basi-tigui*, which means dealers in spiritual and supernatural things. Just as the fetishist priest is *basi-tigui*, so likewise is the Roman Catholic priest, or priest of any religion.[1] Uncle Bird had gone to the hospital, he told me, because he'd thought

---

[1] Protestant missionaries, though occasionally liked and respected by the natives, have never been considered *basi-tigui*.

the proximity, prayers, masses, and protection of the *basi-
tigui* might help him.

Did he know, then, I asked, what was the matter with him?

Oh, yes, he knew, and glanced at Wamba. That was why
he had sent for Wamba. He glanced at her again, and she
nodded her head in assent. It was all right to tell me. So he
told me.

He knew and told me all about why he was dying. Somewhere in the forest, a wooden doll had been carved in his
image and baptized with his name. It had then been wound
round and round with soft scarlet woolen thread which had
been "made to be" his own life-thread. Each day, a little of
the thread was being unwound, while the deadly *basiko* and
dayama incantations were chanted. When the end of the
scarlet thread was reached, he was going to die, he said, and
I, who have no superstition, was convinced that he would.
He was going to die simply and solely because he *knew that
he was going to die*.[2] The only thing he didn't know was
who the witch might be, or where the doll was hidden.

Wamba meanwhile, first whispering with Diisi, was now
moving restlessly around the room, then standing trembling
like a big savage cat when it begins lashing its tail.

"Perhaps you are not going to die, Uncle Bird," she said.
"Have you not been taught that fate is always fan-shaped?
But you should have sent for me sooner."

On our way back to Huan, which had a large native population and the biggest native market in the region, Wamba

[2] To those who believe that concentrated hatred and destructive thought
can send out actual emanations of evil, perceptible through channels other
than the senses—I can only say that while they may be right, I do not believe it.

said to Diisi and me, "With more time, I could handle this in the old way, as such things should be handled. But there is little time, and I am going to handle it by a quicker handle."

The only whites in Huan were the missionary priests, the manager of a "chain-store" trading post, and a French *sergent-fonctionnaire* in charge of a few Senegalese soldiers. Having already "gone native" on this little expedition, I stayed away from the whites. From then on, I let Wamba run the show.

Wamba took a house for us out on the edge of the town, in a compound fenced at the front, but whose back yard was the whole forest. It had mud-thatched outbuildings, including a small fetish house, as these compounds nearly always do, and in this little devil's doghouse, Diisi prepared to go to work on his grandfather's arm. I helped gather pebbles for the altar, and contributed two or three cigarettes which I propped against it. When I went back that night, they were gone, and I didn't inquire whether Diisi had smoked them himself or burned them to propitiate his ancestor. Wamba had made one trip to the market, and servants had returned laden with provisions. Then she went down into the town, and was gone for two days and nights. She returned, worn out and travel stained, looking completely done in. I don't think she'd slept at all in the interval. I gave her a shot of rum from a bottle I'd sent one of the servants to buy from the chain store. She flopped down and slept for a couple of hours. Then drummers came, and we went into executive session with Diisi's grandfather's arm. Before it ended, we had a small, fervent congregation . . . the servants . . .

and other faces I had never seen before. They joined in the prayers, and Wamba seemed pleased. The arm did its stuff, and when it was over Wamba told me she knew everything she needed to know. She knew where the doll was, and the identity of the witch. I suspect that during the two days and nights she'd been absent, working probably as detectives or rival gangsters work in the jungles of Chicago or New York, she'd learned, or bought, the information.

"I am now going," said Wamba, "to save Uncle Bird's life. You can come along if you choose, but I advise you not to. You are one of us, a black man with a white face, but you would perhaps not wish to see what you would see."

Diisi did not accompany us. Wamba and I made a journey, accompanied only by two grim-faced men who she said were her "cousins." "Torpedoes" would have been the name for them in the American jungle. They were forest savages, but I suspected they were Senegalese. They were barefoot now, but I suspected they had worn shoes, and uniforms. There was a mud-and-stone house built into the face of a cliff, many a long mile from Huan. And the house was the masked entrance to a cave. We entered the house, and entered the cave. And there, upon an altar, candlelighted, smeared with chicken blood, I saw the ugly little wooden doll from which the scarlet life-thread had been unwound almost to the last strand. I had expected to see a hag, but the witch, who would unwind no more because she lay quivering on the floor sieved with slugs fired at close range by Wamba's "cousins," was a young wench who spat in our faces as she died. Wamba had no remorse. Wamba was gay and happy as a girl scout who had done her good deed for the day. We later held a festival, a *bamboche*, to celebrate Uncle Bird's deliverance and the beginning of his recovery. He began getting well immediately, and he got well, as I believe, because he *now knew* that he was going to get well.

VI. Sawdust Doll in Brambles

IN contrast to Uncle Bird's whole-souled and whole-minded fear-belief in the infernal, supernatural power of the witch's incantations and the doll, I next present the case of an intended victim who was a disbeliever and had no *conscious* fear at all.

He was a young mechanic from Marseilles, who understood engines and anything he could take hold of with his hands or a wrench, but to whom the complications of modern psychology, much less the idea that a "witch" could hurt him with a doll or by suggestion either, would have been *de la fumisterie*—the bunk.

His name was Louis Bausset, and I got acquainted with him first in a garage, at St. Rémy, where I was living upstairs above a workman's restaurant. He had a girl in a neighboring hill village, and I had a girl in the town. The four of us used to meet occasionally in the restaurant and share the same table. They confided one evening that they wanted to get married and were having a bad time with Marie's doddering old grandmother who had refused to let them. Marie was an orphan, under age, the grandmother was her guardian, and the French laws are tough in such circumstances. Louis wondered if I'd go up with him some day and see if I could help.[1]

There's a turn on one of the main roads well out of St. Rémy where you can look up and see the hill village perched on a steep cliff above the gorge through which the road runs. A winding goat path leads up from that point, but it's a hard climb and people seldom use it to go up, though mountain peasants often come down that way, since it cuts off several miles. Louis sometimes used it, even in going up, but on the Sunday morning set for our visit to Marie and her grandmother, we had borrowed an old Citroën from his garage and rode the long way, roundabout. Marie was waiting for us at a café, beyond the church.

She took us to an old stone *mas*, a dilapidated but massively built farm cottage which had been there for centuries. In introducing me, with peasant formality, she called her grandmother "Madame Tirelouet," but "Mère Tirelou" was the more familiar name by which she and Louis afterward addressed her. Mère Tirelou was withered, skinny in the arms and legs, yet unhealthily plump in face and body, like a withered, half-rotting sour apple. She was civil at first, in the presence of a stranger, and fetched wine with a plate of seedcakes. But when the subject of marriage came up and I began to speak well of Louis, she told me, in a croaking voice, to keep my nose out of other people's business. I tried to point out that it was very much the business of Marie and Louis, the most important thing on earth for them, and that I was Louis's close friend and sincerely believed he would

[1] Years ago, I twisted some of these events into a short story. I never expected to touch it again, but in this context it deserves to be told as it actually happened.

63

make Marie a good husband. I tried to tell her about his work and prospects. Presently she lost her temper and was screaming at us, "Never . . . while I live!"

There was no use arguing with an eccentric old woman in a screaming temper, and as we went away, she fired a parting shot at Louis,

". . . and I may live longer than you do, unless you let Marie alone!"

"I doubt if you'll ever bring her round," I said to Marie as we sat in the sunshine, on the terrace of the café overlooking the gorge and valley. The view was magnificent. I'd never been up there before, and was thinking it would be a lovely place to spend a week in. I was thinking that even though I hadn't been much of a help as a matchmaker, I'd found a spot worth visiting for a while when I left St. Rémy.

"After all, the old lady can't live forever, and, for that matter, you'll be of age in a year or so," I said to Marie. "Why don't you wait a little?"

"We don't want to wait," said Louis. "We want to get married."

I said, "I'd like to come up here and spend a couple of weeks anyway, and if I do I'd be glad to try to get better acquainted with her, and try . . ."

Louis said, "I don't think it would be of any use, but you might try if you are coming up anyway."

That was the situation, and that was the way it still was, when I went up in August and took a room at the inn. The inn owned the café and terrace on the edge of the cliff. The inn was built into the parapet which hung over the gorge.

There was a stone wagon shed which had been converted into a garage, and my room was above it. The motor road came up through the back of the village, and the footpath coming up from the gorge bent round the wagon shed's courtyard walls and joined the road almost beneath my window. Louis had arrived for a few days' vacation, had another room in the inn, and was seeing Marie in spite of the old woman.

In casual conversations with new acquaintances in the village, I learned that Mère Tirelou was supposed by some of them to be a little crazy, and said by others to be a "witch." I pricked up my ears a little . . . but since every village in Southern France has an old woman who sells harmless herbs, tells fortunes in tea leaves or with the Tarot cards, and cures rheumatism, or tries to, with amulets and charms, my curiosity was only mildly aroused. And as for any suspicion that her sort of witchcraft might be sinister, or might have any remote connection with her refusal to let her granddaughter marry Louis, it didn't enter my head.

Then, one hot midafternoon when I lay reading in my room beside an open window, the series of events began which led finally, by paths of ancient evil, to the doll in brambles. I had often heard Mère Tirelou quarreling with Louis, but all at once, down in an angle of the courtyard wall beneath my window, I heard their voices now, and there was a new note in the old woman's. I couldn't catch the words at first, but she was muttering, and he was trying to quiet her, half-amiable, half-impatient and derisive. Her tones, meanwhile, were so curious that I got the unpleasant impression she might be on the verge of convulsions, or a "seizure" as the French call it, and I got up to see what was happening.

They were standing down there in the sunshine, he tall, ruddy, tousle-haired, bareheaded, in knickers and sport shirt; she gray, bent, and batlike in her Arlésienne *coiffe* and shawl, with arms outstretched, crouching, and barring his path. She was now intoning a weird, singsong doggerel, at the same time weaving in the air with her clawlike hands:

> Go down, go down, my pretty youth,
> But you will not come up.
> Tangled mind will twist and turn,
> And tangled foot will follow.
> You will go down, my pretty one,
> But you will not come up again.
> So tangle, tangle, twist and turn,
> For tangling webs are woven.

She kept singing it, and was on her knees, clawing at his feet and ankles, scratching and pulling at his shoelaces. He was bending as if to lift her up, when she hopped aside and arose.

She was no longer barring Louis's path but standing aside, inviting him to pass, so that her back was partly turned to me, while Louis stood so that I would see his face and the expressions which flitted over it—first an interested, incredulous, surprised attention as if he couldn't believe his own ears, then a good-humored but derisive and defiant grin as the old woman began again to mumble her doggerel.

"No, no, Mère Tirelou," he said. "You can't scare me with stuff like that. Better get an honest-to-goodness broomstick when you try to drive me away. Save your cobwebs and incantations for the shepherds."

Then Louis with a defiant, humorous *au revoir* was off down the goat path whistling, while the old woman screamed after him, "Down, down, down you go, but not up, my pretty boy; not up, not up, not up!"

This was years ago, but I already knew, or thought I knew, a good deal about witchcraft. I had known it to produce results, but only in cases when the victim was superstitious and consequently amenable to fear. I knew nothing then about the role the subconscious might play. I felt sure that such complete, hardheaded disbelief constituted a stronger "counter-magic" than any amount of exorcism and holy water, and felt sure that Louis wasn't in the slightest danger.

I have since learned that it's never quite as simple as that. But holding those wrong convictions then, I finished my reading, dined early, strolled to the top of a crest to watch the sunset, and went early to bed.

Usually after ten o'clock the whole village, including the interior of the inn, was sound asleep and silent. It was the noise of footsteps clattering along the stone floor of the corridor which awoke me late in the night. I heard lowered voices in the road, saw lights flashing.

I struck a light, dressed and went downstairs. The innkeeper, Martin Plomb, was talking to a group of neighbors. His wife was standing in the doorway, wrapped in a quilted dressing gown.

"We're worried about Louis Bausset," she said. "He went down the goat path this afternoon, and said he was coming back the same way. It's all right in the daylight, even for a stranger, but it's not safe at night unless you know every inch of it. We thought nothing of it that he didn't come back for dinner, but it's past midnight and we're afraid he may have had an accident."

Already the men, in groups of twos and threes, with farm lanterns, a few with electric flashlights, were starting down the path. It had a lot of "false turnings," they said, which the goats had made, foraging off in the brambles . . . and one turn which led across into another gorge.

Martin Plomb was instructing them to go this way or that and to keep in touch with one another by shouting. I went along with him. It was just before dawn, after hours of fruitless search, that we heard a different shouting from the right. I couldn't distinguish the words, but Martin said, "They've found him." We worked our way across and climbed toward the main road along which we now could see lights flashing.

They were carrying Louis on an improvised litter made with two saplings and pine branches interwoven. He was conscious; his eyes were open; but he seemed to be in a stupor and had been unable, they said, to explain what had happened to him. No bones were broken, nor had he apparently suffered any serious physical injury, but his face was cut and scratched, his clothes were badly torn, particularly the knees of his knickerbockers, which were ripped and abraded as if he had been dragging himself along on his hands and knees. His stockings and shoelaces were torn to tatters.

They all agreed on what had probably happened. He had been climbing bareheaded among the rocks in the heat of the late afternoon, had suffered an insolation, or sort of sunstroke, they said. They'd found him a mile off the path, in a sloping tangle of thornbush and brambles. He should be all right in a day or two, Martin said. They were sending down to St. Rémy for the doctor.

It was dawn when we got to bed, and when I awoke toward noon the doctor had already come and gone.

"He had a bad stroke," Martin told me. "His head is clear —but there's still something the matter that the doctor couldn't understand. When he tried to get up from the bed, he couldn't walk. His legs aren't broken or anything. It's queer. He seemed to twist and stumble over his own feet."

Sharply, as he spoke, the belated certainty came to me that here was an end to coincidence; that I had been wrong; that something evil had been happening here under my eyes.

"Martin," I said, "something happened yesterday that you don't know about. I'd like to see Louis and talk with him. You say his mind is clear?"

"But assuredly," said Martin, puzzled. "He will want to see you."

Louis was in bed, his face and hands zigzagged with scratches.

I said, "Louis, Martin tells me there's something wrong with your legs. I think perhaps I can tell you what—"

"Why, have you studied medicine?" he interrupted eagerly. "If we'd known that! The one who came up from St. Rémy didn't seem to be much good."

"No, I'm no doctor. But I'm not sure this is a doctor's job. You know where my room is. I was at the window yesterday and heard and saw everything that happened between you and Mère Tirelou. Haven't you thought that there may be some connection?"

He stared at me in surprise, and also with a sort of angry disappointment.

"*Tiens!*" he said. "You, an educated American, you be-

69

lieve in that crazy foolishness! Why, I came from these mountains; I was born here, and I know that stuff is silly nonsense. I thought about it, of course, that tanglefoot business, but it doesn't make any sense. How could it?"

"Maybe it doesn't," I said, "but just the same will you please tell me as well as you can exactly what happened to you yesterday afternoon and last night?"

"I went down," he said, "then walked to the crossroads and hitchhiked into St. Rémy on a truck, which brought me back and dropped me there at the same *carrefour* an hour later. I started back up the path, and caught my foot in a vine or something and fell down, and when I got up I saw I must have wandered off the path without knowing it, for there wasn't any path in sight, and I went looking for it. You know how the going is, and how thick it is with thornbush. I stumbled a couple of times . . . anybody but a goat would stumble in that tangle . . . finally fell down a couple of times more . . . and there I was, lost on that damned mountainside. I had the 'stroke,' or whatever it was, afterward. I began to be dizzy, couldn't stand up, everything looked queer to me. I was frightened, I guess, and I kept trying to walk, and kept falling down, and it got dark . . . and that's all I remember. If it's left me like this, I'd rather it had killed me. I'd rather be dead than crippled."

Louis lapsed into somber silence. I had heard enough. People have lain in bed for years because they *believed* they couldn't arise and walk. Medical records show plenty of cases in which such patients have been "cured" simply by being "jolted" out of the neurosis, and it was my job now to jolt Louis if I could.

Neither the old woman nor her granddaughter had been near the hotel that morning. I climbed the winding cobbled street and tapped at their door. Presently Marie reluctantly opened. I said:

"I've come to see Mère Tirelou."

"She is not here," said Marie. The girl was in distress, and I felt she knew or suspected why I had come.

"In that case," I said, "we must talk. Shall it be like this, or would you prefer to have me come in?"

She motioned me inside.

I said, "Marie, I beg you to be honest. You know what people say about your grandmother—and there are some who say it also about you. I hope that part isn't true. But your grandmother has done something I'm determined to have undone. I'm so certain that, if necessary, I am going to see the priest, and have him get the police up from St. Rémy. I think you know exactly what I am talking about. It's Louis—and I can't see how you, pretending to love him and wanting to marry him . . ."

"No, no, no!" the girl cried pitifully, interrupting. "I tried to stop it! I warned him! I begged him yesterday not to see me any more. I told him that something dreadful would happen, but he laughed at me. He doesn't believe in such things. I have helped my grandmother in other things—she has forced me to help her—but never in anything so wicked as this—and against Louis!"

"Well, by god," I said, "no matter what your grandmother has made you help in, it's Louis and me you're going to help now."

"I'm afraid," she said, "afraid of my grandmother. Oh, if

you knew! I don't dare go down there—and besides, the door is locked—and it may not be down there."

I insisted. We broke the lock. The girl went first, and I followed close, lighting our way with the lamp held at her shoulder. The stone stairway curved sharply downward, as in all such farmhouses, then emerged into what must once have been the wine cellar. It now housed various unpleasant objects on which the shadows flickered as I set the lamp on a barrel, and began to look about me. I had heard that witches, practicing in the medieval tradition, still existed in certain parts of Europe, yet I was surprised to see the definite evidence so literally surviving.

Against the opposite wall was an altar surmounted by a pair of horns. Beneath them "I N R I" with the letters distorted into obscene symbols—and there on the floor, cunningly contrived with infinite pains, covering a considerable space, was the thing which we had come to find and which, for all my efforts to rationalize it, sent a shiver through me. Spread there on the earthen floor, like a wild landscape in miniature, was a tangled labyrinth of thorns and brambles. Tangled in its center like a butterfly caught on flypaper, was a doll, a common doll with china head on a stuffed sawdust body; a doll such as might be bought for three francs in any toyshop—but whatever baby dress it may have worn had been removed and a costume suggesting a man's knickerbockers and sport shirt had been substituted. The eyes of this manikin were bandaged with a narrow strip of black cloth. Its feet and legs were tangled, fastened, pierced, and enmeshed in the crisscross maze of thorns and brambles. It slumped, sagging there at an ugly angle, neither upright nor fallen, grotesquely sinister, like the body of a soldier caught in barbed wire. All this may seem silly, childish, when set down in words. But it was not childish; it was vicious, wicked.

I disentangled the manikin gently, examined it to see whether its sawdust body had been pierced with pins or needle. But there were none. The old woman had apparently stopped short of intended murder.

Marie had covered her face and was sobbing her heart out. I picked up the lamp, began again to look around me, and went through a vaulted passage leading to another part of the cellar. Suspended by heavy chains from the ceiling was a life-sized contrivance of wood, with blackened leather straps —as perverse a device as twisted human ingenuity ever invented. I knew its name and use from old engravings in books dealing with the obscure sadistic-masochistic element in medieval sorcery. It was a witch's cradle. And there was something about the straps that made me wonder. . . .

Marie saw me staring at it, and shuddered.

"Marie," I said, "is it possible—?"

"Yes," she answered, hanging her head. "Since you have been down here there is nothing more to conceal. But I have hated it, and it has always been on my part unwillingly."

"Why on earth haven't you denounced her to the authorities? A plain charge of cruelty would have been enough. Why haven't you left here?"

"Monsieur," she said, "I have been afraid of what I knew. And besides, she is my grandmother."

✦

73

I was alone with Louis in his bedroom. I had brought the manikin with me, wrapped in a bit of newspaper. I showed it to him and told him what I had discovered. He was at first skeptical, incredulous, but when I made him see that the manikin had been crudely dressed to represent himself and it became clear to him that Mère Tirelou had deliberately sought to do him a wicked injury, he grew angry, raised up from his pillows, and exclaimed:

"Ah, the old woman! She really meant to harm me!"

I took a chance. I stood up and threw the doll against the wall as hard as I could. Its china head crashed to pieces.

"Did that hurt you?" I demanded.

"Hurt me? What are you talking about? Are you as crazy as the old woman?"

"The doll," I said, "is damned nonsense. Of course smashing it didn't hurt you! Now forget all about it . . . and get the hell up out of that bed! Believe you can walk, and you *will* walk."

He stared at me helplessly, sank back, and said, "I don't believe it. I had a 'stroke.' I don't believe any of it."

I had failed. He lay there, victim of his own unconscious imagination, yet his conscious mind lacked paradoxically the imagination needed to pull him out of it.

I said, "Louis, you still love Marie, don't you? Well, Mère Tirelou has been doing worse things to Marie than she tried to do to you." And I told him brutally, almost viciously, of the cradle that hung there in the cellar, and of its use.

The effect was as violent as if I had hit him in the face. "*Ah! Ah! Tonnerre de dieu! La coquine! La vilaine co-*

quine!" he shouted, leaping up from his bed like a crazy man. "Where are my clothes?" he yelled, rushing around the room.

He'd forgotten all about his "stroke"—and that was that.

Louis Bausset, twenty-six-year-old garage mechanic, was as matter-of-fact and unimaginative an adult as I've ever known. He was not a neurasthenic type. He was devoid of credulity and superstition. I discovered, however, as we talked and wondered, after it was all over, that Louis Bausset at five years of age had believed in all the ghosts, hobgoblins, and malignant witches which infest the fairy tales and folklore of that region, as they do the Black Forest of Germany. He had long ago rejected it rationally, but it had apparently left something emotionally deep down, asleep, as it were, in his consciousness. Psychiatry has a simple name for the not uncommon thing that had happened to him. His "stroke" and subsequent inability to walk had been the result of a compulsion neurosis.

VII. Doll de Luxe in London

I FIRST came indirectly into this tangle when I was invited one night to a dinner at the palatial villa of Alice Crystal Johns, near Juan-les-Pins, during one of my periods of temporary prosperity at Bandol where Dr. Thomas Mann, little Dr. Lion Feuchtwanger, other famous German exiles, and Aldous Huxley were my nearest neighbors, and where D. H. Lawrence had his last illness.

Marjorie and I were driven over by the Princess Violette Murat, then at Toulon, and among the dinner guests were Jean Cocteau, the Comtesse de Noailles, Pirandello, whose *As You Desire Me* had recently been translated into French. Neither Marjorie nor I belonged properly in the group, but some of my books had also been recently translated. I had bought the old ruined Château d'Evenos, which amused these brilliant, wealthy neighbors . . . and they were being kind to us. We were feasted that night superbly on a succession of marvelous dishes, with priceless wines—while Alice Johns sat at the head of the table eating plain, unseasoned gruel from a wooden bowl, with a wooden spoon.

She was beautiful . . . she was always beautiful . . . but she seemed pitifully thin, I thought, and pale beneath her make-up. "I'm on a diet," she had said flatly, as if to avoid comment or need of further explanation. I didn't know that the gruel contained no salt until she later confided her troubles to me privately. It was no secret that I studied black magic, and was supposed to practice it. Alice and I had known each other for several years. She had been gracious to me in London, and it was to ask my help now that she'd invited us to dinner. Later in the evening, on a corner of the terrace looking out over the Mediterranean, she began cautiously,

"Do you really believe that spells can be cast on people? I sometimes wonder, because none of the doctors can find anything the matter with me."

"You've been doing more than wondering," I said, "you're afraid of something specific, or you wouldn't be eating out of a wooden bowl with a wooden spoon. I'm going to ask you something. Was there any salt in that gruel you were eating?"

"No," she said, "it was made without salt." [1]

"You're superstitious as a savage," I said, "and a fine lot of superstitions you've collected! Salt turns into poison when you've been bewitched! You talk like a zombi. Eating from a silver spoon might kill you! You're frightened out of your wits by something."

"I'm not really superstitious," she said. "I guess the bowl and spoon must just be a sort of childish game I'm playing."

"Playing against what?" I asked, and she replied,

"There is something, but it's so idiotic and fantastic . . . so childish and at the same time so crazy . . . that I hesitate to tell you. Do you know a girl in London by the name of Annabel Swain?"

[1] See Appendix, p. 313.

"Yes," I said, "I've never seen her on the stage, but I met her at the Eiffel Tower Hotel, and have seen her around at other places, sometimes at the Fitzroy Tavern."

"Well," continued Alice, "there's a tale going around London that she's got an expensive doll . . . you know how they make dolls now, like window dummies to represent real people . . . and that it's me . . . and that she's had it dressed in a miniature replica of one of my Chanel gowns . . . the green one with gold . . . and that she calls it 'Alice' . . . and amuses herself at night by sticking pins and needles in its stomach!"

"Such things don't generally get about," I said. "Has anybody actually seen it? How did the story start?"

"In that crowd," said Alice, "everybody knows everything. They know that so-and-so smokes opium, that General Tel wears high-heeled shoes and corsets, that Miss Biggs is a mummy-worshiper, and that Arthur has a Negro prize fighter for a sweetheart. Everybody always knows everything. And if Annabel gets *her* nasty little thrill from sticking pins in a doll . . . well, it's silly and loathsome . . . but it isn't exactly anything you could have her arrested for."

"No," I said, "but how do you know the story's true?"

"She was full of champagne one night, wobbly, and when her wobbly friends saw her home, she insisted on their coming up to the apartment and watching her do it. They say she got a quite nasty little thrill out of sticking the pins in, and asking 'Alice' if 'that one hurt.' They thought it made a funny dirty story, and whispered it, of course, all over London."

"She hates you a lot, doesn't she?" I asked.

"Yes, she has hated me for years. She's a strange girl,

vicious as only women of her sort can be, but I suppose I'd better admit that she has her own special reasons for hating me."

That part, I thought, was none of my business. The word "vicious" had caused my memory to click back to another story about Annabel Swain which I'd heard, and forgotten. It was one of those things like the gossip that Lord So-and-So paid little girls to torture rabbits. Only worse. It is not repeatable in print.

I said, "Lady Alice, you've been talking sensibly, almost ironically, about that wretched, silly doll. Why did you ever let it frighten you?"

"But I didn't!" she exclaimed. "I thought it was a nasty, stupid, silly thing, and almost felt sorry for her. I knew you'd think it was silly when I told you about it. I know the doll is nothing but a coincidence. What has troubled me is my own tummy. I'm sure you don't want me to bore you with all the symptoms, but whatever it is is not simple. I'm going to the best doctors and specialists, but they can't seem to do anything, and it's pulling me down. My friends say tactlessly, 'You're not looking well, dear,' or 'You ought to take a cruise,' or '. . . a long rest,' or mention casually that they know a wonderful doctor, and I'm not very happy about it."

I said, "Dear lady, you are lying to me and to yourself. You say you are not superstitious . . . yet the business of the salt, the wooden bowl and spoon; the fact that you have picked me to confide in, all prove that your pretended sense is only on the surface. You believed all sorts of things in Grimm's fairy tales when you were a little girl in the nursery, didn't you?"

"Yes," she said, "and, oh, I'm ashamed of it, but I'm afraid you are right. I'm afraid I'm still that little frightened girl in the nursery, in the dark. I asked you to come tonight because . . . because I am horribly afraid."

"You're beautiful when you're scared," I said irrelevantly. "Why don't you go to London, and let me come along? We'll find out all about that doll. We'll smash it, and smash your precious Annabel Swain too, if we have to. Let's go to the mat on it and end this horrid nonsense."

Alice Johns was something of a power in her international world. She knew a lot of the biggest people in London by their intimate, friendly nicknames, which is an entirely different thing from knowing them by their titles. Yet it had never occurred to her, apparently, to go at this business in the direct way I had suggested. I suppose it must have been because her fears, emotions, and superstitions were in one separate compartment of her mind, while the rational part of her mind still rejected the possibility that a doll could be taken seriously. But now that she faced her fears, there was no stopping her. We flew to London, and I was the one who was a little scared by the highhanded way she plunged into the job. The first thing she did was to phone a Cabinet minister—at his residence. Then she wanted me to go along with her, and help her tell him all about it. She was spoiled, as all beautiful rich women are. Apparently her idea now was to mobilize the Criminal Investigation Department and all the bobbies of the British Empire against the woman who was "trying to murder her." Well, maybe the woman was trying to murder her, but there's no statutory law against sticking pins in dolls.

I said, "Your friend will think you're crazy. You might as well call up the First Lord of the Admiralty and ask him to call out the fleet. We're going to hire some private investigators quietly to find out what we can about that doll, and I'm going to do a little investigating on the side myself, from a different angle."

I persuaded her, and we employed a firm with a former Scotland Yard inspector at the head of it. I told them we wanted to find out if, and when, and how, and for whom, a portrait doll of Lady Johns had been made within the last few months in London, an expensive doll de luxe, with Lady Johns' features and garbed in the miniature replica of a Chanel gown, which she showed them. We didn't tell them why we wanted this information, and they didn't ask. The assumption was that some patent or copyright had been violated. There are "rackets" connected with dressmaking, as with all big international business.

They asked a few questions. They asked if Lady Alice had ever had a plaster portrait cast made of her head. It was a fad some years ago; you probably remember about it; quills in the nostrils for breathing, hair covered with an oiled-silk cap, face smeared with oil, and the plaster-of-Paris mold packed over it. She never had—but there'd been several heads made by sculptors, she said, including amateur friends, and several of them were around London, one in the Renfred studios, she believed, and others owned privately.

Could they have a list? Addresses? Yes, if she could find them.

Next evening a report came by messenger from the detective agency, to say that they were making progress. One of their woman operatives had visited four studios, and in the fourth, whose owner had made a smiling, terra cotta portrait bust some years before, the operative had picked up the trail. A craftsman had come to the caretaker, at a time in February when the artist was on the Continent, and had presented a typewritten letter on Lady Johns' own stationery, apparently signed by her, instructing that a plaster cast be made. The caretaker had of course permitted it . . . had no record or memory of the man's name . . . had supposed he came from Lady Johns.

Alice had written no such letter, and we were evidently getting somewhere. She was still a sick woman, dieting, suffering frequent nausea and occasional "sharp pains." What she believed or did not believe about those "stabbing pains" as she called them, balancing her common sense against her confessed superstitious fear, is a question I am sure she could not have answered.

During the next week or so, our private detectives were tracing and eventually finding the Italian puppet-maker in Soho who had reduced the portrait replica to doll size and manufactured the actual doll. I was at work on the other angle of the case. I was determined to find out, if I could, whether this pincushion doll de luxe had merely been a perverse, vicious whim of Annabel Swain's, or whether there was something fouler behind it. I had a lot of acquaintances in the so-called "occult" underworld of London and its suburbs, which houses more strange cults, secret societies, devil's altars, professional "sorcerers" and charlatans than any other metropolitan area on earth. And I hoped to turn up the other angle in that milieu. London cults include Goat Worship, Cults of Cruelty, Tree Cults, Cults of the Horrible, Rosicrucians, Thugs, Ghost Circles, Black Brothers and Grey

Sisters, Suicide Societies and Mummy Worshipers. The late G. K. Chesterton knew and Arthur Machen knows more about these fantastic, crazy and sometimes wicked circles than they ever cared to write.[2]

These cults include also the Satanists who claim direct traditional descent from the black magic practitioners, sorcerers, and witches' covens which flourished in the Middle Ages. They still practice witchcraft, and celebrate the Black Mass. They also stage occasional theatrical travesties of it which cover its inner meaning and merely exploit the obscene for money. The Black Mass itself, when celebrated solely as a ritual, is not nearly as spectacular as certain lurid accounts of its exploited variations have led readers of witchcraft books to believe. I had seen it celebrated several times, twice in London, in Paris, in Lyons, and once within less than a mile of the Washington Arch, in New York. It has varied little in centuries, and is rather a bore unless one gets a kick out of blasphemy and the defiling of sacred objects. It has attracted, and been exploited commercially in secret, with a lot of pornographic nonsense added, by many a charlatan who is no more of a true Satanist than Bolber or the current witchcraft poison murderers in Philadelphia. It was not these fakers in whom I was interested, but certain real ones whom I knew, and who might be in London. These, in their crackbrained, twisted way, believe in their demonology, and in its infernal sanction, in the same way orthodox Christians believe in their theology, and its heavenly sanction. Their Satan is the fallen Archangel Lucifer, who has always had more power on earth than God, and their ultimate object is

[2] See Appendix, p. 316.

to restore "Him"—they spell it with a capital letter—to the throne of the universe.

Some of them are wealthy, many are otherwise "respectable" and otherwise quite sane. One I know has a degree from Oxford, and nearly all of them are profound students of the Bible, Church history, the Talmud and Kabala. Just as witchcraft is the evil, reverse image of mental therapy, so Satanism is the reverse image of religion. How literally it is a "reverse" image is a thing which should be briefly told, even at the risk of further interrupting, for a moment, the thread of my narrative.

Four essentials are, and always have been, necessary to the ritual: an apostate priest, a consecrated host, a prostitute, a virgin. The false priest is in these days generally a priest who has been unfrocked, kicked out of the Church. The consecrated wafer is obtained by a false communicant who goes to a true mass with his tongue and the mucous membranes of his mouth coated with alum.

Before an altar surmounted by a crucifix turned upside down, and on which the girl who is a virgin lies naked, the black-robed priest intones parts of the true mass *backward*, in dog Latin, substituting the word "evil" for "good" and the word "Satan" for "God." The prostitute, robed in scarlet, performs the duties of acolyte, the goblet of wine is placed between the breasts of the recumbent virgin and a part of the wine is spilled over her body. At the supreme moment, the sacrament, the consecrated wafer, which they believe has become by its previous true consecration the body of Christ, is debased instead of elevated, and subsequently defiled. Efforts were made to "convert" me at one time, which explains how I know so much about it. I have spent

84

entire nights talking and drinking Scotch with leaders of the Satanists, have had them in my studios and have been in theirs; have even helped draw the pentagrams with chalk upon the floor when they were trying, as the spiritualists try with ghosts of the departed, to evoke the materialized presence of Beelzebub or Ashtoreth. The only materialization we ever got—and which scared the wits out of all of us including the Satanist leader—was a stray cat which had wandered in from a Chelsea fire escape one night in summer.

It was this Satanist leader I thought of now. If he was still in London, he might have the information I sought. I had little difficulty in locating him, and he agreed to meet me that evening at the Fitzroy Tavern. At a table in the long alcove beyond the bar, I put it to him flatly. I said, "You know from experience of over ten years that I'm not a spy, informer, or reformer, and that I have no connection with the police. Nor am I engaged in any investigation into present activities. I want some private information about one single private individual. I want to know whether Annabel Swain is, or has ever been, a Satanist, and if so how deeply she got into it."

"Is there any police-court angle in this?" he asked. "Blackmail or anything of that sort?"

"No," I said, "and there won't be."

I had done him some favors in the old days when I was a student of diabolism, and he said,

"All right, if it's my turn to do you a favor, you'll keep my name out of it. She's in it. I've seen her in the procession of communicants, both here and in Paris."

"Has she ever been a student of the other stuff?"

"Oh!" said he, with a grunt, "so that's what she's been up to! If she's a real adept I'd be surprised to learn it. But I could find out for you . . . or perhaps you know enough already."

"Yes," I said, "I think I know enough."

And by that time we did. Worshiping the devil and sticking pins in dolls are indeed not statutory crimes, but now that we knew where we stood, Alice Johns had the necessary influence, and the necessary ruthlessness, to put the screws to her enemy. She was literal-minded.

"You tell me that if I hadn't been superstitious, I might never have been ill," she said, "but superstition or no superstition, I'm going to have that doll and Annabel Swain's hide!"

She knew an excellent angle from which Annabel Swain could be attacked, and though it came close to being the equivalent of "framing her," we didn't have the slightest qualms of conscience in doing it. The actress was known to be what's called in that decadent set, as it's called too now I believe in Hollywood, a "druggist." She wasn't a dope victim or dope maniac, and might never be, but she was on and off cocaine and heroin, consequently had to buy it from peddlers who could be located if necessary and made or bribed to talk. She must have small supplies of it from time to time, in her apartment, and if there didn't happen to be any there just now, it could be "planted." Not a very savory business, but the whole thing was unsavory. And when a couple of beautiful women in that ruthless group are deadly enemies, out for each other's scalps, it's been my lifelong observation that they willingly use weapons which would make an honest gunman blush.

Three nights following, around one o'clock in the morning, a licensed detective named Yarborough, accompanied by two gentlemen with badges who *said* they were members of the narcotic squad, returned from Annabel Swain's apartment with the doll, and with a brief scrawled note on violet paper, which said,

Darling, it was only a bad joke, of course, and I'm terribly sorry you took it seriously. But you never had a sense of humor! Am sailing for New York tomorrow and if I never see you again, I hope you choke.

With all my love,

A.

"It was a very bad joke indeed," I said. "She was merely trying to kill you, and since you seem to have been almost as superstitious as she was, she might have succeeded."

The doll was a lovely object to have been put to so foul a use. It was a perfect little masterpiece of boudoir art, and its startling, perfect likeness made me shiver a little. It was Alice Johns in miniature. She was emotionally affected too. She was dubious at first about touching it, then burst into hysterical laughter, clasped it to her breast, began hugging it and kissing it and comforting it.

"Are you going to burn it?" I asked. "That's usually the classic procedure. We could have a little ceremony, and if it amused you, I could recite the old formula of purification."

"I am not!" she retorted with a laugh that was still hysterical, but had relief and a spark almost of gaiety in it too. "I'm going to keep it and feed it gruel without salt . . . from a lovely wooden spoon!"

The memory of the agonies she had gone through sobered her, and she said presently, "If she hated me that much and really wanted to see me dead, why didn't she have me poisoned and be done with it?"

I said, "She did. Haven't you realized yet that you were poisoned? They hang people for poisoning your body, but no law can touch them when they inject the poison in your mind."

VIII. Nail-Studded Doll in Toulon

TO poison the mind of an individual *against some other individual* is an easy, all-too-common practice—so common that the phrase describing it is familiar in all languages. "His mind was poisoned against her." Thus friendships, loves, and family ties are broken. Thus Othello, his mind poisoned by Iago, murders Desdemona.

Poisoning group minds against other groups is an equally familiar phenomenon. Common metaphors frequently conceal deep metaphysical truths. The term "spellbinder"—originally applied only to the actual witch or sorcerer—has become a common appellation for the rabble-rousing orator. Baboon talk, direct in its appeal to the emotions, short-circuiting the mind and substituting "feeling" for "thinking," sets nations at each other's throats. Adolf Hitler is a bloodier witch and weaver of evil incantations than the foulest witch in any German fairy tale. The poisoning of minds *against somebody or something else is so familiar* that no more need be said about it.

But the art of poisoning an individual's mind in a way that will cause the poison to *eat inward* is a more obscure phenomenon. The witch—whether male or female, for the word properly is sexless—has had a monopoly on its technique from time immemorial.

By consorting with witches in primitive jungles, and in "jungles" even more sinister existing under cover in most civilized cities and countrysides, I have learned most of their secrets.

I have always been afraid of using what I know—whether to help a friend or hurt an enemy. Only once have I ever employed it as a lethal weapon, and fortunately for such conscience as I may possess, the thing stopped short of actual killing, though it came close to it.

One day after I had come back for a third time from Africa, and when Marjorie and I were living in the Villa des Roseaux, near Toulon, a distinguished ecclesiastic whom we were proud to call our friend brought a new acquaintance to visit us. My friendship with Monseigneur Delatour, extending over years in Paris, on the Riviera, in Algiers, and in Rome, had become so intimate that we called him affectionately by his first name, Rafael, and once, for some house guests who had come down for Christmas, he had celebrated the Midnight Mass on Christmas Eve in the little chapel of our villa. Afterward, in the old tradition, he had laid aside his vestments to go into the kitchens and superintend the basting of the wild boar on which we banqueted.

Because of that friendship, we were cordial now toward the newcomer, a certain "Abbé Penhoël," whom he brought to lunch one day in April. Our Monseigneur explained that the Abbé, from Brittany, had been engaged for several years in experiments connected with extra-sensory perception, mental telepathy, and clairvoyance—somewhat the same sort of laboratory work, I supposed, that British and American universities are conducting. I gradually began to suspect, however, during our first luncheon conversation that our visitor was involved in other and more dubious branches of the esoteric. So that I was not surprised when Rafael confided to me in the garden later that the Abbé possessed or believed himself to possess—in some degree, a kind of supernormal power far beyond anything the universities were investigating. And Rafael had added:

"I think he does possess something extremely interesting, but I don't altogether like it. I hesitated quite a while before bringing him out here today, but I knew you were keen on that sort of thing wherever it is real, or seems to be, and he wanted to meet you."

I was interested, and liked the Abbé Penhoël well enough, so that, vacationing in Toulon, he came back to Les Roseaux often. He enjoyed swimming, canoeing, walking. I was finishing a book. His frequent presence was an agreeable diversion for Marjorie who found him interesting and liked him pretty well, too.

He and she often sat on the beach in front of our terrace, after swimming, and talked mysticism by the hour, engaged sometimes in harmless "palm-reading"—and then, for reasons which it didn't occur to me were any of my business at the time, she seemed to take a sort of dislike to him. He continued coming to the house, and it was only long afterward I learned that he had made a violent "declaration" to Marjorie. He had tried to force his attentions on her, and her refusal was probably the motive for what followed. I knew nothing of this at the time, so that we all kept seeing each other.

One afternoon—this was in late April—the Abbé Penhoël, with our Monseigneur, a couple of French authors, and a publisher, were having *apéritifs* and tea. The talk turned to work. The publisher or somebody asked Marjorie what she was working on now, and she told, with eager enthusiasm, about a novel she was planning, of how she looked forward with real pleasure to writing it; of how she meant to begin that very week, and intended to have it completed by the last of October.

They had all gone away and it was getting toward dinner-time, and I was down on the beach watching the sunset when our maid, Anna, came and said, "Monsieur, you had better come to the house. Madame Marjorie is crying."

I found her on the sofa of the funny little French parlor, off from the big living-room, seldom lighted and almost never used. She was shaking with sobs, her face buried among the pillows.

She lifted her wet face and sobbed, "Willie, I am so terribly unhappy."

I got it out of her very slowly, partly because I think she was afraid it would make me unhappy too. She said, "Do you and Rafael believe those things? Do you believe the Abbé can foresee things?"

I said:

"I don't believe it. But nobody knows for sure. That's what the psychologists and so many of the big universities would give their shirts to know. I don't mean about the Abbé Penhoël in particular, I mean about the whole thing in general."

She said, "I'm so unhappy. I'm so afraid."

I said, "Let's get this out on the carpet. What has he told you?"

Then it all came out. He'd not only been reading her palm a while back, but had made her horoscope, done a lot of monkey business with astrology, numerology, chiromancy, and the devil only knows what. He had just now told her that he was "terribly sorry," heartbroken about it, but had finally decided that it was best to tell her: *that she was going to die in October, before her book was completed.*

"He said he was sure?" I asked.

"Yes, he said he was sure. And I am so unhappy. I am so afraid."

I had trouble locating Rafael, but finally got him on the telephone at a club where he was dining in Marseilles. I said:

"I must see you immediately. You must come back out here, or I will come in to Marseilles if you prefer it. But I must see you tonight."

He said, "I have to go to Paris on the midnight train. You'd better come here."

We met at the Cintra, and I said:

"Now tell me all you know, tell me everything you know or have ever heard, about this Abbé Penhoël."

He said, "I am glad you ask me, because if I had known everything I now know, I would never have brought him to your house. He has been dabbling in magic, and if he were not a priest—I know nothing actually or officially about what he is, and it's not always easy to find out—I would call it black magic. I don't like it. What has happened?"

I said, "I thought so—and plenty has happened."

I told him what had happened, and he crossed himself. I said:

"You can't go to Paris tonight. You must find the Abbé Penhoël tonight, or tomorrow morning. You must find him immediately, and bring him to me."

He said:

"You know, the parish of St. Sulpice has its exorcist, a powerful man of God, a good, almost holy man. I know him. I can bring him down here."

I said, "No, I'll handle this myself."

This was after midnight, and it was about six o'clock the same morning that Monseigneur Delatour arrived at Les Roseaux with the Abbé Penhoël. He had routed him out of bed at the Grand Hotel in Toulon, and they had had coffee on the way. We awakened Anna and had some more coffee. Marjorie stayed upstairs in her bedroom.

I said to the Abbé Penhoël:

"Even if it is true, it seems to me it was a rather dreadful thing for you to tell her. Moral obligation is a tangled problem in such a case, but even if it is true, it seems to me that you should not have told her. If you are not absolutely certain, it was a wicked thing to tell her."

He said:

"I am terribly sorry, tragically sorry, but I am sure that it is true."

I said:

"You are absolutely sure?"

He said:

"Alas, yes."

I said:

"I beg you to go all over it in your own mind here and

now. Take all the time you want. Rafael and I will go into
the garden if you like, or you can have my study if you want,
for quiet. But I beg you to consider whether there isn't something you have overlooked, which makes it uncertain, which
makes it a possible misreading of your signs and omens, or
whatever you call them!"

He said:

"No, I struggled and suffered with it all night after I left
you. I am terribly sorry."

I kept repeating. I said:

"Are you absolutely sure that it is sure?"

He said:

"Yes, I am sure."

Then I knew what I was going to have to do. I said:

"Monsieur the Abbé, in these deep esoteric delvings of
yours, have you ever heard of fan-shaped destiny?"

He said:

"No, what is it?"

I said:

"Well, it is not in any book. I learned about it from the
black witch, Wamba, with whom I lived, on the Ivory
Coast."

He looked at me level-eyed, and repeated, "I have never
heard of it."

I got up and whistled a silly tune, *Les Gars de la Ma-
rine*, which the sailors sing when they are drunk and gay. I
lighted a cigarette and offered him one.

He was a little disturbed, but not much. I said, lightly:

"*Au revoir*, Monsieur the Abbé. It was nice of you to
have taken the trouble to come out this morning."

He got up to leave, still suave, grave, polite, impeccable,

but I knew he would ask me about the fan shapes before he went away. And he did.

I said, carelessly, "You've really never heard of them?"

He said, "No."

I said, "Well, that's just too bad for you, Monsieur the Abbé."

And he said, "Why?"

And I said, "Because Marjorie is going to be well and radiant in October—but whether *you* will be alive then is going to be extremely doubtful."

Rafael said, "What are you going to do, my son?"

I said, "I want you to keep your clean hands off it. It's a dirty business."

He said, "I still think you should let me bring the exorcist, and you know that I shall have an impersonal, unpleasant duty to perform later if this so-called Abbé has ever really been ordained, which I begin to doubt, but, in the meantime, it shall be as you wish."

"Thank you," I said. "And in answer to your question, I don't know what I'm going to do yet, because I'm not sure yet what I'm fighting. It's a dangerous thing for a clairvoyant, even though he is a man of good will and a Christian, to be playing also with black magic. It is intrinsically evil because the clairvoyant, even though he be a man of good will, is under the temptation, consciously or subconsciously, of using his magic to bring about the fulfillment of his prediction. Simply perhaps as a protection to his ego, his human vanity, his prestige. It may be that this is a case of that sort. But it may be that it's something even more wicked. It may be that our Abbé determined to bring about the death of

Marjorie because he wished her dead, and 'foresaw' her death anteriorly. If it is this latter, he deserves, of course, that I should kill him, deserves it as much as if I saw him trying to stick a knife in her. If it is the former, I would not want to have his death on my hands. I don't know yet what I am facing or what I may have to do, but I am very much afraid of this Abbé Penhoël—and being afraid of him, I'm going to attack him."

Rafael said, "It is all very dangerous."

I said, "I know it's dangerous and I'm terribly sorry, but you must keep your hands off it."

Before going to Paris, Monseigneur Delatour asked me to tell him about Wamba's fan-shaped destiny, and I did so to the best of my ability. Wamba believed and taught me that all possible future events exist already in time and space. This sounds like pure fatalism, but it is not. For she believed also that the future, if foreseen, might be to some degree controlled. And the real purpose of fetish consultation and divination is to decipher and control the future. Those of us whites who are fatalists at all usually believe in a predestination, providence, or kismet which cannot be changed, from which there is no escape. What is going to be, will be. But Wamba believed differently. She believed that fate, though written, projects itself into the future not as a straight line, but fan-shaped, in myriad alternate paths, multiplying to infinity. She had conveyed to me this difficult concept of fan-shaped destiny by an ingenious analogy: I am walking in an unknown forest. There are as many directions to walk as there are points of the compass. I know nothing of what awaits me in any direction, but in all directions *fate* awaits me, things already written in the sense that they embryonically exist already, and are there *inevitable*, but *alternate*, depending on the path I take. In one path there is a tree from which I will pluck refreshing fruit. In another, a panther waits to leap upon me, which, if taking a side path, I shall kill instead of becoming its predestined victim. Beside another path, there is a good spring of water. In another direction, there is an elephant trap into which I will fall and be impaled on the stakes. In still another, a friendly camp where I will be well treated. And all these things are written fan-shaped in the future. Wamba taught me—as is so often the case in the deeper "jungle" of all human life—that no process of logic or reason can disclose whether it is better to turn right or left. And since we are continually moving in some path or other from the womb to the grave, since even stopping to stand still is also a form of moving, no tiniest choice in the most trivial matter, no event, itself however trivial, is without its potentiality to change one's future life. Therefore the Negro primitive consults the fetish; therefore he devises charms and grigris to protect him in the labyrinth. If we have no faith in his methods, we can at least begin to understand why he deems it necessary to try something. We whites often recognize, and sometimes with a shock, that despite all our processes of logical foresight, we also walk in this blind labyrinth, not knowing where any path will lead. The gate clangs shut and you miss your train by a split second because you fumbled for pennies when you bought a morning newspaper; and next day, in another paper, you read of the wreck, with a list of the dead . . . a list that would have contained your name inevitably. Usually the drama is less sudden, less spectacular, less final, but seemingly pointless hazards or decisions change all our lives.

"Come over and make a fourth at bridge this evening?"
"Sorry, I've got some work I ought to do." You are hesitating, and your friend has almost hung up the telephone. Just before it clicks, you say, "Oh, well, I'll come over anyway." During the evening a girl drops in whom you have never seen, nor heard of, and six months later you marry her. Tomorrow, for all I know, I may go to the corner for a pack of cigarettes, and be run over by a truck—or start another sequence that will make me five years hence a millionaire, or put me in the gutter. Now the basic difference between Wamba's mind and mine, or yours, is that while we regard all such blind sequences as unpredictable and therefore uncontrollable, she believes they form a mysterious pattern which can be to some degree deciphered, and hence controlled. This, I think, is one of the fundamental elements of black primitive psychology and sorcery. In the fan-shaped labyrinth of life where neither logic nor consciously directed will seems adequate, the savage seeks for supernatural guidance in his fetishes, as the Christian seeks it on his knees in prayer.

Rafael was actually on his knees before he said good-by to us, and unless you choose to call his prayers an interference, he kept his hands off everything until the finish, except that on his advice I had Marjorie gone over by a couple of the best doctors in Marseilles. He wasn't wanting me to have a possible murder on my conscience if it turned out that the Abbé had really been clairvoyant, had really sensed intuitively that the Angel of Death, through no human wish or guilty volition of his own, was actually at the threshold of Marjorie's door, already tapping, if ever so gently.

But the doctors said, "Organically and functionally, she's

sound as a bell. Her normal life expectation is fifty years
. . . a half a century . . . anything you choose to guess.
Has she been sick? She seems nervous. What's all this about,
anyway?"

I said, "Oh, nothing. She just got nervous about something."

As a matter of fact, she was terribly frightened, already
depressed, acutely conscious of all her physiological processes,
and imagining all sorts of things. That's the way it always
begins. If you become acutely *conscious* of your visceral organs and functions, heart, kidneys, respiration, no matter
how sound they are, they'll soon begin to bother you. Add
ordinary fear, and you'll be ill. Add superstitious terror, and
you'll crack up completely.

In the practice of witchcraft and black magic, one can have
"bad breaks," and "lucky breaks," just as in anything else.
I hadn't decided exactly yet on my whole plan of action, but
almost immediately, before three days had passed, Basil Orlet
came tearing down from Paris in his little Bugatti, to see me.
Something had happened which was good fortune for me,
and the reverse for the Abbé Penhoël. The Abbé had confided what he was justified in calling my "threat on his life"
to my friend Orlet. It was natural that he had done so, since
he knew nothing of our close friendship. Orlet was reputed
to know more about black magic and white magic, their history, technique, mechanics, limitations, than any other man
in Europe. A hard-boiled, brilliant, and successful journalist,
this had been his lifelong hobby, as some people go in for
Sanskrit or porcelain . . . except that he was more than a
dilettante. Back in 1927, dabbling in the black side of it, he
had got mixed up with one of the Satanist groups down in

Lyons, which had later wanted to use him for some purposes of their own that were definitely criminal. They had refused to release him, and when he defied them, had made the threat that they would destroy his little daughter. Orlet, devoid of superstition and knowing that magic has nothing supernatural in it, nevertheless highhandedly employed their own technique against them . . . in reverse . . . and beat them with it! It was as beautiful as a Christmas festival in the Orlet apartment on the Champs Elysées, and the little daughter thought it was a lovely new game her papa had invented to amuse her. On the face of her nursery door there hung a great Crusader's sword, reversed so that it formed the Holy Cross, and around its keyhole and hinges were festooned sprigs of laurel. On the windows and in the chimney were other herbs and symbols, some of them Christian white magic, some pagan, from the ancient, elder formulas. And around the whole nursery area, running through, in, and out of the other apartments, was laid down in white enamel instead of chalk the sacred pentagram. In addition to this, the child and the Breton nurse wore necklaces beneath their garments on which were tiny sacred medallions, and other amulets, ancient before Christ ever cast out demons by the shores of Galilee—so that they went regularly outdoors to walk in the park as usual. On top of this he sent messengers down to Lyons to tell them all about it, adding that if they didn't instantly lay off, he would cease merely defending—and destroy them utterly!

"It was nonsense," had said Orlet, with savage cynicism, "but it was the right nonsense. If you engage in that sort of 'nonsense' you must go the whole hog, and leave no loopholes. They didn't dare to strike back . . . then or ever."

They were afraid of him and "it" because none of it was "nonsense" to the Diabolists, who are as sincere fanatical believers as any other superstitious sect, or any jungle savage. They didn't dare touch the child any more than you would have dared to touch a hooded cobra.

The lucky break I now had was that Orlet knew what I had learned and done down on the Ivory Coast, and being my devoted friend, and no friend of the Abbé's, and sensing that there was a war between us, had had no mercy and no scruples. He had said:

"Good god, man, I don't know what you've done, whether you were sincere, or right, or not, or where justice lies, but I'm sorry for you, and I don't know what to advise you. I had rather you didn't tell me anything more about it."

The Abbé had asked, "Why?" and Orlet had said:

"Because I think you are probably going to die in the month of October. You might as well have stirred up all the black witch-doctors of the West Coast, and if you've ever been down there, you know what that means! That American, crude as he is, has learned more than a white man ever ought to learn. I'm afraid he's going to kill you—and don't misunderstand me. He won't do it by any method the police could stop!"

"Do you believe those things, Monsieur Orlet?" the Abbé had asked.

And Orlet had said:

"I don't believe them, I know them. Just the same, unless I misread your nature and psychology, there's one piece of advice I can give you. Unless *you* know more about them than I think you do, your only possible protection hangs right there around your own neck—your crucifix."

And then, Orlet told me, the Abbé Penhoël had admitted, in a moment of panic:

"Alas, Monsieur, *I cannot use that.*"

And that was really what Orlet had come down to tell me. Also, he had come to help me. We knew what we had to do—and ruthlessly set about doing it. I knew, of course, as Orlet had known about the swords and laurel, that some of the things we did were in a manner of speaking "nonsense," but also knew that they would not be nonsense to the Abbé Penhoël. Orlet—who was stronger, more self-confident, and a better man than I am—had been content to defend. I was afraid, and was attacking.

I bought an ugly little doll, and dressed it as a little false priest in black robes, with a little crucifix reversed dangling from its neck, with a tiny little symbol of a toad. I drove some brass-headed tacks into the region of its kidneys, and a couple more into its little belly. Then I photographed it, made one print, destroyed the negative, and had the print mailed to the Abbé Penhoël—from a house of prostitution in Marseilles. What I did with the doll afterward, and for a number of successive weeks, involves a seeming contradiction to my major thesis and belief that the ugly little doll intrinsically is utterly harmless; that it couldn't harm the Abbé Penhoël except through his direct knowledge and desperate fear of it; that the sole power of witchcraft lies in the open field of suggestion; and that the suggestion can be implanted and intensified *only* through the channels of the normal, ordinary, direct senses. I found myself now, inconsistently . . . like any thirteenth-century coven witch . . . like Wamba in the jungle . . . weaving the old nursery-rhymed hatred "incantations" around that ugly, silly, inanimate little doll. I spent a lot of concentrated time and effort—which takes the juice out of the man who's doing it—*wishing* and *willing* the Abbé Penhoël to suffer and waste away.

How can I explain or justify that inconsistency? How afterward continue the assertion of my reasoned belief that there is absolutely nothing even supernormal—much less supernatural—in the power of witchcraft?

I can only answer as Chesterton did when asked if he believed in ghosts. "Absolutely not," he replied sincerely, and added with rare candor, "but I'm afraid of them!" Well, I was afraid—afraid I might be wrong. I was sure there was nothing supernatural in the hocus-pocus—but afraid I might be wrong in denying any power to the supernormal. If Professor Rhine and his colleagues are on the right track—if extra-sensory emanations, telepathy, clairvoyance, etc., are authentic phenomena, if ordinary playing cards or cards marked with circles, stars, and wave lines, can "send out" any emanations whatsoever that can be "picked up" in any manner whatsoever, other than through direct impact on one of the five normal senses—then a witch's doll can send out extra-sensory emanations too! If Upton Sinclair can focus on the penciled drawing of a cat or kitchen fork and reach his wife by telepathy across an ordinary room, it is possible the witch can focus on the doll and reach his enemy with concentrated, poisoned thoughts and images, with evil and destructive images, across Africa, or France. I intend to give my full reasons later for doubting that anything of the sort has ever been conclusively proved, but it remains the final open question—the last veil of mystery after the veil of superstition has been torn away. And in this ugly combat, with Marjorie's life at stake, I wasn't taking any chances.

I spent all the emotional force I had, with the doll as my unholy symbol—precisely as believers in the pure white magic of religion spend hours before their images which are sometimes "dolls" too, but clean and sacred, bathed in the pure light of faith and love. I was saturating mine with darkness and evil, if I could.

I cannot know, and indeed must doubt, that I succeeded in projecting any psychic "poison," any extra-sensory aura of evil and destruction which could cause my enemy to feel it through any mysterious channels of the supernormal. Indeed, I had seen to it—by devious but normal means, with the indirect help of Basil Orlet, that the Abbé, who *believed* implicitly in all of it, believed in a way that neither I nor most of my readers can, was kept fully informed, and progressively informed, of everything I was doing to "him" in that doll-effigy.

In August a letter came by registered mail from the Abbé Penhoël, saying that he was dreadfully sorry, wanted humbly to ask forgiveness for the terrible mistake he had made and to reassure Marjorie; that there was something he had misread, wrongly read, about Marjorie's predestined life-cycle; that he now *knew* he was wrong, and would never forgive himself—though he prayed that we would—for having needlessly frightened us. He was begging me to cease. But this was only August. October was still two months away. The end of October was three months away. And I was afraid to answer him.

In September he was in a hospital in Paris, and the doctors thought they knew what was the matter with him. He was suffering excruciating pain *in the region of the kidneys,* and they were thinking of operating. I repeat, that I am devoid of superstition, and I guess I was devoid of pity too. I was elated, and it seemed to me that Marjorie who had lost weight, lost her healthy glow, and been a sort of *malade imaginaire* all summer, was picking up and beginning to be herself again. I wanted no needless homicide on my conscience, but I didn't know what to do. Marjorie was no longer deeply unhappy or in terror, but she was still unconsciously, if not outspokenly, afraid of the month of October.

In his extremity, as I learned finally, the Abbé had sent for Monseigneur Delatour to confess that he'd been guilty of commerce with things that were anathema, to beg Rafael's intervention in the saving of his life and his soul, which he was now convinced were both in mortal danger. Rafael came south to talk with me, and the talk was very solemn. He said:

"The wretched man is penitent and sick to death. There are two sides of this both of which concern me deeply, and which I must try to explain to you. Not even witchcraft and not even murder . . . if he had caused Marjorie's death . . . is the sin against the Holy Ghost. The infamous dabbler in magic, Gilles de Retz, once Joan of Arc's field marshal, who was guilty of a series of atrocious murders, made a full formal confession, was granted the last rites of the Church on the eve of his execution, and masses were said for him after his death. You may not believe in the immortal soul, but I do believe in it, and I want to tell you solemnly that you may not only have his physical death on your conscience as truly as if you had shot him, but may be the instrument of his soul's damnation. He has already taken his demission, of course, is no longer a priest, if he ever was a true one, expresses an abject repentance; and, if he has time on earth to prove his sincerity, may yet be saved from an eternity in hell."

I said, "Whether I believe literally in those things or not is beside the question, isn't it? You believe in them, and I suppose the Abbé, believing in Satanic supernatural forces which transcend reason, must believe in the other face of that coin too. If that is so, his demission and confession must have already eased him a little?"

"That is true," replied Rafael. "Long before the doctors ever learned it, we men of God have known that an in-flamed conscience can often have as fatal consequences as an inflamed appendix. But mind you, he is also suffering from a deadly horror-fear of you and your machinations. . . ."

"All right," I said, "you can go back and tell Penhoël that I've laid off it. You can assure him that I've 'cleansed it' . . . he'll know what that means . . . and that I'm will-ing to wash it up forever. But you must add, and I mean it, that unless Marjorie is blooming and in perfect health on midnight of the last day of October, I'll see to it that he dies writhing in agony!"

October came and passed, Marjorie was radiant, and the former Abbé was still alive, recovering. I was the one who was sick. It is always like that. What I had been doing always injures one, weakens one, debilitates and wears one out, in-evitably. Discard and forget, I beg you, the demons, dolls, and mumbo jumbo. What you are actually doing is tearing out your own emotional guts at the same time you're trying to tear someone else's emotional guts to pieces. I have paid a heavy price for learning these things. And I shall never practice that sort of magic again, whether for good or evil.

Despite these overtones, I believe that a true way of recounting this entire story would be to say simply that the Abbé Penhoël sought to bring about Marjorie's death by arousing her fears through the piled-up forces of suggestion, and that I saved her solely and simply by tossing the ball back to him.

Part Two

THE VAMPIRE AND WEREWOLF

I. Concerning Vampires and Werewolves
in General

THEY are harder to collect than dolls. Like the ground hog, they emerge infrequently. Like the hedgehog, they discourage familiarity. One doesn't intimately encounter vampires and werewolves at every hex-infested crossroads or find one hidden in every witch's cellar. Though a considerable part of my life has been spent following twisted roads and descending into darkened cellars, I have met only one vampire, one panther man, and two werewolves. Those encounters, however, were more than sufficient to confirm my worst beliefs about them. Here again are phenomena—never supernatural—but just as dangerous and deadly as the doll.

In fiction, the vampire is nearly always a gaunt, sinister ghost-man, cousin to Bram Stoker's Dracula; or a supernaturally pale but lovely woman with green eyes and red hair, cousin to Hanns Heinz Ewers' Alraune and Balzac's Succubus, who pierces tiny, neat holes in the victim's throat and drinks the blood.

In classical and pagan superstition, in medieval church lore, in the thundering anathemas of Krämer and Sprenger for the Holy Inquisition, in *Malleus Maleficarum* ("Hammer Against Witches"), in the Bull of Pope Pius VIII—and still today to the Reverend Montague Summers—the vampire is a dead man or dead woman who breaks out of the coffin, as did the Algerian monk from his cell in the scandalous limerick, goes about neatly puncturing plump victims' throats, and returns to the grave feeling better—as full of fresh new blood as a Jersey mosquito. But, being already dead as it were, the vampire is not nearly so easy to kill as the mosquito. You must dig it up, exorcise it, sprinkle holy water over it, and bury it again at a crossroads with a wooden stake driven through its heart.

In fact—that is, in fact as opposed to fiction, hocus-pocus, ecclesiastic tommyrot, and superstition—the vampire is a diseased and sometimes hallucinated human being, psychotic rather than criminal, with a pathological taste for human blood—but not necessarily a taste for murder. Vampires usually belong in Bloomingdale or Matteawan, but seldom in the electric chair. Vampires generally do not raven or rip, but prefer to feed daintily on blood, as does the hummingbird on nectar from a flower. If the victims die, as did those of the lovely Countess Elizabeth Bathory, it is just too bad—but murder is never the vampire's objective, any more than it's the objective of the hummingbird to kill the hollyhock.

Now the werewolf is a somewhat different animal. In fiction and superstition it runs a pretty close four-footed parallel to the vampire—except that instead of merely sipping blood like cider through a straw, it ravens, kills, and devours the flesh of its victims. To Krämer, and to Reginald Scot who wrote the classic *Discoverie of Witchcraft* for King James I, Royal Inquisitor of Scotland—and to dear old Dr. Baring-Gould who more recently wrote "Onward, Christian Soldiers," as well as to our Reverend Montague Summers in this Year of Our Lord 1940—the werewolf is a human being supernaturally transformed into a beast, and capable of changing back and forth, from two-legged to four-legged, at will, with the help, of course, of the devil.

Now the werewolf in actual, bloody fact—and here we're getting somewhere—always turns out to be two-legged, unfurry, and unsnouted, no matter how gory its human jaws may be. The werewolf is a pathological case, a hallucinated human being, like the vampire, but too savage to be caged in Bloomingdale or any sanitarium. He'd better be shot down like Pretty Boy Floyd and Dillinger, and often is, but if he's captured alive the only safe place to put him is in the strongest cell at Matteawan, or in the electric chair, if the jury is unsympathetic toward "criminal insanity."

Explosion of the two superstitions that the vampire is an unlaid corpse and the werewolf a man changed supernaturally into a snouted beast never brought back any mangled victims or mitigated the grief of their families. Yet we have over and over again in scores of books written by supposedly sensible commentators and historians, the same silly non sequitur which has made of most modern books denouncing the old superstitions of witchcraft arrant trash. Because the vampire and werewolf are not supernatural creatures, if you please, they consequently don't exist at all!

Pages of substantiated history, both lay and medical, reliable encyclopedias including the *Britannica*, and the verified reports of reputable news agencies including the Associated Press contain hundreds of cases which corroborate my rational thesis that vampires and werewolves, i.e., diseased, hallucinated humans with a lust for blood or human flesh, exist and always have existed, and frequently *themselves believe* that witchcraft and the devil are mixed up in it.

I have no intention of cluttering this book with interminable warmed-over cases. Instead I'm going to get on with it, first giving you, as a preliminary to my own encounters with these phenomena, one full-length portrait from the past. The lady deserves to be included despite the fact she died long ago. She is par excellence the world champion lady vampire of all time. Her score was 80—and she fits into my thesis for the additional reason that she practiced witchcraft and black magic all her life.

II. World Champion Lady Vampire
of All Time

CLEOPATRA, Greek queen of Egypt, bathed in the milk of wild asses. Pope Sixtus V, on advice of his physicians, bathed in the blood of oxen. Anna Held, French wife of Flo Ziegfeld, bathed in Grade A milk from contented cows. Earl Carroll's girl bathed in a tub of champagne—and police promptly raided the party.

The spoiled and beautiful Countess Elizabeth Bathory bathed habitually in the blood of young maidens. The then more tolerant police finally got around to raiding her party, too, but only after she had "milked" of their life's blood somewhere between 80 and 300 serving damsels.

She had begun, apparently, by merely drinking human blood, as is the custom of the more dainty vampires—and as Earl Carroll's girl doubtless did with the champagne—but presently she was using it for beauty baths as well, and eventually she became the messiest lady vampire in all history.

She also practiced magic and was a witch. Though mistress of vast estates, chatelaine of Csejthe, kin to kings and cardinals, cousin to Count Gyorgy Thurzo, then prime minister of Hungary, and destined to become family namesake in reverse of the luxurious ocean liner Bathori which plies, or rather did ply, between Hoboken and Danzig, she trusted most in her own witchcraft . . . and depended on her coven and familiars, rather than her family power and wealth, to protect her from arrest.

Most of all, she depended on a certain incantation, written on parchment, kept continually on her person. By one of those curious coincidences which foster the survival of superstition, this parchment was lost or stolen on the day before she was arrested. It has never been found, but it's easy to guess what was in it. For on discovering its loss, she hurried to the forest, gathered the witches of her coven, waited until night when clouds and stars were in the sky, and returned to the château with a new incantation, similarly inscribed on parchment, and which is a matter of court record:

Isten, help me! *Isten*, help me! You little cloud, help me too! Give health, protection, and long life to Elizabeth. You little cloud, when I am in danger, send ninety-nine cats! I order you to do so because you are supreme commander of the cats. Give orders to the cats. Tell the cats to gather from wherever they be, on mountains, water, rivers, seas. Order ninety-nine cats to come with speed and bite the heart of King Matthias. Order them to bite the heart of Moses Cziraky, and to bite also the heart of my cousin the prime minister. Command them to claw and bite the heart of Red Megyeri. And keep Elizabeth safe from harm.[1]

It's pretty good as incantations go, and if the government officials had been sufficiently superstitious, they might never have dared touch her. A guess is that the police may have stolen and burned the original incantation, and didn't know this duplicate had been concocted. At any rate, the new one

---

[1] The names are those of the government and police officials whom she feared.

didn't work. On New Year's Eve, 1610, the Castle of Csejthe was raided, the New Year's Eve party interrupted, and the countess put under arrest.

The army of cats failed to arrive in force, but by another queer coincidence, the village priest who had denounced her and who came with the police was attacked, severely scratched, and bitten by a corporal's guard of cats, as he mounted the interior staircase. Six "enchanted cats," accompanied by a flurry of "enchanted mice," which also tried to bite him, were chased all over the castle and finally disappeared into "thin air."

My own four cats here in Dutchess County, 1940, have a way of disappearing magically just after they've clawed the dog, stolen the meat, or knocked over the vase of flowers; so that the village priest in Niyatra County, 1610, who was a reputable if credulous old gentleman, may easily be forgiven for believing the countess's cats were phantoms. And for adding the enchanted mice!

These cats and mice, by the way, have been hiding for three centuries in a gold mine whose vein I discovered in the New York Public Library, with the help of Hungarian translators.[2] Neither English, French, German, Italian, nor any

---

[2] Dezsö Rexa, *Báthory Erzsébet, Nádasdy Lerencné*. Based on the old court records. Published in Budapest by the Gyula Benko Royal Bookshop, 1908, in Hungarian, and never translated into any other language. A seventeenth-century Hungarian Jesuit Priest, Father Turoczi, did a learned speculative monograph on the psychotic—and to him perhaps diabolic—nature of her vampirism and blood bathing. A German psychiatrist, R. A. von Elsberg, published with S. Schottlaender, in Breslau, 1904, a volume entitled *Elisabeth Báthory (Die Blutgräfin)*; *Ein Sitten- und Charakterbild; mit einem Titelbilde*. He apparently had no access, as Dezsö did, to the original documents. All he does is to rehash the facts recorded by Dezsö and the Jesuit, and then base his psychiatric opinions on them. Apart from a few romances and a couple of plays, superstition stuff and

of the more generally known and more easily translatable languages, have ever given much space to the Countess Bathory. The encyclopedias, including the *Grand Larousse*, give only this brief mention:

Elizabeth Bathory, wife of Count Nadasdy Bathori, slew 80 peasants in her château in Csejthe, Nyitra County, Hungary, to bathe in their blood. Surprised in the act (1610), she was condemned to life imprisonment.

The untranslated material, including the biography by Dezsö, is authoritative, scholarly, and rich. The Countess Bathory [3] was born in 1560 on one of the vast Bathory family estates, on the edge of the Carpathians. The family was for centuries one of the wealthiest and most outstanding in central Europe. One of her relatives was a cardinal, another was Prince of Transylvania, and one became king of Poland. It included also bishops, sheriffs, governors of provinces, judges. They had always been a hard and cruel, if able, family, and by the time Elizabeth was born, were a decadent and degenerate, though still powerful, side branch of royalty. A favorite aunt of hers was a notorious lesbian. An uncle was a diabolist and practiced witchcraft. Her brother, oversexed, was a satyr. Elizabeth was betrothed as a child to Count Ferencz Nadasdy, a great soldier, who became afterward the famous "Black Hero" of Hungary. They were married on May 8, 1575. She was fifteen and he was twenty-one. The Emperor Maximilian of Hapsburg attended the wed-

horror stuff, all in the untranslated Hungarian, there is nothing more. The only basic, correlated source material is contained in the old court documents, the volume by Dezsö, and the monograph by Father Turoczi.

[3] Twice a countess since she was born one and afterward married Count Ferencz Nadasdy—she was apparently a Lucy Stoner, for she survives in history not as a Nadasdy, but under her own family name.

ding. King Matthias of Hungary and the Archduke of Austria sent wedding presents. They went to live in the castle of Csejthe, in the hill country of northwestern Hungary, still famous today for its vineyards, red wine, ghosts, and werewolves. The superb ruins of the castle are still standing, and there are steel engravings which show it in its heyday. It was like one of the dream castles drawn by Howard Pyle or Maxfield Parrish. It was like an inland Mont St. Michel. Vast walls on a hillside, above a village, dungeons, caves, cellars, surmounted by turrets and spires.

Count Nadasdy was soon off to the wars, and presently the countess eloped with a pale young nobleman who was said to be a vampire. It seems he was a vampire who in this case had bitten off more than he could chew, because presently the girlish countess returned, licking her chops, while the young nobleman was never afterward heard of. She was forgiven by her hero-husband, who returned occasionally to sleep with her, but for the first ten years of their marriage they had no children.

The one touch of normalcy in this dangerous young lady was that she detested her mother-in-law, who had come to live in the castle. She preferred to associate with her serving maids and occasionally amused herself by torturing them, aided by an old nurse named Ilona Joo, who was, like herself, immersed in witchcraft. Count Nadasdy was a bit of a savage himself, a leader of mercenary troops, and apparently had no objections to his wife's torturing her little playmates, to while away the long winter evenings in the lonely castle. He doubtless reasoned that it would keep her out of other mischief . . . such as eloping with visiting vampires.

Count Nadasdy seems to have been aware also that his

young wife was a witch. She bore him no babies in the early years, and he encouraged her in the concoction of charms to induce pregnancy. These were successful, and they later had four children. That he knew she was engaged in blacker magic is evidenced by one of her letters to him in which she wrote:

. . . Thorko has taught me a lovely new one. Catch a black hen and beat it to death with a white cane. Keep the blood and smear a little of it on your enemy. If you get no chance to smear it on his body, obtain one of his garments and smear it.

Little black hens, however, were mere caviar to the voracious countess. For several years prior to her husband's death she had been vampire bleeding and murdering peasant girls. The count and countess remained on as excellent connubial terms as any two loving Gila monsters, and probably understood each other perfectly. A couple of years before he died, she wrote him this touching, domestic, dutiful letter:

My dear Husband,
    I am writing, as you asked me to do, about our children. Little Anna is healthy, thank goodness, little Orsik is well except for his sore eyes, and Kato is cutting her new teeth. Thank goodness I am in good health, except for occasional headaches, and I pray that you are in good health too, my beloved husband.
                                        Your obedient wife,
                                            Elizabeth.

In 1600 her husband died, at the age of forty-seven. He was in the prime of life. It is too late to wonder whether she'd perhaps smeared one of *his* shirts with the blood of a little black hen. There was no inquest. The mother-in-law was sent packing, of course, on the day after the funeral, and from then on, for ten whole years, the Countess Elizabeth was free to indulge her fancies. She was at that time approaching forty, and was still extremely handsome. There's an excellent oil painting, three-quarters length, which shows her, in the style of Holbein, in an immense starched ruff, jeweled stomacher, pannier skirts of Burgundy velvet with an apron and puffed sleeves of sheer, white lawn. Her hair, elaborately coiffed, drawn back from her broad forehead, is meshed in a jeweled snood, above big, dark, wide-set eyes which are heavy-lidded, hard, and cruel. The nose is classic Greek; the chin is a bit heavy, the mouth curved, dimpling, and sensual, like that of the Mona Lisa.

Among her retainers and subsequent companions in crime, in addition to her old nurse, the witch Ilona Joo, there was a sort of major-domo by the name of Johannes Ujvary; another manservant named Thorko who practiced sorcery; a second witch named Dorottya Szentes; a forest witch named Darvula. Accomplices among the permanent serving maids were the Demoiselles Barsovny and Otvos.

It was a diabolic household with expert devil's disciples as its minions. The countess, entouraged by them, never lacked for diabolic advice and suggestions when her own imagination flagged, but the inception of the blood baths ran parallel with the case of the little girl who was mentioned some years ago in the *New Yorker*. The child had a tantrum in which she screeched, wept, tore her copybook to tatters, stamped on the floor, paused out of breath, and then spat like a cat or a sailor. Her kindly, Christian mother said, "The Devil gets into little girls sometimes. The Devil put you up to that. The next time you feel a fit of temper coming on, be a brave little girl and say, 'Get thee behind me, Satan.'" The little girl reflected, and replied, "The Devil may have made me tear the book, stamp my feet, and scream—but the spitting was my own idea."

Blood baths were the countess's own idea. I doubt she'd ever heard of Pope Sixtus V or Cesare Borgia, either. The idea came to her as the result of an accident, which occurred one day while she was having an elaborate hair-do. She was vain, sensual, narcissistic, probably lesbian, also took pleasure in the embraces of the black-bearded husband when he returned between battles—and consequently spent a lot of time having herself beautified. Since Helena Rubinstein and beauty parlors hadn't yet been invented, her own maids worked overtime at it in the boudoir. On this particular morning, a maid pulled her hair with a comb, and the countess slapped her in the face so hard that the maid's nose bled. Blood spilled on the countess's hands, and it seemed to her that where the blood had fallen, the skin became more smooth, more youthful, and more beautiful. So she began bathing in human blood to keep her youth and beauty.[4]

For the next ten years the castle of Csejthe was an abattoir and human "dairy" in which she kept scores of peasant girls chained in the dungeons and cellars, like cattle, to be "milked" of their blood until they died. Whisperings and even direct accusations had been rife in the countryside, but the victims had all been peasants, serfs, and it was less strange than it may now seem that the authorities were so long a time in taking action.

[4] In those days, blood baths, though never before involving human blood, had a double phony sanction of magical buncombe plus medical buncombe. Cesare Borgia bathed in ox's blood, on the recommendation of his doctors, as a cure for pimples, and Pope Sixtus V took similar treatments as a tonic.

On New Year's Eve, the night of December 30, 1610, Count Gyorgy Thurzo, her own cousin, the governor of the province, accompanied by soldiers, gendarmes, and the village priest, raided the castle and arrested everybody in it. They had interrupted an orgy of blood. In the main hall of the castle, they found one girl drained of blood and dead, another living girl whose body had been pierced with tiny holes, another who had just been tortured. In the dungeons and cellars they found and liberated "a number" of other girls, some of whose bodies had already been pierced and "milked," others intact, plump, well fed, like well-kept cattle in their stalls. The dead bodies of some fifty more were subsequently exhumed.

The countess, being a noblewoman related to royalty, was kept prisoner there in her own castle, while the other members of the household were taken to the jail at Bitcse. They included the major-domo, Johannes Ujvary; the sorcerer, Thorko; the old witch-nurse Ilona Joo; the witch Dorottya Szentes; the forest witch Darvula; several maids who were accomplices; and a couple of manservants.

The trial took place at Bitcse, in January and February 1611. Theodosius Syrmiensis de Szulo, judge of the Royal Supreme Court, presided, with twenty associate judges assisting. The Countess Bathory was included in the indictment and evidence was taken against her, but she was never present in the courtroom. She had been caught red-handed, refused to plead, and was permitted to remain during the whole time a prisoner in her own château. The charge against all of them was straight murder. It was a criminal trial, not an ecclesiastical trial, so that it was not complicated or cluttered with the issues of vampirism or witchcraft.

Johannes Ujvary was first examined. A part of the testimony ran as follows:

Q. How many years have you worked for the Countess Bathory?

A. I have been sixteen years in her household.

Q. How many women, to your personal knowledge, were murdered by the countess and her associates?

A. No women. That is, no married women. Thirty-seven girls were killed, within my direct knowledge.

Q. Who obtained the victims?

A. I got six of them myself. We told the girls we wanted them as servants. Miss Barsovny and Miss Otvos enticed others in the same way.

Q. How were they killed?

A. Well, their arms were tied behind them, then twisted with tight cords, tourniquet-fashion, and the veins cut with scissors.

Q. Were they ever otherwise tortured?

A. Sometimes the two old women, Ilona and Dorottya, would torture them, and when they did it well, the countess would give them presents. Sometimes the countess tortured them herself.

Q. What were the tortures?

A. They were beaten with whips and cut with knives. Sometimes we froze them in cold water afterward.

Q. When did the Countess Bathory begin these practices?

A. She began long before her husband died.

Ilona Joo's testimony came next:

Q. How long have you worked for the countess?

A. More than ten years. I was the family nurse.

Q. How many girls did you help the countess in murdering?

A. Many, many.

Q. How many?

A. As many as forty.

Q. More than that? As many as fifty?

A. No, about forty.

Q. Were any of them tortured?

A. Sometimes we put heated keys and coins in their hands. We smeared one girl's body with honey. When they fainted, we used to put paper between their toes and set it on fire. Mostly we opened their veins with scissors. Sometimes when the flesh was drawn tight, blood would spatter the walls.

Other servants testified similarly, added details, helped run the score up to a hundred or more victims, but only eighty bodies were ever traced or found. At no point did witch hysteria, vampire hysteria, superstition, or forced confession enter the deliberations or ultimate court findings. The incantations, etc., were embodied in the record, but would have been a matter for the Holy Inquisition. And the Inquisition was never called in. There was no need. The servants testified to the truth because there was no possible way of escaping it, and in hope that complete confession might mitigate the court's severity.

As a matter of fact, those of the defendants who were accessories, or procurers, got off "lightly," as court sentences went in those days. They merely had their heads cut off, and their dead bodies were burned afterward. The two old women Ilona Joo and Dorottya Szentes were convicted as principals, and had a worse time of it. The fingers of their hands were torn off, one by one, and they were burned alive.

The disposal of the Countess Bathory supplies perhaps the strangest touch of all in this history of hallucinated post-medieval horror, in which perhaps only the victims and the judges on the bench were completely sane. Yet, viewing the Countess Bathory in the Leopold-Loeb light of modern psychiatry, her personal case couldn't have been more fairly handled if she'd had the late Clarence Darrow as a lawyer, with a battery of alienists and the most enlightened jury of today. What they gave her was a medieval version of a padded cell in Matteawan for life. They accomplished this by simply never sentencing her! The only sentence they could have inflicted from the bench was death. Her cousin, the prime minister, interceded and they invoked red tape. She stood convicted, but they simply delayed passing sentence, and no sentence was ever passed on her. She remained imprisoned in her own château, and in order to make sure that she would continue imprisoned, they sent stone masons to Csejthe. They walled up the windows and door of the countess's own bedchamber, with the countess inside, leaving only slits for air where the windows were, and leaving where the door had been only a small hole in the wall through which food and drink could be passed. The king, Matthias II of Hungary, had felt at first that she should be executed, but finally agreed to the indefinitely delayed sentence, which was tantamount to solitary imprisonment for life. She died four years after she had been walled in, on the twenty-first of August, 1614.

Dezsö and Father Turoczi guess that one of the reasons they walled her in, instead of merely keeping her locked up, is that they were afraid of her witchcraft. But whether it was that, or merely the reluctance of honest judges to sentence a madwoman to execution, they did a pretty sensible job of it, as things went in those days. The superstitious element of vampirism was hallucinated tommyrot in 1614 as it is in 1940, but she was the bloodiest wholesale murderess who ever lived. And they had put her where she could commit no more murders. If they were a bit superstitious about her, they had sense enough to know—if some of my distinguished contemporary colleagues and supposed authorities have not— that one of the things no witch or vampire on earth can ever do is to walk through or break down a solid wall.

III. Vampire 1932 from Brooklyn, N. Y.

I'D been walking in the hills behind Le Trayas, on the Riviera, with Eugene Bagger, the stocky little Austrian journalist who worked for the New York *Times* some years ago and later wrote *Eminent Europeans*. We'd returned to the town, where he had a house and where I was staying in the hotel, which contained that summer a number of other writers, painters, musicians, including some Americans.

It was late afternoon. I was hot, and went down to the shore for a swim. There was a rocky, pebbled cove, a sort of inlet deep among the pine trees, closer than the sand beach. Seated on the pebbles, alone and with her hands clasped round her knees, was the girl I knew as Mary Lensfield. She painted a little, and translated children's books. She sat all alone there, staring out toward Porquerolles where the steamers passed. She was a queer type, striking without being beautiful. She was extremely thin and pale, with flaming hair and the sort of greenish eyes which frequently go with pale skin and hair that is naturally red. I had known her off and on for quite a time, but never very well. I'm not sure anybody knew her very well. She was friendly enough, but never very gay, and apparently not very strong. She said hello in an absent-minded sort of way. I dived from the top of a rock. In making the turn of the cove, I swam a bit too close to another rock just under water, and scraped my shoulder on the barnacles. It wasn't scraped badly, but when I came out there was a streak of bright, shiny blood glistening on my wet shoulder.

"You've cut yourself," said the girl. I sat down beside her, twisting my head to look at the scratch, and said, "It doesn't amount to much. I doubt if I'll need to put iodine on it." I asked her how her work was going. She was translating some of Comtesse de Ségur's juveniles. When she made no answer, I glanced at her. She had bent closer and was staring with wide, dilated eyes at the scarlet abrasion. Then she jerked convulsively toward me, and her teeth were in my shoulder, and she was sucking like a leech there—not like a leech either, but more like a greedy half-grown kitten with sharp-pointed teeth. It hurt sharply, but astonishment held me motionless for a second, and then a mixture of surprise, curiosity, and sheer amazement made me grit my own teeth and let it ride. She had deepened the abrasion, and was literally drinking blood! I am properly ashamed of it, but I sat there tense, perversely fascinated, and let her slake her thirst.

A big truck roared past on the Corniche road above us, behind the trees, and it was this noise, I think, that brought her out of it. She slumped back, terrified, her nerves torn to pieces, sobbing, shaking all over, with her face buried in her hands. I said nothing. I had been frightened too by the glimpse of her smeared, red mouth. But I said nothing. When she quieted a little and realized that I was silent, she said,

"Seabrook, what shall I do? Shall I have myself locked up? Shall I kill myself? Or what?"

Everything I'd ever known about the girl had been racing in that silence through my mind, and some of the things, which had seemed pointless when they occurred, seemed now to have a possible new significance. I'd met her first a couple of years before at a party in Bob Chanler's weird house, off Gramercy Park, in New York. She lived in Brooklyn Heights, and seldom came to Manhattan, but Bob wanted to paint her portrait, so she returned several subsequent times to his house, which I was then frequenting, and once or twice stayed over in the evening. On one of the evenings a queer episode had occurred. Bob never went in deeply for the esoteric, in fact had a slight contempt for it, but his friend Stanislaus Ivorsky was a student of the occult, and had brought there a certain Madame Ludovescu, who claimed to possess supernormal powers, physical rather than psychic, including the ability to heal cuts and burns, and to staunch the flow of blood. She was a dowdy woman, dressed pretentiously—velvet, a big picture hat, long, black kid gloves and bangles. Stanislaus had brought a medical friend to the party, and the doctor had consented to be the subject for the blood-staunching experiment, but Bob, whose skepticism was mixed with a vast, Gargantuan curiosity and childish egoism, roared,

"I want to be the goat in this miracle!"

So it was agreed. The doctor got a saucer, turned back the sleeve from Bob's left wrist, held it over the saucer, dabbed the skin with alcohol and nicked the transverse superficial vein with a small scalpel. It wasn't any pinprick either. The blood trickled in a slight but steady stream, as we all crowded round the table. Madame Ludovescu bent her head, as if nearsightedly studying the puncture, wiping her unrouged lips meanwhile with a handkerchief, which she kept held to her mouth for an appreciable moment. I guess she thought we had our attention safely fixed on Bob's wrist. Then she pressed her lips tight to the wound, seemed to breathe upon it precisely as I had seen Hindu fakirs do. We heard a faint mumbling as if of muttered prayer or incantation, and the muscles of her mouth were moving. It took fully a minute or more, and seemed longer. Then she raised her head, saying, "It has ceased. You can see."

It was then the queer interruption had occurred which now brought the whole thing back to me in memory. The woman's mouth and cheek were reddened, a tiny thread of scarlet trickled from the corner of her mouth, and as she lifted her face, saying, "It has ceased," Mary Lensfield, who had been watching with the rest of us, moaned and keeled over in a dead faint. "It's nothing serious," said the doctor in a moment, lifting her to a couch. "She'll come round in a minute or two. The sight of any blood sometimes affects people that way." And she did, and we thought nothing more of it.

The flow from Chanler's wrist had ceased completely, and the others had exclaimed now in awe and admiration, when Bob had shouted,

"Didn't you see? Prayers my eye! She licked it like a puppy! I licked it myself just now, and that's what's caught her cold! I might as well have been licking green persimmons! Make her give you that handkerchief, if she dares. You'll find it stinks of tannic acid, and probably Adrenalin.

Hey, Paul! Give this bitch ten dollars and a drink of gin, and throw her out!"

I'd forgotten all about the Rumanian woman and her cheap tricks. It was only the memory now of how Mary Lensfield had moaned, shuddered, and dropped to the floor that brought the episode flashing back. And it made me remember another episode which had occurred more recently at Antibes. It had a queer angle too, which had seemed merely a casual coincidence at the time. The Lensfield girl had shared a room there with a friend, also an American girl, and the two had seemed to be inseparable. The friendship had suddenly been broken for reasons that nobody knew. The girl had moved to another *pension*. And I now sharply recalled that at the time of the quarrel, or of whatever had happened, this second girl had cut herself with an ice pick, or said she had. At Chanler's, Mary Lensfield had gone to pieces and fainted at the sight of blood on another woman's lips. In this second instance, I began to wonder if there had been an accident with an ice pick, and if so, whose lips might afterward have been stained.

For here was Mary Lensfield now, her own pallid mouth smeared with blood—afraid that she was going mad. I said, "Has it ever happened to you before?"

She said, "I was visiting a friend at Vassar. She cut herself on broken glass. I helped bandage it. She slept soundly that night. I had persuaded her to take a triple bromide. I wanted to kill myself next morning."

I said, "Was it something like that when you had the quarrel, if it was a quarrel, with that girl—I don't recall her name—at Antibes a couple of years ago?"

"Yes," she said, "it's as bad as that. *I am what you think.* It has happened more than once."

I said, "What did you mean by saying you were 'what I think'? I don't think anything except that you're a sick girl who ought to see a doctor."

And then it was she, mind you, who whispered the old, ugly word "vampire." While she talked on now, as if a floodgate were opened, spilling out her sick and tortured soul, I think I realized for the first time a truth which has never been clearly stated, so far as I know, by anybody: that the persistence and bolstering of superstition not only fosters fear (and cruelty) in the public mass mind, but also helps spawn and foster the very horrors it attacks. Let me explain exactly what I mean, with reference to the vampire. The unsuperstitious individual who becomes afflicted with this craving for blood either sees a doctor or goes out and commits crimes easily dealt with by the police. Which of those two simple things he does depends simply on his moral balance. But the superstitious man or woman, so afflicted and superstition-ridden besides, reacts entirely differently. If he, or she, is a morally bad type, the next step is, "Oooooooooh! I'm a vampire!" or "Wooooow! I'm a werewolf! I'm superman now, and nothing but a silver bullet or a stake driven through my heart can stop me! So I'll go to town!" He or she, superstition-ridden, but with a moral conscience, as in the case of the wretched young lady with whom I was now talking, says, "Woe is me! I have become a horrible and awful thing. And I can do nothing to resist it. Better I were dead! Better I had never been born!"

It made me sick to learn, as we sat there and talked, of how this otherwise mentally normal girl!, afflicted with blood-craving and inclined toward a belief in heaven and hell inherited from overly religious parents, had wallowed in the obsessed reading of everything she could find on the subject of vampires. There's a vast bibliography, containing lots of honest stuff of course, but cluttered with learned, stupid, pious, horrid fantasy and supernatural doctrine, written by professors, esoterics, cultists, crackbrained preachers and priests, including also certain celebrated modern doctors of theology. She had read them all absorbedly, and in three fourths of the medieval stuff she had found that among the marks of the female vampire were pallor, thinness to the point of emaciation, red hair, and green eyes! Pure, crazy coincidence! Yet you can imagine how she must have stared in her own mirror. She knew, since the coincidence hadn't driven her completely crazy—though it might easily have done so in conjunction with her secret knowledge of her own blood lust—that she'd never been dead and buried, and that she didn't crawl back at night to sleep in a vault or coffin like Lady Vere or Dracula. But that hadn't helped her any, because part of the learned, superstitious hogwash on the "nature of vampires" explains that if you're bitten by one (and this, of course, can occur in your sleep without your knowing it), you're in danger of becoming one yourself, before you die, in your own natural lifetime—just as a person bitten by a mad dog is in danger of hydrophobia. She asked me whether I believed what all those learned writers did, or whether I thought she was crazy.

I gradually realized that she was not only pouring out her fears to me, but was close on the edge of confessing her complete belief in all that horrid nonsense, "confessing" herself to be of that unholy kin.

And I realized too as we sat there in the twilight that if this same misadventure had happened in this same Mediterranean cove a couple of hundred years before instead of in the twentieth century, not only would the man have fled in terror and reported her to the ecclesiastical authorities, but the girl would have made a full confession, voluntarily without need of any torture, that she was a true vampire. She would have died believing in the justice of her condemnation, and would have been buried at a crossroads with a stake driven through her heart. I came out of those reflections angry—but not at her.

I said, "For Christ's sake, forget all that crazy nonsense. *You're* not crazy, but all those goddamned supernaturalists are as crazy as hell. Agreed, you're a 'vampire' if you insist on calling it that—you're a sort of baby vampire who *could* grow up into a monster, but you're not a supernaturally doomed creature, and you're not a criminal either, yet. You're not even wicked, yet. You're just an ill, hallucinated girl, and you ought to see a doctor. See a doctor first, and get him to find you a good psychiatrist, one who is an M.D. too . . . here or back home in America."

My advice was sound enough, but it came too late. Miss Lensfield followed it literally, returned to America, and put herself in the hands of doctors, specialists. She never succumbed again to her tragic craving, but within a year she was dead—of pernicious anemia. The red blood cells in her body, the erythrocytes, had been disintegrating. Her whole chemical organism had been involved in a terrific struggle to balance itself and survive, and it had been discovered too late for transfusion or anything to save her. This desperate physiological maladjustment had been at the bottom of her mental maladjustment, of her awful craving, and she'd been no more morally responsible for her monstrous yearnings than midgets, dwarfs, and giants (innocent victims of their pineal and thyroid glands) are for their monstrous shapes. It all makes part of the picture tied up with the now commonplace certainty discovered in the twentieth-century merging of clinical medicine and psychiatry, that anomalies in the realm of psychology and behavior are often traceable to chemical-organic causes.

IV. Panther-man from the Ivory Coast

CONFIDENTIAL interviews, exchanges of cigarettes, and mutual confidences with caught, convicted werewolves are fairly rare. Werewolves and their kin aren't often caught alive. The werewolf, along with his African prototype, the leopard-man, panther-man, hyena-woman, are usually killed on the spot or escape to commit subsequent depradations, and die generally—as generals do—in bed.

My little friend Tei, petty chief of the Yafouba, and sometime white-collar clerk in the administration offices at Dakué, was an exception. He had been caught red-clawed, confessed, been sentenced to die, and now sat in the shade of the jail-yard wall, chewing kola nuts, smoking cigarettes, waiting while the official papers came from Bingerville to confirm the sentence. When not engaged in werewolfery, this Tei was a beguiling little scoundrel, and had become, indeed, a sort of pet werewolf, now that he was caught. Clouzet, the local administrator, was almost beginning to be sorry they were going to have to shoot him. I spent hours with Tei, smoking interminable cigarettes, chewing kola, listening to him talk. He was a skinny little runt, wrinkled face, bright eyes, keen smile, with a wisp of a billy-goat beard that bobbed up and down as he chewed. He was naked now except for his loincloth, amulets, beads, crocodile teeth, and little leather bags strung round his neck. When he'd worked up in the office, he'd worn store clothes and shoes, had a fountain pen, a watch and chain. Time no longer made any difference to Tei, as he wiggled his toes and kept insisting,

". . . but I tell you I *do* turn into a panther. No—I can't do it now for you! I can't do it like that—whenever I want to. I can't *do* it ever. It isn't anything *I* do. It's something that *happens* to me. But when it happens, I *am a panther.*"

"Do you like it?"

"Oh, yes," he would always answer, "it's nicer than being a man."

"But if you really do turn into a panther," I kept badgering him for the four-hundredth time, "then why do you have to put on that panther skin—those mittens with iron claws?"

"It's a part of the fetish," he'd repeat, "it's part of the magic. It's like rubbing the panther fat, and eating the part of the panther's liver, and dancing the panther dance, crouching and leaping. It's when you make the leaping that you become the panther. . . ."

Once he'd added hopefully, when I'd brought him a bottle of sweet vermouth, of which he was inordinately fond, "I don't know whether a white man could do it or not, but I'll be glad to teach you the leaping . . . and you could always try."

"All right," I'd say, getting back to the point which interested me most, "but after you've leapt and become the panther, if you really become a panther, why don't you leap out of the disguise? You don't need *two* panther skins, and you don't need the iron claws, if you've got real ones!"

To this, Tei had a variety of answers, the best one being that you never knew when you might suddenly change back into your human shape—and be recognized.

In the end, I became firmly convinced of Tei's sincerity, convinced that his hallucinations about actually turning into a panther were completely real—as hallucinations. I got to thinking about the whole queer business of subjective and objective reality, and it occurred to me that in the typical panther-man murder-drama as it usually occurs in the jungle —and as it had occurred in the death of Blito to which little Tei had confessed—there is a three-way illusion, a three-way subjective reality which spreads out beyond the mere illusion in the panther-man's one individual brain. I'm not turning mystical, either. By "three-way subjective reality," I mean simply that three separate individuals, or groups, participate simultaneously in the hallucination:

1. The panther man,
2. The victim,
3. The witnesses, if any.

So it had surely been in the killing of Blito, which occurred as she walked in the twilight along a jungle path leading from her village to a spring, and of which we had full circumstantial knowledge.

Tei, in his panther garb and iron claws, believing himself to be a panther, completely victim of the subjective reality of his own frenzied illusion, had leapt, probably yowling, down from a branch on her shoulders, and had torn her throat out with the claws.

What had Blito seen and felt in that fleeting instant as

she died? If she had seen anything, it had been the flashing form of a panther, leaping as a panther leaps. What she had felt is sure. She had felt a lithe, *furry* body landing on her shoulders, and claws tearing at her throat. She had died in the complete subjective certainty that she had been slain by a panther.

When there are witnesses to these murders, as in this case there were, what do the witnesses see? They see a leaping panther, engaged in a kill, and flee screaming to raise the village.

The dead Blito will never know that the panther was human—a were-panther. The witnesses will only learn it was a were-panther when the hunters come back. When it's a real panther, they can easily trail and find the mangled, partially devoured body, and the real panther's tracks. In the absence of normal beast marks, they suspect now it was a panther-man—and to them, in this completed circle of subjective reality, it was a man not in human form, but in a panther's form.

These same villagers now came often to the jail yard to see Tei in his familiar, human form. Sometimes they brought him mangoes. They bore him no malice. They believed, as he did, that he couldn't help sometimes turning into a panther. They were sure that this would happen, for a last and final time, when Tei was stood up against the jail wall and shot. After he'd been shot, he'd no longer be there, as Tei. There'd be a dead panther lying there, its body pierced with bullets. They were all coming, from miles around, to see it, because Tei's case—a curious mixture of comedy, monkey-shines, and horror—had had our whole part of the jungle, including whites and blacks, in a dither for weeks on end.

Blito, you see, had been Tei's own jungle love—and also Clouzet's—in a district where the blacks, and whites too, bought, sold, and swapped young Yafouba girls, wives, concubines, and slaves, as we do puppies, cats, and hunting dogs. I bought one once for three dollars and a pink celluloid mirror. When Tei became a government employee, Blito, who was young, handsome, jangling with bracelets and trinkets, had caught Administrator Clouzet's roving eye. The foxed-face little village chief, who had as many girls in his harem as he had chickens in his hencoop, was delighted. The natives are never jealous in such cases. The best thing that can happen to them, and they know it, is when a daughter or any other female member of their household can get into a white man's house, and bed. The perquisites always add up to more than the original "gift" or purchase price. Sometimes when Blito danced on the lawn of Administrator Clouzet's compound to the accompaniment of tribal drums, for our amusement, Tei would be sitting on a stool near Clouzet's chair, and enjoying it as much as anybody. In those days, Tei was a cocky, active, intelligent, likable little savage, who had feathered his nest with the French. Though he still wore amulets beneath his store clothes and the teeth of wild animals braided in his hair, he sported a golf cap, yellow shoes that might have come from Harlem, and was "Monsieur Tei of the Administration" to the barefoot ones back yonder in his village. When the servants brought vermouth and Pernod, Clouzet occasionally handed Tei a glass too, with a grin.

That was the way things had stood at Dakué when I went north to join Administrator-General Bercole on a hunting trip. Returning to his headquarters, we heard there'd been trouble down in Clouzet's district. First we heard there'd been a raid of Liberian leopard-men from across the river. These Liberian leopard societies are group versions of the Ivory Coast "panther-man," [1] the European "werewolf," and generally hunt in packs. They are criminal secret societies which practice a sort of mass lycanthropy, working themselves up to a state of frenzied hallucination in groups. First we heard that Blito had been *among* the victims—and then we heard the straighter report, that Blito had been the only victim, while on a visit back to her native village, which was, in fact, near the river, the Liberian border. Clouzet, we heard, had called out a platoon of *tirailleurs,* and Tei, whose village district it concerned, had been put in charge of the investigation.

"It's a queer story," said Bercole. "Of course Clouzet has always been a fool, but it's a queer story. Only Blito murdered. Who says there was a raid? Who says anybody came across the river? I'll be interested to hear what happens."

A week or two later, we had word from Clouzet that the crime had been pinned on three marauding Liberians. They had been captured, and there was more than enough evidence to have them condemned and shot. Bercole, responsible for the whole region, still felt there was something queer about it, and the next day we went down to Dakué. Bercole dissimulated his suspicions, was mild as a lamb, congratulated Clouzet, had a casual look at the prisoners, and presently, as we dined with Clouzet, began asking innocent questions.

How had they caught them? How identified them? Had they confessed yet? No, said Clouzet, they hadn't confessed.

[1] See Appendix, p. 316.

They even claimed an alibi, of all things, but you knew what native alibis amounted to, and there was enough circumstantial evidence to satisfy any court anywhere. Bercole repeated his congratulations, and Clouzet said,

"Well, the credit really belongs to Tei. The *tirailleurs* and constabulary helped, but it was Tei who really pulled it off."

"So," said Bercole mildly, and I noticed he was scratching his head. "By the way, who had the Liberian idea in the beginning? Who had the original leopard society hunch?"

"It was Tei," replied Clouzet, "he's a smart little headman."

"Yes," agreed Bercole, "he's one of the smartest. I'd like it, though, if we could get a confession out of those Liberians. I think I'll see what I can do about that if you don't mind."

Bercole saw the prisoners, separately, and together, several times, then was gone from Dakué for two days, came back, and said,

"They didn't do it. They couldn't have done it."

"Are you sure?" said the astonished Clouzet.

"Yes, I'm sure—and you know what it adds up to now, don't you?"

"*Mon dieu!*" said the astonished Clouzet, "it couldn't be! He's been a good government employee for years. . . ."

"Ah me," said Bercole wearily. "I like you, Clouzet, but you're a baby. This case stunk long before I found out those poor apes you arrested couldn't have done it. It still stinks. It smells. It smells so loudly that I got a little sniff of it when I first heard, a hundred miles away. And now I'm sure."

So the highhanded Bercole had acted on his "hunch," arrested Tei, torn Tei's fetish house to pieces, discovered hidden in the thatching the panther disguise, skin, bloody-clawed mittens—and Blito's anklets, bracelets, likewise stained with blood. Tei confessed readily, since the jig was up. He'd been turning into a panther, he said, from time to time, for years.

The *rigolade* of the industrious and faithful little government employee who'd been a part-time panther on his evenings off, illogically mitigated the ghastliness of the hallucinated crime, but rightly failed to mitigate its expiation.

The French have never gone in for hangings. They do it with a firing squad in Africa. The natives had come from miles around to see the execution, convinced that the body would turn miraculously to its panther form in death. But the body which lay crumpled there at the foot of the yellow wall outside the jail yard was merely the body of little Tei. I felt a little sorry for him, for I'm sure he would have been surprised, as they were, that no miracle had happened.

V. Lady Hyena with Jeweled Earrings

IF I am convinced, and hope to convince you, that many witches, vampires, werewolves, panther-men, and their kindred, are hallucinated humans who believe in their own hocus-pocus and are frequently guilty as hell of murder and worse, I don't mean to imply that all unhappy creatures so accused are thus deluded or guilty, or both.

One of the by-products of superstition, whether primitive and savage or a medieval hang-over among us supposedly enlightened whites, is that in addition to providing a contagious culture-medium for epidemic witchcraft and lycanthropy, it makes witch fear, witch hysteria, similarly epidemic, with the result that innocent individuals are frequently accused unjustly, persecuted, and destroyed. Also it offers a foul field for private plotting.

Innocent, for instance, as any Hawthorne heroine, or screen-warmed-over Maid of Salem, was the handsomest and youngest daughter of a Mossi chief in the Upper Volta who was "framed" by native priests, and subsequently murdered by them. The priests had convinced the countryside that the wretched girl was a demon-hyena, and nearly got away with their crime.

I'd been up toward Ouahigouya, looking at some hippopotami, with Bercole, who was a naturalist as well as a hunter, and who would as soon have shot his own pet goldfish as one of those amiable and lumbering water beasts. We had dropped in to see his colleague, Monsieur Maillard, administrator in one of the Ouahigouya districts, to tell him about the hippopotami. It was while we were playing three-handed cutthroat bridge afterward, at the administration residence, that we first heard about the mysterious "lady hyena," and I recall that my friends were excessively impatient about it—at first.

The black Moslem butler had come to say in faultless, discreet French that a British gentleman had called who seemed disturbed about something, and "wished earnestly" to see the administrator tonight.

"Name of a pipe!" said Maillard, "tell the British gentleman to come back at ten o'clock tomorrow morning . . . or tell him to go jump in the Niger. Don't you see that we are playing cards?"

Government functionaries in these isolated regions, where no hotels or public restaurants exist, are terribly imposed on by sportsmen, "explorers," tourists, until they learn to be inhospitable for self-protection. Ordinarily the butler would have taken it on himself to tell the stranger to come back next day, and now when the butler still stood there uncertain, reluctant to withdraw, I sensed something unusual. "What are you standing there for?" growled Maillard. "Whatever his business is, it can wait. Get on out now!"

But the butler strangely held his ground. It wasn't, the butler explained timidly . . . well, it wasn't exactly business. The British gentleman was quite perturbed. You see, he had shot a hyena. . . .

"Name of a name of a name!" It was Bercole who swore this time, pushing back his chair. "Tell the fool to go out and shoot a thousand hyenas! Does he suppose there's a closed season on shooting hyenas in Africa? If he'd shot one of my hippos . . . But who cares about hyenas!"

"Monsieur Commandant," said the now trembling butler, "it was a young female hyena, and there were jeweled earrings in its pierced ears."

"The Englishman is drunk?" asked Maillard, mildly.

"No, Monsieur Commandant, he is not drunken, and he has the hyena outside. I have seen it."

"I've always been told that *anything* can happen in Africa, but I've been here so long that I don't quite believe it," said Maillard with heavy sarcasm. "You may now bring in the English milord and his milady hyena."

The Englishman was dignified, middle-aged, stuffy, and, as we soon discovered, also quite annoyed. He was anything but apologetic for disturbing us. His attitude definitely implied that hyenas never wore earrings in properly run British dependencies. He explained that he'd been hunting at night, for lion, on the cliffs toward Bandiagara, and that he felt it necessary to report so "unreasonable" a happening to the authorities. In night hunting, you wear an electric bulb, with a reflector, fastened round your hat or forehead, with the wires running to a battery in your pocket. When the light picks up a pair of gleaming eyes, you shoot, and sometimes it's a lion. If you've misjudged the distance, and, in consequence, the space between the eyes, it may be a wildcat, or even a rabbit. This can happen to anybody on a dark night. In this case it had been the hyena which the Englishman's porters now lugged in and deposited, at a sign from Maillard, on a trestle table so that we could examine it. It was just a dead, two-thirds grown young female hyena, but the lobes of its ears had been pierced as women's are, and set in the ears were a pair of beautiful native gold earrings encrusted with semiprecious stones of the sort found in the neighborhood of Gao.

The butler brought Pernod and whisky. The Englishman became a bit less stuffy. We all unbent and agreed that here was a fine how-de-do.

The Englishman was put up in the guesthouse, the dead hyena locked in the office, and next morning, Maillard sent for the local Mossi chief and his *féticheur* priests, the local witch-doctors, the native gendarme sergeant, the interpreters, who all came presently, rubbed their eyes—and were dumber than they should be. No, they knew nothing about it. No, they had never heard of such a thing ever happening before. No, they could guess nothing about it. No . . . absolutely not . . . none of them had ever previously seen that particular pair of earrings. They presently departed, but Bercole, who had helped conduct the investigation, was sure they were lying. They'd been dumber than was necessary, he said.

No charge could be brought against them, or against anybody. It's no crime to put rings in a hyena's ears and turn it loose on the mountainside. And when no crime is involved, it has always been the policy of the French not to interfere with the *féticheurs,* their native temples, and their native shenanigan and superstition.

No further official investigation was made at this time, and it was plain curiosity, I think, rather than a suspicion of anything sinister, that prompted Bercole before leaving the region to pay an informal visit to his high-up native colleague—that magnificent old patriarch and reprobate, His Negro Holiness, the Yatanga Naba, Black Pope of all the Mossi. These two oddly assorted tyrants—the cocky, little French administrator-general who took a twisted pride in his petulant, shabby informality, and the superb Yatanga who weighed three hundred pounds, wore gorgeous robes of silk and gold, and claimed descent from a black high priest of the Egyptian Pharaohs—had been intimates and allies for a long decade. Both were completely cynical, equally contemptuous of French red tape and jungle mumbo jumbo, yet both loved West Africa, and both worked in their own devious ways toward the furtherance of its tangled destinies.

The Yatanga's palace was at Ouahigouya. Thither Bercole went with the jeweled earrings in his pocket, and the intrigued Yatanga Naba, after seeing them and hearing Bercole's story, promised he'd get to the bottom of it. The Yatanga, who knew that a lot of the forest priests were rascals, was never loath to catch them out on limbs and put the fear of the devil in them. It was he who really uncovered the murder for us. It proved to be a double story, with plausible superstition motives on its surface, and plain crime underneath.

The jeweled earrings, as subsequently proven, had originally adorned the ears of a certain Sarab'na, youngest daughter of a native "king" named Sanou. In this territory, with French consent, every big tribal chief is a "king," while the native temporal ruler of all the Mossi, the effeminate Moro Naba, is an "emperor." The titles are less ridiculous than they sound, for the Mossi have walled towns, adobe palaces, fine horses, and affect magnificent garments of brilliantly colored leather. So that Sarab'na had been in native parlance, a *moso-masaké*, "little princess," though it helped her not at all when her dreadful fate came upon her. The surface story had been that when she had come to the age of thirteen, the priestly witch-doctors and fetish-women attached to her own household had discovered, in the portents and omens which resulted from the incantation ceremonies surrounding her initiation to womanhood, that she was not a woman at all, but a demon-hyena—which means according to their myths that a hyena had magically taken up its abode in her human body. If this were true, according to the belief of the Mossi, it constituted a deadly danger to her own family; for when the hyena possession came upon her, as it would some day inevitably, she would, first of all, slay her own parents—her own human father and mother. To kill the girl would have been no use, by their belief, for that would simply release a disembodied, demoniac hyena spirit, against which there could be no protection at all. Consequently, she had been turned over to the priests, who undertook to make the hyena come out of her in its material form.

The procedure is the same as the driving out of devils used to be among Greeks, Romans, Jews, and Christians. The incantations and mumbo jumbo differ, but the essence of it is to make the body of the possessed person such an uncomfortable habitation that not even a devil or wild beast cares to remain in it.[1] Superstition is never completely logical, even within its own false premises, and in the case of the demon-hyena, they believe it will either abandon the body and try to escape, when it can be clubbed or shot down in its animal

---

[1] See Appendix, p. 322.

form—or that the human body itself will become magically transformed into the ravening beast, and must then be slain.

The sour note that aroused Bercole's suspicion concerning this surface version based on superstition was that the girl's own sisters had helped in the procedure. As to what they had actually done to the unhappy girl, Bercole had some details from the Yatanga which are too dreadful to write or print. They'd kept her in a cellar, and the sisters had worked on her in relays while the priests howled their incantations and exorcisms. All this, it seems, went on for the best part of a month, in the subterranean vault of one of their mud temples, and Sarab'na had become a demented creature, scarcely indeed human any more except in form, crawling on all fours, slavering, cowering, snarling at her tormentors— but the hyena refused to be driven out, nor did the girl's form ever change.

What threw it out of the already bad-enough field of superstitious persecution into the same crime-for-gain category as our own recent witchcraft-arsenic murders was the fact, finally dug up and proven by Bercole and the Yatanga, that the girl's jealous sisters, abetted by other relatives with an eye on the family succession, lands, and cattle, had bribed the priests to fake the omens; had cooked up the plot to get Sarab'na out of the way. She had been her father's marked favorite and he had planned an early marriage for her, to a "prince" of the Songhai, with half his holdings thrown in as a dowry. Because she was his favorite, they hadn't dared risk an ordinary murder, but had evolved the horrid plot which would put him in terror of Sarab'na and make him believe she was a menace to his own existence.

When the unfortunate girl was completely demented, they went to Sanou, invited him to see for himself, and what he saw was a whipped, starved, and tortured creature who went on all fours, completely mad and ravening, who devoured chunks of raw meat when they were thrown to her. This convinced him so fully that they were easily able to obtain his acquiescence to their further plans. They persuaded him with childish logic that the reason they hadn't been able to exorcise the hyena, to make it come out in its own form, was that it realized, shut up as they were in the cellar, that it would be cornered and killed the moment it showed itself. So, after further conference, Sanou agreed to let them take her out among the cliffs, and try it in the open.

What they did, of course, was simply to murder her out there, and throw the body in the river, which swarmed with crocodiles. And if they'd let it go at that, it would have been just one of those things in Africa that no white man ever hears of. But the wily priests, who planned to go back and say that the girl herself had *become* a hyena and fled into the bush, had played their too smart trick with the earrings. They had trapped a young hyena alive, "planted" the earrings, and turned it loose, on the long chance that sooner or later somebody might glimpse the marvel fleeting in the moonlight, might even kill it, as actually had chanced to happen, thus "proving" that the wretched girl had been a real demon-hyena; thus increasing the prestige of their priestly craft and magic. This is precisely what would have happened, had the hyena been seen or shot by any superstitious native. The almost impossible long chance they had overlooked was that it might be bagged by a white man and carried to the administration. White hunters almost never shoot hyenas. The hyena is carrion, and its hide is worthless. Nor could white men alone have ever got to the bottom of it and brought the priests and their accomplices to justice. Bercole had a long talk with Maillard about that. And it was agreed that it would be a mistake to try to make it stand up in a tribunal. Justice was left to the Yatanga Naba, who took a savage pleasure in seeing it was administered—in the savage fashion the savage crime deserved.

VI. The Caged White Werewolf
of the Saraban

"THE last two times they brought her back to the plantation," said the mahogany exporter, and he was speaking of
his own wife Marthe, whom he had married in Marseille
before coming to the Ivory Coast, "her mouth [*son museau*,
he called it, which properly means a wild beast's snout] was
smeared with blood."

He was begging Bercole and me to understand that he
had done the only thing he could, and we were wondering
what other solution could have been any better.

No roads or regular safari trails led up into the Saraban,
and no white Frenchman, not even Bercole on whose district it abutted, had ever been up there officially until now.

A lot of native rumors had kept seeping down to the coast,
and Bercole, forced finally to investigate, had invited me to
go along with him. He'd been in a bad humor about it, for
if there is any one thing, other than sunstroke, that gives
your seasoned African colonial a sharper pain in the neck
than something else, it is precisely any tale about mysterious
white women gone jungle mad, or held prisoner and made
to officiate as voodoo priestesses. They generally turn out to
be there of their own free will, from one of the brothels

behind the old port in Toulon, near the Senegalese barracks, or from the Kasba at Algiers, where no color lines are drawn —and seldom thank you for butting in on their new racket.

If there was a white woman "held captive" in the Saraban, Bercole had been sure it would be something in that category. Yet the queer rumors had persisted, and there were natives who swore they had been there . . . had seen with their own eyes. They said there was a man up there, on the banks of the Cavally, on the other side of the mountain, who kept a woman, with long, straight hair, in an iron cage, "*kai gaibou*," that is, "like a panther"—like a wild beast in an iron cage—and Dioula peddlers, who claimed to have actually seen the woman, swore she was a white European.

Bercole had been long years in Africa. "It could be," he'd said to me, "that this is a drawing, painting, or carving that has taken hold on the imagination of some isolated tribe back there. Their belief in animism, you see, means that nothing is ever necessarily what it seems. It could easily be a wooden image or an idol; it could even be some animal, or even a stone or a tree. When you live here in the jungle twenty years, you begin to understand that what you first mistook for fantasy, or deliberate lying to mystify us whites, is often something different and quite sincere. My Senegalese chauffeur who served four years in France as a sergeant, who can take my motor to pieces and put it back again, who has a phonograph and can read Morse code, once took me to see his grandfather at Konakri. I'd said, 'I thought he was dead.' The chauffeur said, 'No, he's come back.' So we went to see his grandfather at Konakri, and his grandfather was a goat! My Baoule housekeeper Ouia, who has more hard common sense, as you know, than nine tenths of the white functionaries down in the governor's palace, keeps a sea shell which is her dead sister. Half the time, to them, a tree is not a tree. A broken monkey wrench you've thrown away is a snake—or somebody's cousin. And it's more tangled even than that. It takes deeper twists no white man can follow. In those twists *a man's way of wearing a hat* can be his grandfather, or a herd of elephants. So God knows what we'll find, if anything, when we go up the river."

Next day, as Bercole's truck took us toward the mountain, he said, "We'll see no literal *kai gaibou* panther-woman in a cage . . . depend on that . . . but I'll show you more baboons than you ever dreamed were in the world. We had a telescope trained on the mountain a couple of years ago when the chief surveyor was up from Bingerville, and the rocks were swarming with them, like maggots in a cheese."

We camped and slept at the base of the mountain, and left the truck there next morning. We packed light, went afoot, with his cook, his boy, six porters, and by late afternoon were up among the apes. The rock ridge lay like the gray carcass of a mile-long whale, emerging from the green jungle sea, and its clefts literally swarmed with baboons. It was a baboon metropolis. On some of the slopes, they were thick as flies. Bercole and his Negroes treated them like people. They were not afraid of us . . . quite harmless, as long as we remained polite to them—and as long as we were not afraid of them. They chattered with interest, but not in anger. Bercole said that if we killed or wounded one, or even threw stones at them, they'd mob us, submerge us, and tear us into little pieces.

We camped next night on the further slope, above the Cavally, and in the morning a petty chief appeared, drawn by our smoke, with a dozen men armed with spears, to see who we were and what we wanted. They were *Ouabé*, like Bercole's own porters. We went down with them, gave them three big salt bars and some tobacco. They found us a pirogue above the rapids, and manned it with paddlers. We went for three days up the river, with the Saraban on our right and the Liberian hinterland on our left. On the fourth day we came to a worked mahogany clearing, and soon to a plantation, in a lagoon, on the French side. Apart from its remoteness, it looked ordinary, commonplace. It could hardly be what we were looking for, yet the paddlers said it was. We tied up, and as we were unloading, the proprietor came down to the water. He was a surly but not stupid-looking fellow, brown-bearded, middle-aged—a Luxembourgeois, it turned out. Bercole always dressed shabbily, without insignia, and the man, not knowing whom he had to deal with, made it plain he was not glad to see visitors. He offered us no welcome, and was surly. It was always a mistake to be surly with little Bercole. Bercole said in a sharp, clipped, official, nasal twang:

"So here you are, whoever you are, playing that old game in my territory! One foot in Liberia, the other in French territory, cutting mahogany on both sides of the river, evading taxes, probably paying no concession. I am Bercole, you understand, administrator-general of this district. . . ."

"I'm sorry," said the proprietor, "I could not know who you were. I am Joseph Hecht, formerly of Luxembourg and Marseille. My papers are all on file, *Monsieur l'Administrateur*, in Bingerville. I regret . . ."

"*Hein,*" said Bercole, "so that's who you are . . ."

"I regret . . ." the man began again, when Bercole interrupted, this time deprecatingly, almost amiably.

"It wasn't that anyway. That wasn't what I came up here to see you about. I came up here to put an end to a crazy, idiotic story the tribes are circulating. I hesitate to mention it."

"How does it concern me?" asked Joseph Hecht, and added, "The tribes are making me no trouble."

"They say," blurted Bercole, "that you keep women in cages!"

At this, an extraordinary change came over the bearded man. His former aggressiveness dropped from him. It was not so much that he wilted. His face softened, rather, and with the softening was a sort of queer, bitter resignation.

"Ah, monsieur," he said, "it is just as well that you came. I would have spared you the invitation, but I must beg you now to come to my house. For you see, it is true. I keep my wife . . . yes . . . I suppose cage would be the name for it. In this climate, she would die if kept locked in a close room. And if I did not keep her confined, where she cannot break out nor others break in . . . Yes, monsieur, it is true. I keep my wife—in a cage."

Bercole is a difficult man to surprise, but his mouth had dropped, and he was staring at Hecht as if he thought the man was crazy. "No," exclaimed the planter earnestly, "I am not mad, nor is my wife insane in any ordinary sense. I do not know what you believe about such things, but from time to time my wife becomes *demoniac, possessed*. She becomes a wild beast. The jungle madness got into her, and the witch-doctors themselves are afraid of her! If she had been one of their own, they would have killed her. They have told me.

The last two times they brought her back to the plantation, *her jaws were smeared with blood.*"

"*Mon dieu, mon dieu, mon dieu!*" said Bercole. We had reached the veranda. House boys brought bottles and refreshment. Bercole said, "I have lived for twenty years in the jungle. . . . I have heard of it happening to jungle women . . . but a white European . . . I do not know what to think."

"There are worse things in Europe than in any jungle," said Hecht. "Before I ever met my wife, before she dreamed that she would ever live in Africa, she had already become entangled."

"Entangled in what, in God's name?" asked Bercole, muttering more to himself than asking the direct question to Hecht.

"I will try to tell you," said the man. "I want to tell you. She confessed it all to me in Marseille, and wanted to get away from it; and it was one of the reasons we came to the colonies."

Here, concisely, is what he told us, with the first evil roots back in the center of civilized France.

He had first met the girl in Valence, near Lyon, where she taught in the *école normale.* He had fallen in love with her— was still in love with her despite everything—and they had married. Honeymooning in Marseille, she had become frightened at someone she saw in the street, who she believed had followed her down there, from Lyon. She had confessed what she was afraid of, and begged Hecht to take her out of the country. The "Center," the Valley of the Rhone, has always been the stronghold of a deep, medieval religious mysticism, which has—as such medievalism always has—its demonology,

159

black superstition, and weird cults growing out of them. One
of these cults had pulled the girl in, and taking advantage of
her perverse, neurasthenic temperament, had made her an
adept, an *illuminée*. She had participated in the sacrifice of
animals, had drunk the sacramental blood, had lain naked on
the altar, and had once or twice become *possessed*. In her
usually normal state, she feared and hated it, but they had
her hooked, and didn't want to let her go. It was to escape
that she had married Hecht, and then persuaded him to take
her thousands of miles away, to a new life. Like all the pro-
vincial French who want to make a new start, they had naturally gone "to the colonies."

All had gone well for a while, and then one night she had
disappeared. Her bed was empty. The tom-toms had been
throbbing all night down in the forest. Before Hecht could
get a search organized, the blacks themselves had brought
her back, already a little afraid of her, but bowing down before her with reverence, and giving Hecht to understand
they thought she was a sort of goddess. It was only later that
he learned what had happened on that first night. They'd
been holding an invocation of their jungle gods and demons,
with the drums, masks, chants, and dances, when she suddenly appeared in the light of the torches, swayed, began
screaming, tore off all her clothes, and rushed into their
midst, galvanized, illumined, shrieking. The natives had
milled around her, throwing themselves at her feet so she
could trample on them, howling *"G'nouna! G'nouna!
G'nouna!"* which is the feminine incarnation of *Gla*, the
Great Demon of the forest. These topmost demons in their
pantheon are worshiped as much as feared, are regarded as

gods rather than devils, and rarely, as they believe, become incarnate.

But again one night she was gone from her bed, and this time when he found her, her mouth was smeared all over with blood. The natives were in utter terror. They told him it was the blood of a sheep. But they were so terrified he did not believe them. They were no longer worshiping her. She was one possessed, they said, with an evil spirit. A third, more definitely horrible thing had happened soon afterward, and then the witch-doctors had solemnly come to tell him that his wife was *kai gaibou*, possessed by the spirit of a panther.

So the husband, who had made previous unsuccessful efforts to prevent her from slipping away when the jungle madness came upon her, had contrived the cage, to bar her in, to make running away by night or day impossible, to protect her against herself, as he said—from her own madness. She was as sane as anybody, he said, between these awful lapses.

Yes, he said, the cage was here in the compound. It was a part of the house, really, built on as a sort of wing. We would go there now, and Monsieur the Administrator would do whatever he judged wisest.

So we went, no longer antagonistic toward the man, filled more with embarrassment and pity than with any morbid curiosity. And there it was, just as the Dioula peddler had said—the white Frenchwoman locked in an iron cage, *kai gaibou*, like a panther, like a wild beast in the zoo. As for the cage itself, it was roofed, comfortable, clean, and large as a room, built sheltered against the bungalow, with mats on the clay floor, a divan in one corner piled with cushions, and in another corner a shower with toilet arrangements—the same Hecht had for himself in the main house.

As for the woman who came forward to the bars, sullen but less embarrassed than we were, wrapped in a silk *pagne* twisted round her body in the Arab manner, inhaling deeply the smoke from a cigarette, she was a heavy, dark-complexioned, coarsely handsome creature, sensual rather than beautiful, definitely volcanic, neurasthenic. I wondered whether she had ever really been a schoolteacher—whether she hadn't been in an older and commoner profession before her marriage.

"My wife, Marthe," said the planter, making the weird introductions. She stared at us, almost insolently, and the conversation, as the French say, refused to begin. It was damnably embarrassing. Bercole sought refuge in the strictest official formality.

"Madame, I am the administrator-general with full police authority in this district. I have men with me. I have heard what this man here has recounted. I take note of what I see in the presence of this gentleman as a witness. I take note, and I am ready to act. Do you make complaint against this man who says he is Joseph Hecht, and says he is your husband? Are you held here against your will? Do you wish to be released first, and then charge him?"

The woman inhaled again deeply and stared at Bercole.

"He is my husband," she said, and stopped, and then went on. "I have nothing to say, and no complaint or charge to make. You'd better talk with him about it."

"As you wish, madame," said Bercole, saluting punctiliously.

We were halfway down to the rapids next day, sliding with the current, in the pirogue, when Bercole said:

"It looked crazy, but it wasn't a stupid idea, you know. She's better off, probably, than in an insane asylum. And I don't believe she could be judged insane anyway. Apparently, she's not, except for that blood lust which sends her off at intervals. Maybe she is bewitched, *ensorcelée*. I don't know what I believe about sorcery, but there's one thing I do know about it. No magic, my friend, can twist or break an iron bar. Maybe Hecht has not been stupid. But if she were my woman, assuming everything he told is true, I give you my word of honor, I'd shoot her through the head and believe I'd done the right and moral thing about it."

VII. Werewolf in Washington Square

IN esoteric lore and old theology, the difference between black magic and white magic is that Satan and his devils help you with the first, while the Lord Jesus, saints, and bright pure spirits, including that of your dead aunt from Hawkinsville, Georgia, help you with the second.

In applied witchcraft and applied occultism today, the only difference between black and white is in the *intention*. If you're doing it for evil, it's black; if you're doing it for good, it is white. All magic, whether white or black, is dangerous—and there are sometimes lamentable kickbacks.

Treating patients with ultraviolet rays or radium is dangerous too. And so are strychnine pills. Unless the doctors know their stuff, somebody, occasionally both the doctor and the patient, get burned or poisoned. It's the same in occultism and white magic. Even when it's "only a game," like tabletipping or the ouija board, it can take dangerous turns, and when you get deeper into it . . . into the *Yi King*, for instance . . . it can sink you.

The *Yi King*, oldest of all books on divination and magic, was written in China long before Confucius, and long before dialectic theology was invented. It is neither black nor white. It is magic, *tout court*, and I was employing it, with friends from Columbia and Cornell, neither for good nor for evil, but out of sheer curiosity to see how far we could make the cat jump—if we could make it jump at all. The cat remained poised and indifferent, but the experiments had various violent effects on the two-legged professors, and on other human beings whom we persuaded to shuffle the tortoise-shell wands. In the end I realized again, belatedly, that magic is a thing you'd better let alone unless you have the protection of a pure and guileless heart like Parsifal's. My heart was far from pure, and I'd have materialized Lucifer himself, if I could, as readily as any of the unfallen archangels. But my experiments in reverse-orthodox, pentagrammed diabolism had never materialized *anything*. And I'd gone on to the *Yi King* to see what poltergeist high jinks *it* might uncork, if any.

The adventure I propose to relate occurred in John Bannister's studio, looking out on the Washington Arch, in the summer of 1923. He kept himself out of the newspapers, but had a curious word-of-mouth reputation which was international. Some people considered him the greatest living secret master of esoteric mysticism and magic; others insisted he was no more than a crackbrained charlatan. At any rate, he had a small private fortune, and never founded cults or exploited his hobby commercially. I knew him intimately and wavered between two opinions.

Our active monkey business with the *Yi King* (pronounced, by the way, Yee Ching) dated back to 1922 when we had chanced to find and buy the first actual set of wands I'd ever seen. We'd been playing chess one afternoon at Mouquin's, and later in the afternoon were strolling up Fifth Avenue when something in the window of a Chinese curio shop caught our eye. It was the shop on the east side of the Avenue, above the old Brentano's, around 29th Street. We went inside, and the clerk took from the window a little bundle of flat, dark-colored tortoise-shell wands, fastened together with a bit of string. There were six, and they were all identical. Each was about the size and shape of an ordinary foot rule, slightly smaller. One face of each was blank, and the reverse face of each was cut crosswise in two with an inch-wide strip of inlaid white ivory. We recognized them immediately for what they were, but Bannister said casually to the Chinese clerk,

"Do you happen to know what they are?"

The clerk shook his head. "One game like fan-tan maybe. Maybe he part lost. If you not know, you not buy."

We bought them at a reasonable price, took them down to Bannister's studio, got the books out. We had the translation by Professor James Legge of Oxford, published by the Clarendon Press, among the Sacred Books of the East, edited by F. Max Müller. Also a volume in French, by Harlez of the Royal Belgian Academy, and a German treatise which I couldn't read.

The wands themselves are supposed to be the key to the great book. When shuffled and tossed in the air so that they fall, each "heads or tails" as it were, they are then laid parallel and will form (like the Heinz pickle products) one of 57 varieties of the mystical hexagram.

Here they are. The ringed one, No. 49, the *ko* hexagram, is the one that got us into trouble. We should have been warned by Confucius who said, "If some years were added to my life, I would give fifty to the study of the *Yi*, and might even then fall into grievous errors."

THE HEXAGRAMS, in the order in which they appear in the Yî, and were
arranged by king Wăn.

8	7	6	5	4	3	2	1
pî	sze	sung	hsü	măng	kun	khwăn	khien

16	15	14	13	12	11	10	9
yü	khien	tâ yü	thung zăn	phî	thâi	lî	hsiâo khû

24	23	22	21	20	19	18	17
fû	po	pî	shih ho	kwăn	lin	kû	sui

32	31	30	29	28	27	26	25
hăng	hsien	lî	khan	tâ kwo	î	tâ khû	wû wang

40	39	38	37	36	35	34	33
kieh	kien	khwei	kiâ zăn	ming î	zin	tâ kwang	thun

48	47	46	45	44	43	42	41
zing	khwăn	shăng	zhui	kâu	kwâi	yî	sun

56	55	54	53	52	51	50	49
lü	făng	kwei mei	kien	kăn	kăn	ting	ko

64	63	62	61	60	59	58	57
wei zî	kî zî	hsiâo kwo	kung fû	kieh	hwăn	tui	sun

In addition to being the key to the book, the wands were also supposed to open other magic doors through which the spirit could stroll into the past or future, walk through walls, across the ocean, over mountains, to heaven, hell, or Honolulu—depending on which hexagram you tossed. To "send your soul into the infinite," you shake and toss your tortoise shells like poker dice, then arrange the wands parallel and fix the resulting hexagram firmly in your visual memory. Next, you must visualize an imaginary closed door with this symbol painted on it. All you know about the imaginary door is that if it swings open at all, it will open away from you—as if pushed. Next you kneel, or sit cross-legged like a Buddha, or squat on your haunches, if you choose, like a Chinese bandit waiting for his head to be cut off. You try to make your mind a blank, simply staring in imagination at the door and at the symbol. You do it either in the dark or blindfolded or simply with your eyes closed, if you have the will power to keep them closed for what may be a long time.

After a while, maybe in a half hour, maybe in seven or eight hours, maybe not at all in any single given trial, the door will seem to swing slowly open. Then, in your imagination, you go through it. You don't merely look through it. You go through it, in your imagination. You "arise out of your body," as the book says, and "walk through the door." What you see, encounter, and experience on the other side is believed by the esoteric to be seen by the soul's eye—to be experienced by the astral body.

I believe soul's eyes and astral bodies are boloney, and that here is again merely another—if one of the oldest and most complicated—methods of rapping at the door of your own subconscious. But it certainly bangs on that sometimes, like a hammer on a brazen gong. Whatever bell it rings, it rings it. Some of the university professors were amiably interested in our experiments, and I shall never forget the night when Morris Bishop of Cornell went through the door to become a monk in the old Abbey of Solesmes, and chanted pure Gregorian in the old Latin. It was no proof of the old reincarnation tommyrot, because he was a Latin scholar (which is the crux generally left out of such recounted episodes), and had sung Gregorian plain chant long before he started writing *Limericks after Lear*. My own unhappy adventures beyond the door consisted always in seeking something I could never find, and are consequently not worth mentioning. What happened to various others beyond the door was often dull, but sometimes astonishing, and not always entirely respectable. There was one memorable night when a chubby professor of Greek from Columbia—who in his state of normal consciousness disbelieves in one sort of fairies and heartily dislikes the other sort—became a wanton young female Corybant.

In the hair-raising adventure we had at the last with Nastatia Filipovna, there was a disturbing element of coincidence —absent in the Greek professor's case—between the transformation she experienced and the esoteric meaning of the particular hexagram she was concentrating upon. I'm not trying, however, to play this account two ways against the middle. It is true that she had tossed the *ko* hexagram by pure chance, and knew nothing of its special significance—but despite that fact, which is of the sort the esoterists love to harp upon until the cows come home, I stand solidly on the side of those who believe that such coincidences, no matter how sensational, are never anything but—sheer, gratuitous coincidences. The Chinese ideograph for *ko* is ⌗. Both

Harlez and Professor Legge translate it as meaning: "Skin; hide; fur; leather; also to skin; to flay. Also, figuratively, to undergo change; to be made different." Among the magical properties ascribed to *ko* in the *Yi King,* quoting from the Legge translation, are these:

> The common man may change his face; the sage may change his whole being as does the leopard.
>
> Two sisters may live together in the same skin, differing and opposed, yet the same.
>
> The great sage may change himself as the tiger changes its form and stripes.

I had known Nastatia Filipovna in the days just after the World War. She was a Russian refugee who had dropped her title, had come to New York, had gone through the usual vicissitudes, then married a Cleveland manufacturer, and dropped out of sight. I'd heard nothing from her for a number of years when there came one morning in my local mail, scrawled in an imperious yet childish hand, a note from the St. Regis. It said, "Take me to eat lobsters. And bring me that Bannister of yours if you can find him."

I phoned Bannister, and we took her to luncheon. He had met her in the old days, when she was singing with Balieff, and she wasn't the sort one easily forgets. I suppose "violent" would be as good a single descriptive adjective as any, and I'm inclined to believe that her physiological savagery, perhaps as much as her psychology and temperament, had a bearing on the course things took when her atavistic passions were unleashed. Nastatia was an aristocrat—and a savage. She was far too handsome in an animal sort of way to be in good taste in civilized bourgeois Anglo-Saxon society. All her physical traits, though superb, were exaggerated. She was tall, narrow-waisted, full-breasted, had coarse but beautiful brown hair. Her tawny, brown-flecked eyes were enormous and wide-set under a powerful but low forehead. She had a large nose, and a big, full-curved mouth with teeth that flashed magnificently when she smiled but became ugly when she lost her temper. As for her manners, they were those of an eccentric grand duchess, or a savage, depending on how you choose to differentiate.

At luncheon, she told us of some experiences she'd been having. That was why she wanted to see Bannister. She'd known Rasputin, had dabbled in occultism, and had found a Russian fortune-teller in Cleveland who had initiated her into crystal gazing. She had begun to be able to go into self-induced trances, but hated everything that happened to her in the trances. To begin with, she didn't like Cleveland, she didn't like her husband, she didn't like America. Trance stuff and the occult are escape mechanisms, just as drugs and liquor are. She didn't like reality. But she didn't like what she'd encountered in the crystal-ball illusion world of unreality either! She kept "sliding across," she said, into a camp of Mongols, where she herself, with some other women, was engaged in cutting up the carcass of a bear with a stone knife.

In these trance experiences she suffered cold, discomfort, brutal treatment. She hated the "hard work," the "dirty skins" she wore, the smells, the "burned food." And the worst of it was that now, every time she sent herself "across," she kept "sliding back" to that brutal life. She talked in commonplace, petulant terms, as if complaining about having to live in one sort of house when she wanted to live in another.

"I don't want to live in Cleveland, but I don't want to sleep in caves either, and be clubbed about by cave men!" she protested, as if we were to blame for it.

"It's jolly well good for you, you know," said Bannister. "Clubbing is what you need, and I hope every time you go back there they beat you black and blue. But speaking seriously, my dear, I'd give my eyeteeth for a real throwback of that sort, if it's real. They are extremely rare. I don't suppose you've thought to make notes or check your experiences against what is actually known of cave life? You don't know what this stuff of yours may tap!"

Bannister was off on his hobby.

"It's stupendous, if it's real! If you weren't so selfish you'd realize it. But no, you want your castle in the Caucasus. Or you want to be Catherine the Great. And you think I'll help you do that, my dear? Well, I won't. But I'd love to help you in the other direction—farther and farther back."

Nastatia flew into a rage. "Of course!" she retorted angrily. "You have always been a filthy swine. I come to you unhappy, and all you think about is your own rotten experiments. You ought to know that I won't be anybody's Trilby. To hell with you! I am not interested in adding to other people's knowledge. I am interested in myself."

"Come, Nastatia," Bannister protested, "don't lose your temper. I apologize. You'll never be anybody's Trilby. But if you want to try a different door from the one you've been using . . ."

We told her all we knew about the *Yi King,* and of course she wanted to try it. So we invited her down that same night to Bannister's vast apartment-studio, hung with crimson curtains and black drapes, stinking with incense, cluttered with

Tibetan idols, Hindu Durgas, prayer wheels, gongs, demon masks, and magical gimcracks from every corner of the globe. What we were doing was in one sense as completely respectable as the Sunday evening table-tippings my aunt used to participate in with other credulous members of the Methodist Ladies' Aid Society. There's no more intrinsic evil in the *Yi King* than in a ouija board. And we had in the party a thoroughly decent young British vice-consul, Edward Gay, who had spent a lot of time in the Orient and whose interest in these matters was as honest as that of my friends at Columbia. Yet what we were doing now was dangerous, as it turned out. Nastatia was a neurasthenic, hyperimaginative type, already addicted to occult escape mechanisms.

On the night the thing happened, she had been kneeling for a couple of hours, on the floor in the center of the crimson-draped studio, with her eyes closed, in semidarkness. The three of us sat quietly waiting to see whether the door would open for her or not. She said petulantly, "My knees hurt. I am getting numb." She presently groaned, let her legs slump, and was on her haunches, sitting on her heels, but with her body still upright. Her head sagged, and after another full hour had passed in silence, we wondered whether she had gone to sleep. Then she said:

"The door is moving. The door is opening. But it?s opening into the outdoors! I supposed it would open into another room. It's beautiful out there . . . and yes . . . I'm going.

"Snow . . . everything's white . . . everywhere snow," she kept murmuring, "and the moon . . . the moon on the white snow . . . and black trees over there against the sky. Yes, I'm outside now, I am lying in the snow . . . pressed against the snow . . . I am not cold . . . I am wearing a fur coat. I am lying naked in a fur coat . . . and I am warm in the snow . . . flat with my belly and chin on the snow I lie. It is good to lie warm in the snow. . . ."

"Do you get what it's about?" I whispered to Bannister.

"Not the faintest idea," he replied. "Do you?"

Nastatia was talking again, and quite apart from its trance-like dreaminess, her voice sounded puzzled too: "I am moving now . . . but I am not walking. I am crawling on my hands and knees . . . why am I crawling? . . . but I'm not crawling now, I'm running, on my hands and feet, lightly . . . now! now! now! . . . I'm running lightly like the wind . . . how good the snow smells! I have never smelled the snow before. And there's another good smell. Ah! Ah! Faster . . . faster . . . faster. . . ."

She was breathing heavily, panting. Her big handsome mouth was open, drooling. And when she next broke the silence, it was with sounds that were not human. There were yelps, slavering, panting, and then a deep baying such as only two sorts of animals on earth emit when they are running—hounds and wolves.

"My God!" whispered Bannister. "She's turning into one, there on the floor! Her face is changing! See!"

"You silly ass," said the Vice-Consul sharply, "she always had that face . . . big teeth . . . pointed nose." He snapped on the lamp nearest him. No horrid physical miracle was occurring, but it was bad enough and ugly enough, without that. Nastatia had always had a predatory, vulpine face, as many humans have, and now it was horrible. Gay went over to where she crouched, took her by the hand, slapped her smartly on both cheeks and cried, "Come out of it, Nastatia! Wake up! It's all right. Wake up! You've been dreaming."

The girl snarled hideously, her eyes wide open now, and leaped for his throat. She would have torn his throat with her teeth if the long-crouched position had not numbed her so that she lurched and fell heavily. And now, literally on all fours and crawling, she slithered, still snarling, into the dark shadows of the corner. We had the lights on, snared her in big blankets, wrapped her tight as she struggled like a maniac, put ammonia under her nose, and she came out of it.

We helped her to a couch. We brought a towel and a basin. We didn't talk much. We brought her brandy. In a few minutes she made us find her handbag with powder and make-up. She went into the bathroom. She came out and sank into an armchair and lighted a cigarette, and said, "What time is it?"

Presently she yawned, and said, "I'm hungry."

It was about two o'clock. She lighted another cigarette. We found a taxi and went over to Siegel's place under the Sixth Avenue L for sandwiches and coffee.

A week passed, and then she telephoned that she wanted to try it again.

She remembered what had happened—and she liked it!

She told me that as a tiny child, she had seen wolves coursing over moonlit snow in Russia, had thought it beautiful, and wished with all her passionate baby soul to run with them. It was a nice rationalization, but if the thing had happened a few centuries before, in the full flower of inquisitorial superstition . . . and had become known . . . we might all have been thrown in the bonfire for it.

Part Three

WHITE MAGIC, PROFESSOR RHINE,
THE SUPERNORMAL, AND
JUSTINE

I. Presentation of an Open Question, to Which a Negative Answer May Not Be the Final Word

THE veil of the supernatural which once shrouded witch-craft and black magic has been pretty well pierced from many angles.

The veil of the supposedly supernormal, however, still shrouds more than one deep mystery. Those who believe we have pierced it a little, and are convinced by what we have seen that there is nothing supernormal behind it, may not have pierced the holes deep enough, or may not have poked them in the right places. Those who believe they have pierced it deeper and glimpsed authentic phenomena which can only be explained in terms of the supernormal may have seen distorted images or may have interpreted them wrongly. By the supernormal, in this context, I mean anything which occurs contrary to the fixed known laws of time-space, the fixed known rules of logic, or endows its supposed possessor with senses and powers outside those laws and rules, as known up to now. It is "supernormal," of course, in a different context, for a man to play perfect blindfold chess, or add six-column sums by lightning calculation at a glance. But I am dealing only with the first connotation in this book.

The veil of the supernormal cloaks witchcraft, telepathy,

clairvoyance, occultism, mystical excursions into the past and future—only incidentally. It is indeed the veil which shrouds all life in mystery.[1] Religion has sought to illuminate the shadows by the light of faith, and philosophy has sought to do the same thing by the light of reason. The two lights have somewhat neutralized each other. I happen to stand with those who believe that life—including witchcraft incidentally, and including also all phenomena of the so-called supernormal—can be interpreted in terms of reason. I believe that seers, mystics, clairvoyants, telepathists, spiritualists, readers of the future, fakirs, yogis, and dervishes,[2] whether in cells, séances, or laboratories, can reveal nothing beyond what has first entered their consciousness through the channels of the five normal senses, and has subsequently been churned over, sifted, reshuffled, trance emotionalized, and frequently distorted by their own unconscious and subconscious minds.[3]

[1] See Appendix, p. 324.

[2] Most of our progress from ape, to cave, to man, has been built on sensory foundations. In the world of mysticism there have been exceptions such as Jesus Christ, Gautama Buddha, Lao-tse—and possibly Mahatma Gandhi in our time. But the average oriental swami is as inferior to the average Rotarian, in power, brains, intelligence, harmonious adjustment to life, co-ordination, and capacity for active happiness, as the barnacle is inferior to the baboon. The average dervish or yogi, squatting immobile for a year, or for a thousand years, in his lotus posture, with his heel stuck in his anus, is as inferior to the average American business man on his hurried commercial-airline-flagship way to a Chicago convention as is a bullfrog on a lily pad to Nicholas Murray Butler. If you prefer a bullfrog on a lily pad to Nicholas Murray Butler—you are a mystic. I don't know whether I am a mystic or not.

[3] The term "unconscious" or "subconscious" is interpreted differently by different schools of psychology. All admit that the human, and animal mind too, consists of something more than the conscious experience of the present moment. And all admit that this "something more" contains at least the framework of instincts or inborn drives and the system of memories or residues of past experience. Each momentary sensation resulting

God knows they produce plenty of authentic *abnormal* "psychic" phenomena, sometimes physical phenomena—faintings and fits, convulsions, catalepsy, rigidity, glazed eyes, hypnotic trances. I've even seen them froth at the mouth. A lot of them are absolutely sincere. They cannot know—even if rationalists are right about it—that what froths up must be derived from their own subconscious—no matter how beautiful it may be as in the cases of certain epileptic saints; or how wicked and abominable, as in the cases of certain esoteric sinners.

All hard-boiled rationalists felt that way about it—and felt they had a right to feel that way about it—up to and through

from an external stimulus derives its "fringe" of primary and secondary meaning and its capacity for significant and intelligent reaction from the pre-existing or unconscious part of the mind. It is agreed to be mainly responsible for ordinary dreams and for creative imagination. But when you turn from a consideration of the functions or effects of the unconscious to a consideration of its intrinsic nature, you enter the arena of a free-for-all dogfight—a scrambling and scrambled conflict of not always amiably diverging opinions. At one extreme are the behaviorists who insist that the unconscious or subconscious is only a somewhat misleading name for that part of the brain structure consisting of association or conduction paths produced by previous experience; and that as such it is purely physiological, with nothing mental or psychical about it. At the other extreme are the psychological mysticists, following the late William James, who regard the unconscious mind as a sort of entity similar to the conscious mind, but vaster in extent, a great sea of fears, hopes, desires, and thoughts more or less insulated from the conscious mind but more or less united to the "cosmic mind" and endowed with metaphysical powers, from which might derive telepathy, clairvoyance, prophecy, etc. Between the materialistic view of the behaviorists and the "idealistic" view of the mysticists, there are a number of intermediate positions. I am not committed to, or meaning to defend, any of these positions, whether intermediate or extreme. I am using the term "unconscious" or "subconscious" merely to designate tentatively and in its purely functional sense, any capacity or power or manifestation that would seem by its character to be a product of the individual's mind but not of his conscious mind, in the sense that the term conscious is generally accepted.

the beginning of this twentieth century, while the phenomena were still confined to monastic cells, spiritualist prayer meetings, fortune-tellers' booths and mediumistic séances; and while such "scientific" investigations as went on were confined mostly to cranks on the one side who wanted to be convinced by the swamis and mediums and on the other side to honest debunkers like the late Houdini. Such unprejudiced individuals and organizations as really investigated it—including the *Scientific American* and Houdini—got negative results and publicly exposed a lot of fraud and charlatanry.

The picture has somewhat changed, however, within recent years. A basic phase of this subject, along with its supposed phenomena, has been rescued by Professor J. B. Rhine of Duke University, Gardner Murphy of Columbia, the late William McDougall of Oxford, Harvard and Duke, from the half-world of Indian guides, tipping tables, tambourines, and trumpets, and been lifted for purposes of prolonged and honest study into the completely respectable world of the scientific laboratories and scientific examination, in many of the big universities. I don't believe they have yet proven anything conclusive,[4] or that they will, by their present methods. But I can be wrong about that—and whether I'm right or wrong, the whole thing has become, for the first time in the world's history, a scientific problem, scientifically stated, with an honest solution being honestly sought for.

In less orthodox ways, and with no possibility of laboratory control, the investigation of these same phenomena has been a part of my lifelong obsession in witchcraft and magic. If the orthodox laboratory research gentlemen have a justifiable

[4] See Appendix, p. 327.

contempt for the sort of hot and sweating, rough, occasionally dangerous plowing I've been doing in this field of the supposedly supernormal, I must admit to having a slight reciprocatory contempt for their unheated, surface scratching, which has broken no deep earth up to now—for their efforts to prove or disprove something in so deep and emotionally fox-fire-glimmering a swamp field with cold little decks of cards, guessing games and adding machines. I don't think they've yet taken off their gloves and grabbed the dragon firmly by the tail—if there is any dragon.

Whatever there is to it, if only illusions, delusions of coincidence, in which you and some millions of others *have remembered* the one time you had a premonition that Aunt Sally would be run over by a truck or Uncle Charlie drowned at sea (and she was run over or he was drowned) but have *forgotten* the equally strong premonitions you have had when nothing subsequently happened—these supposed telepathic extra-sensory flashes that did pan out, almost always occur when you are consciously or unconsciously under some worry, stress, or strain; sometimes mental, sometimes physical, sometimes both. Real and provable or not—they almost never occur "cold." They almost never occur to people who are indifferent, whose emotional condition prior to their occurrence is that of calm, cowlike normalcy.

I think Rhine and his associates have handicapped themselves by the utter calmness which prevails in the extra-sensory excursion trips on which they conduct calm, unworried excursionists by the hundreds of thousands in calm and full possession of their five ordinary, normal senses. If there is such a thing as extra-sensory perception, I don't think they'll ever awaken it to startling positive performance in that way.

If there is such latent power, I think it's much more likely to be stirred up by such experiments as the swamis, mystics, yogi engage in—prolonged sleeplessness, fasting, numbness, anaesthesia—anything not too dangerous that may short-circuit or lull to abeyance the five normal senses and leave the door wider open for extra-sensory phenomena (if any) to kick through. And I go the whole hog on it.

That's how the long-kneeling adept of the *Yi King* taps on the door. Hindu fakirs lie on beds of nails or stare into the sun till they go blind. The Arab Rufia, a sect of Moslem mystics allied with the Melewi, hang themselves up by one wrist and dangle like bats in the darkness for hours until they go into a trance, or faint. The Eskimo witch-doctors described by Peter Freuchen have themselves tightly bound with thongs, and go into their trances only after the long-cramped posture has worn out and dulled their normal senses. The more civilized Melewi, the most cultured mystic sect of Islam, whirl until they're dizzy. The completely civilized mystical mandarin sits cross-legged, bends his head down over his fat belly, and stares at his own navel. They're all the same thing, really. If you have the will power to sit motionless for eighteen hours or so, in an ordinary chair, keeping your mind as open and empty as possible, and stare fixedly at the point of a lead pencil, you'll end by having all sorts of exciting, sometimes beautiful and sometimes terrifying "revelations"—even though they're nothing but illusions.

If, as I suspect, these revelations, messages, experiences, in telepathy, clairvoyance, spiritual vision, are never extra-sensory or supernormal, but merely well up from the depths of the experimenters' released subconscious, they can be nevertheless violently exciting and have been known to produce (as a sort of by-product), sublime masterpieces in poetry, religious and mystical prose, etc.

If anything more important "comes out," it's more likely to come by hammering at the door, by breaking the door open, if there is such a door, than by discreet, cold tapping, followed by the insertion through an imaginary crack of a spook visiting card printed with stars and circles. If and when the door does open, the subject is sure to see more clearly with his extra-sensory vision, when he has baggage-checked his normal five senses in the waiting room outside.

Dr. Rhine's technique in seeking to "baggage-check" the normal senses, is for his subjects to be calm, at ease, relaxed, comfortable, both physically and mentally—the body completely calm and the mind as calm and empty as possible. Cats, dogs, saints, cows, savages, primitives, old ladies on rocking chairs in the country, can do this, but it's next to impossible for most of us. It's easier in a way than bending over and staring at your navel till your neck is numb and your brain empty or dreamy—but in another way it's harder. "Blanking" the mind so that *anything* can come into it is the one thing nearly all of us are desperately afraid of and incessantly struggling against. Hence crossword puzzles, anagrams, contract bridge, knitting, reading. We have to be at something every waking instant, if it's only mechanically reading the label on a tube of toothpaste . . . for fear . . .

Dr. Rhine's results seem to show that his subjects seem to do less well when they're tired. My guess about that, and I think it's a shrewd guess, is that they simply don't get tired enough. All five of their normal senses are still functioning normally. Their minds cannot be completely blank of sensory things. Yet it has always seemed to me the simplest sort of common sense that a vital step toward extra-sensory perception consists in breaking as far as possible—or at least wearing thin—the connection with the five ordinary senses that we are normally completely slaves to.

Rhine and the ESP investigators, it seems to me, are undertaking to do with telepathy, clairvoyance, and what was once "spook" stuff, the same job that chemistry and physics did with alchemy—but with one perhaps important oversight. Just as the chemists and physicists lifted the search for the elixir of life, the philosopher's stone, the transmutation of lead into gold, from the dark hell's caldron of the alchemist, who was a magician and sorcerer, into the clean test tubes and crucibles of the scientific laboratory—so Rhine and his associates have lifted the search for supernormal, extra-sensory vision out of the dark, veiled atmosphere of the modern, mediumistic witches' caves of Endor, with their trumpets, tambourines, "Indian guides," and phony ectoplasm, into the clear light of controlled psychological laboratory experiment.

But they might learn something by remembering that the same hot fires burn beneath the crucibles of science as burned beneath the caldron of the alchemist. The caldron still boils and seethes in chemistry. The night skies over Bethlehem and Pittsburgh glow with as red a light as ever did the night skies over cave and forest when the old alchemists tossed in the fat of toads, bat's blood, and sometimes a murdered baby to make the lead turn into gold. Physical sciences abandoned the crazy superstitions, but still turn on the heat. Rhine and his associates light no fires. They never turn on the heat. Their mental test tubes are always cold.

It is true that chemistry, with even hotter crucibles than

the magicians had, has never been able to turn lead into gold, or find the elixir of life—but it has turned pitchblende into radium, and found vitamins.

Now Rhine—even if he turned on more stress, strain, warmth, more mental and emotional excitement, more psychological and mental heat than the Greeks once did in their wild orgies around the oracles of Delphi and Dodona, or in the Mysteries of Eleusis, or Ezekiel when he prophesied and saw the wheel, or the great Saint Theresa in her long ecstasies—might never in my opinion turn the dross of mediumistic buncombe into pure telepathy or pure clairvoyance; but if he warmed things up and kept the fires controlled, he might discover and learn more about whatever latent mental, psychic powers may lie dormant and unused in the modern Western world.

The late William James, probing the same problems as Rhine's but from a different angle, experimenting with the "mystical vision" and the "anesthetic revelation," turned on the heat in Harvard, experimented with loss of sleep, with ether, laughing gas, fatigue, strain, hashish, analonium. He uncorked experiences more baffling and exciting than have the current extra-sensory laboratories, but was never able to persuade himself that they came from any other source than the subconscious, or that they ever contained any elements that postulated extra-sensory perception or clairvoyant power.

This supernormal stuff is all in the same bag, you know, whether you split it into telepathy, clairvoyance, mystical vision, fourth-dimensional excursions, or the metaphysical corollaries of the Einstein theory in which space if not time curves round and back on itself like a serpent swallowing its tail. Dr. Rhine is not merely experimenting, you know, with telepathy and clairvoyance confined to the immediate instant, to the "nick" of time. He is experimenting also with precognition, previsionary clairvoyance, seeing into the future. Also with retrocognition, i.e., seeing back into the past clairvoyantly.

If and when the laboratory people produce anything as worth recording, as lasting and exciting as have the world's great white magicians, prophets, sages, seers, and mystics, or as Margaret Prescott Montague recounted years ago in the *Atlantic Monthly*, only then will I believe their cold test tubes constitute as good a method as the red-hot, fire-illumined crucible.

If and when either Rhine or the Grand Lama of Tibet, working cold or hot, produces *one* individual authentically possessed of telepathic or clairvoyant power, and *capable of really using it*, I will then believe that it exists, as an extra-sensory power, outside normal consciousness, outside the normal senses—and also outside the limits of the subconscious as we know it up to now.

If it ever does happen, it won't make the slightest difference whether I believe it or not, or whether you do either, any more than it makes any difference whether you believe in dynamite or not—because *one* person authentically possessed of telepathic or clairvoyant power, and *capable of pragmatically using it, could make the world his toy for good or evil, wreck all the stock markets in less than a week, smash governments with their secret diplomacy, control the outcome of all battles, whether in the Baltic or in "big business."* He could begin by breaking the bank at Monte Carlo, all the baccarat banks, three-card monte and "Russian" banks in the world, pick up the Union Pacific *en passant,* then go on and break the Bank of England.

Clairvoyance is believed by many to include not merely the power of projecting the extra-sensory vision through space, and through opaque objects, the pasteboard of Rhine's cards, through solid walls, across hundreds of intervening miles, to perceive things occuring elsewhere in the *current instant* of time; but also the power to project it both backward and forward in space-time.[5]

If space-time is curved, and if time and space are interdependent, as Einstein holds in theory, then, by one of the metaphysical corollaries, the past, present, and future instant are perhaps space-time illusions—the future already existent in space and the sum total of the past still spatially existent in the current instant.

Light travels at the speed of 186,000 miles per second, and many of the great fixed stars are hundreds of light-years distant from the earth. Beetle-Goose (Betelgeuse) is more than 150 light-years distant. The Swan (Cygnus) is 1,290 light-years distant. Andromeda's Whirling Spray, that spiral galaxy which is another "universe" beyond the Milky Way, is more than 800,000 light-years distant from the earth. If you were somewhere out there, and could see light carried there from here, bringing you visual images, what you would see in the light-waves would be our ancient stone age with its cave men, Pharaoh building the first pyramid, Caesar's legions marching—depending on how many light-years distant you stopped off—all occurring as images *in the present nick of time.* If you were sitting today on a remote planet

[5] See Appendix, p. 332.

revolving around Betelgeuse, and had a telescope sufficiently powerful to see what was occurring here on this earth—you would see George Washington crossing the Delaware. If you went to one 450 light-years distant and looked back, you'd see Columbus crossing the Atlantic. The light and visual images which reached your eye could bring you nothing later than the length of time it took the light to travel, so that you'd see those things happening again in distant time-space, in what would be for you the present nick of time. In visual terms and terms of light, to this hypothetical earthling space-projected to distant planets, if he went to a planet 75 light-years distant, our Civil War would have concluded yesterday, and the shot which killed Abraham Lincoln would not yet have flashed. As for our present nick of time, with its Manhattan skyscrapers, streamline trains, airplanes, Hitler's madness, current on the instant here, it would still be veiled in a 75-years-distant future, to a visual observer 75 light-years away.

A final curious, purely Einsteinian corollary of the queer space-time relation in terms of light is that if you could travel through space with a speed *greater* than light, you could stop off like excursionists or God, live in any period of the past you chose; and so, it would seem, could likewise go scooting into the future. To May Sinclair, philosopher and metaphysician as well as novelist, is attributed the limerick which caps these scientific fantasies:

> There was a young lady named Bright,
> Whose speed was much greater than light;
> She went off one day
> (In a relative way),
> And returned on the previous night.

If Einstein's theory is sound, and if such speed were attainable, the young lady could literally do it, while telepathy and clairvoyance, including the reading of the future, would become as simple as television and the radio.

If tranced esoterics, cataleptic dervishes, or your Aunt Sally ever do get glimpses of the hidden past or future, they probably get them in some such fourth-dimensional manner, piercing through and beyond what Jung and Fulton Oursler call the "slit" in time.

If anything happened to Kipling's Brushwood Boy or to Christopher Isherwood more recently in Connecticut,[6] where he saw his niece playing tennis *next* summer and read a birdcage catalogue published in 1949, it must have been something like what happened to the young lady in the limerick.

I got some extraordinary results in this category which I'll describe in a later chapter . . . with a young lady named Justine. If they consisted of anything beyond delving, dreaming, and wandering in the rich caverns of her own deep subconscious mind, it must have been in that mysterious category.

One thing only is certain, and that is that the *illusion* of it, frequently more startling and vivid than any present material reality, is something nearly all people have experienced once or twice in a lifetime, usually under nervous strain, fatigue, or stress. It is a condition which can be deliberately produced, increased in frequency, prolonged in time, by deliberate technique and practice. I believe the possibility of experiencing these illusions, or whatever they are, to be inherent in all humans. Anybody can go through that "door" with training and patience. I've been through it, like all who have experimented with magic whether white or black. I

[6] See Appendix, p. 332.

think anybody, as I've said, is potentially able to do it. But it isn't easy. If you think concentration is easy, "blanking" the normal activities of the surface-conscious mind, staring with closed eyes at nothing, or staring with open eyes at a globe or pencil point, sitting cramped for long hours—just try it for *one* hour! In the East where they've been at it for five thousand years, only the highest adepts can do it without mechanical aids. Only the greatest mystic seers and saints can do it by sheer will power alone.

And even then, the memorable experiences seem to come almost by accident, as my most memorable seemingly supernormal experience did one night on Harrison Smith's yawl, the *Cossack*, in an Atlantic storm off the New England Coast —off Monhegan Light.

II. "Astral Body" on a Boat

THE *Cossack* is a 42-foot yawl, teakwood-finished, built in Germany in the great days of Kaiser Wilhelm—and was owned for a while in America by the New York publisher and yachtsman, Harrison Smith. He sold her not long ago, and now has a newer boat, the *Cossack II*.

During the summers when I was crewing on the old *Cossack*, in the late twenties, she used to lie at the Yacht Club in Port Washington. She was a grand boat and, before my time, had crossed the Atlantic more than once. She had cruised in the Isles of Greece, outridden North Atlantic storms, and come through high adventures in the Bay of Biscay. We sailed her frequently in the Sound, occasionally up through the Cape Cod Canal, occasionally to Martha's Vineyard, Nantucket, and Bar Harbor. Hal himself was skipper, and we generally sailed with an amateur crew of three or four. One August he and I alone took her out of Port Washington, planning to pick up the other members of the party at New London. Arriving at New London, we found a wire saying they hadn't been able to catch their train on the day they'd planned, but would join us later, up in Maine. So we decided to go on. Normally it would have been nothing for the two of us to handle her. Hal was a veteran skipper. Being shorthanded, we could put in anywhere we pleased to anchor and sleep at night. But we got caught in a memorable storm off Monhegan Light, and he wisely decided that the safest thing was to run for it, way offshore, and ride it out. The *Cossack* could take it. The *Cossack* could take anything in open water. And there would have been no sense in risking piling her up inshore, trying to make a harbor. It was never dangerous. It was merely an exciting little adventure, in which we didn't risk losing anything but sleep. But the storm continued; the wind came mostly out of the northwest. We were blown well out to sea; and stayed out there three days and nights. Nobody worried. There was nothing to worry about—except provisions. We had been going to buy them later when the party was complete, and the only reserve we had aboard was some old cans of corned beef. The goddamned stuff must have been aboard for a couple of years. But we weren't very hungry. We were both walleyed from loss of sleep, for close to ninety hours. The boat couldn't take care of herself in that weather, even running before the wind. One of us had to be continually at the wheel, with the other continually on call. Most of the time we were both on deck. Then, when it had quieted a little, we took alternating four-hour shifts, one of us at the wheel, while the other tried to snatch four hours of sleep below. What with the excitement, our liking each other, our talk of Moby Dick, our struggles to heat the goddamned corned-beef hash and keep the coffee pot from turning over, I don't think either of us ever thought about being physically tired; and I don't recall that we were ever tired, in a body-muscle sense at all. But we were walleyed, dopey, and at the same time keyed to a sort of supersensitivity, from prolonged loss of sleep. We felt, thought, and saw things with a sort of acute superlucidity which made it seem as if a veil or fog had been lifted from our minds and from the normal outline of the masts against the thick sky. We talked about it. Anybody who has, in the war or elsewhere, gone for an abnormally long time without sleep, under exciting circumstances which make sleep still impossible, will know what I am talking about. It gives the same sort of seemingly mystical clarity of inner vision that dentist's gas or anesthetics sometimes do, in the transitional moments, going in and coming out.

At eight o'clock on the evening before what was to be the last day of the storm, Hal relieved me at the wheel, and I went below to lie down and try to sleep. I found I couldn't sleep. My mind was racing. In thinking of the curious abnormal state our minds were in, I began to recall a period I'd spent, engaged in long study, with a famous group of Eastern mystics who have been specialists for a thousand years in curious, abnormal states of mind. While in Arabia, I had served a novitiate in the celebrated Melewi Monastery in the mountains behind Syrian Tripoli. The Melewi, known only as "Whirling Dervishes" to our Western world, are the highest order of the Sufi, and are considered to be the most learned of all the mystical religious groups of Islam. Their whirling, which has caught the outside world's eye, has been circused, toured, and exploited—just as the Sistine Chapel Choir has, and for the same simple reason that its music, vestments, and its dancing, too, are beautiful. But to them, whirling is a way of inducing the mystical trance states in which they believe themselves endowed with supernormal senses, vision, and power. But it isn't all dancing and music by any means in a Melewi Monastery. A lot of it is plain, hard study. And I was thinking now of the efforts they had made to teach me the elemental principles on which they base their belief that the mind (or soul) and the body can be separated, that the mind (or soul) can go out beyond the body, can "shuffle off this mortal coil" temporarily, as it were, leaving it and returning to it, as one does with a house or a garment. By study, I don't mean that you memorize abracadabra or the ninety-nine names of Allah backward. They don't go in for hocus-pocus. In one of the first lessons, the monk in charge of my instruction had held a lighted candle to my hand, so that the flame touched, and said,

"Tell me what I am doing."

"You are burning me!" I yelped like a resentful kid.

"No," he said, "flame cannot touch *you*. You might have answered that I was burning your hand. And that, in a sense, would be moving toward the truth, but not far enough. Your hand is not you. And neither are the nerves running from your hand to your brain. And neither is your brain. Nor is your body you; nor any part of it, nor the sum total of it. If you devote your life to this, as I suppose you won't, you can reach the point where it would be *a* hand, rather than *your* hand that was being burned."

Presently he had reached over and deliberately torn the sleeve of my robe. Again he said,

"Tell me what I did."

I was going to say, "You have torn the sleeve of my robe," but recalled that they had handed it to me when I began the novitiate and had not let me pay for it, since everything in the monastery was common property. So I replied,

"You have torn the sleeve of a robe."

"That is better," he said. "And your body is no more you, no more your property either, than this robe is. Your body is simply a material object which you inhabit temporarily as you inhabit this garment. It is like your worldly wealth, if you happen to have any. You use it. It is, of course, not *you*. But it is not *yours* either. Nothing is you or yours, except your *self*—your *I*."

"Suppose," I had said, "that instead of a candle, you had lighted a bonfire and burned my body to ashes. . . ."

"Suppose," he said, "I threw this robe of yours in the bonfire instead. In that case you would be naked—of your robe. If your body were burned, you would be naked—of your body."

"It would hurt like fury," I said, and he replied, "It would indeed, unless you had become an adept. Have you forgotten that your own Christian saints have smiled and felt only the calm ecstasy of purification and deliverance as flames devoured their bodies? It is the same with our highest adepts."

"I'd hate to have to try it," I said, and my monk had answered with smiling candor, "I shouldn't like to try it myself. I doubt that I am sufficiently holy. But under easier circumstances, I have learned to detach the *self* from the material body, and if you remained with us long enough, we could teach you to do it too."

Of course, I hadn't remained in the monastery long enough —since "long enough" might have meant twenty years, a lifetime—but they'd taught me quite a lot, and once, I vividly now recalled as I lay there wide-eyed, sleepless, I had put a part of that teaching into practice, in America. I'd begun to be bothered with an impacted wisdom tooth. It turned out to be such a honey that my own dentist sent me to that emperor of tooth-pullers, Hasbrouck, who gave me gas and cracked it loose and pulled it out in pieces, along with some slivers from the jawbone. He'd poked novocain or something in it too, so that when I came out of the sleep, I felt nothing more than a slightly sore jaw, as if I'd been hit with a club. He'd said,

"In two or three hours when the shock wears off, it's going to hurt you, probably badly. I'm giving you these three morphine pills. . . ."

He told me what to do, and how to take one or more of them if need be. I went home in a taxi, feeling as if I'd been in a barroom fight, but feeling pretty good about it, with the morphine pills in my pocket. I lived in an apartment at Floyd Keeler's house, 52 West 12th Street, and Katie was South at the time, if I recall correctly. At any rate, I was alone there, midafternoon, still feeling pretty good. I lay down, as I'd been told, put a compress on the jaw, laid out the little box of pills with a glass of water, regarded their protective presence with contentment, and nearly dozed.

Around five P.M., it began. It wasn't much of anything at first—just a dull, increasing ache, but enough to make me think I'd better be taking one of the pills pretty soon. Then, all of a sudden, with no other warning, it started really doing its stuff—and it wasn't like anything I'd ever felt or dreamed of. I'd had my thumb caught in a car door once, but it couldn't touch what was happening now. It knocked me upright, as if my head had exploded, and I let out a screech. Before I could grab for the pills and glass, it subsided, and then began coming back, this time in waves instead of explosions. The pain was god-awful, but I felt astonishment, surprise, almost a slight detachment, about the waves. They suffused my inner universe. They began bright red, then began to glow, became white flame, and then turned black as the wave receded. I wondered if anything like that happened to women having babies. Was it like that when they screeched? There was nobody to hear me, so I let out a couple of good screeches. I thought, "If the black continued black, if the edges of light round the black went completely away . . . I suppose that would be fainting." The red waves came . . . turning to flame again. I thought, "God almighty, if I could get outside this, it would be really interesting." I remembered what the Melewi had tried to teach me, and thought now would be a time to try it. I'd just about forgotten the morphine pills. I hate pain, and am as much of a coward as anybody, but what was happening to me was one of the most violent and interesting things that had ever happened to me in my life. So I tried to do what they had taught me. There's no incantation hocus-pocus in it. There's a bit of technique which they call "shifted concentration," but what it boils down to is simply the persistent use of the will, toward detachment. I set about trying—and ended by never touching the morphine pills, because in a very few minutes, I had done what they taught me, completely. There it was—the waves and the pain, the red, the glow, the white flame; the stabbing pain and then the ache making everything turn black—the sequences kept occurring exactly as before—but instead of experiencing them in the sense of being torn by them, it was like calmly *remembering* them.

This part is perhaps a little difficult to describe. But it

had seemed to me it was exactly like going through violent, secondhand experiences, in reading a novel, or in calm remembrance. It doesn't give you any physical pain, or any psychic pain either, to remember when your thumb was caught in a car door, or when you had an inflamed appendix, or if you're a mother, when you had a baby, but you can remember all the details, how much it hurt, how it waved and varied. You can become fully re-aware of the pain, but the re-awareness doesn't pain you. Well, it was almost exactly like that, except that the awareness and the occurring were taking place simultaneously. They continued simultaneously for several hours, during which I lived in that truly "magical world" of Melewi detachment. When it finally died down, I was merely tired, and went to sleep. If I'd had a scientific mind, which I lack, I think I'd have sacrificed a thumbnail by banging it once with a hammer, while in that state, to see whether the detachment held—whether it would be *my* thumb, or just *a* thumb I whacked. But I overlooked the opportunity.

And now I lay sleepless, keyed nervously to abnormal tension, with my mind racing back to those experiences, while wind and wave pounded the *Cossack*, held on her course by Hal up there on deck at the wheel; I looked at the luminous dial of my watch to see when I'd be going to relieve him. It lacked only ten minutes to midnight when it would be my shift up there. I was about to go in the galley and make some coffee first, when I thought, or rather felt, with a sudden quick flash, Well, if I could do one of the things the Melewi taught me, perhaps I could now do another. Suppose I can. Suppose it's true. Suppose I try. Suppose I do it!

I lay back in the bunk, and closed my eyes, and began forming words. I can *send* my body up there to the wheel, a body with its eyes to watch the compass, a body with its hands to steer. I will send it. But *I* am not that body. *I* will remain here, to sleep. *I* will repose here, lying in the Melewi astral body, to sleep.

It was bright, cold daylight, with the sun glaring through the morning haze. The wind was still high, but the storm was abating. I was there at the wheel, and the boat was steady on her course. Hal, I learned later, had been shouting at me, then pounding me on the back, then trying to pull my hands away from the wheel. They were cold and blue like the hands of a dead man.

I said, "Good morning."

Hal said, "Good morning hell, Willie, what on earth happened to you? I thought you had passed out. Your eyes were wide open, and the boat was steady on her course . . . the wind hasn't changed . . . and she's been on it all night. But when I came on deck, I thought you had passed out. I should have come up at four, you know, but I went sound asleep, and you didn't call me. I guess you must have passed out with your eyes wide open, just before I came on deck."

I said, "What time is it?"

He said, "It's long past six."

We looked at our watches. It was nearly seven o'clock. He said, "Are you sure you're all right now? Can you get below all right?"

"Yes," I said, "I'm fine. By the way, did I come up last night, or did you come down and get me?"

He said, "What do you mean, Willie? It was just midnight, and I was just going to yell down when you came up. Don't you remember?"

I said, "Did I say anything to you?"

"No."

"Did I do anything strange?"

"Not unless your not saying anything was strange. I asked you if you wanted some coffee, and sort of wondered why you didn't answer."

So that was that. Whatever I'd done, I had done it. I had no recollection of anything that had occurred in the seven-hour interval since I'd repeated the word "sleep." One part of me, with feet, eyes, muscles, hands, functioning like a robot's, had gone up on deck and been there at the wheel doing its physical-mechanical job. Another part of me had been in deep and dreamless slumber—somewhere. I'm not insisting where, because I don't know where. The Melewi teach that it had been asleep in an "astral body" which was left lying below in the bunk, while the soulless, three-dimensional body of flesh and blood climbed up on deck. They teach that the astral body would have been invisible and intangible to the normal eye and touch, but that an adept could have literally seen its shadowy outlines. They teach that Hal —that is, any person with senses and perceptions solely normal—could have sat, or slept, in the same bunk, completely unconscious of any other presence. But that a cat or dog would have known. I'm not sure I believe any of that part of the Melewi teaching. I am inclined, on the contrary, to doubt it. I know simply that a part of me had slept soundly through the night, while another part of me, steering by wheel, wind, and compass, had held the *Cossack* steady—and had kept her on her course.

III. Our Modern Cagliostros

LOOKING back for my limited purpose upon Cagliostro simply as a man who claimed to be the greatest white magician of his epoch, sponsored by kings, princes, Marie Antoinette, and Cardinal de Rohan; idealized by Houdon, immortalized later by Dumas in *Joseph Balsamo* (and specifically leaving out my comparison his connection with affairs like that of the Queen's necklace, since none of the current gentlemen I propose to examine at length has ever been accused of swindling)—there are three outstanding Cagliostros, white magicians, alive and active in our modern Western world today, with a fine new crop coming up in 1940.[1] By calling them "white magicians," I mean they traffic in magic and the occult, claiming to help rather than harm their fellowman—and woman. By calling them "Cagliostros" [2] I

[1] See Appendix, p. 335.

[2] In using "Cagliostro" as a generic term applied to these famous modern occultists, I have no intention of asserting that any of them are charlatans. Whether an individual who traffics in white magic is a charlatan, or not, is always a matter of opinion, depending on whether or not you believe in his magic. To an atheist, for an extreme instance, a vested Roman Catholic priest celebrating the mysteries of the mass is technically a charlatan. To many rationalists, all white magicians are charlatans. Concerning the three gentlemen I propose to discuss, your opinions on this point will be your own.

mean that in process of doing this, they have variously won
fame and fortune; have consorted with and been sponsored
by the modern democratic equivalents of kings, cardinals,
princes, their wives and mistresses—on Wall Street and Park
Avenue, Park Row and the Champs Elysées. I have known
two of them fairly intimately at intervals over a long period
of years. The three are:

George Gurdjieff, founder of the Gurdjieff Institute in Fontainebleau and New York, which in its heyday is said to have had
twenty-nine schools scattered about in Europe and America.

Aleister Crowley, founder of the Great White Brotherhood,
the Order of Oriental Templars in England and America, and
of the College of the Holy Ghost, sometimes referred to as the
Abbey of Thelema, in Cefalù, Sicily.

Pierre Bernard, known as "Oom the Omnipotent," founder
of the wealthy Brae Burn club and cult at Nyack, New Jersey.
I have never met Mr. Bernard, who is sponsored by Rutherfords,
Vanderbilts, Dukes, the former Mrs. Ogden Mills, and many
other distinguished people, including the prize fighter Lou Nova.
I have, however, all the material publicly available on him, and
am including it in my appendix notes.[3]

George Gurdjieff, in my opinion, is, or was, the greatest
of the three. He first came to America in January, 1924, sponsored by the late Alfred Richard Orage, formerly editor of
the *New Age;* by the world-famous Russian mathematician
Ouspensky; by Muriel Draper, Zona Gale, Claude Bragdon,
Ernest Poole, and other variously celebrated or influential
Americans.

I was taken to meet him, privately, on the night after his
arrival, in a palatial suite in an old-fashioned uptown hotel,
and was so deeply impressed by his brains and brute strength

[3] See Appendix, p. 354.

that we sat talking until nearly dawn. Whether his power lay simply in the fields of hypnotism and autosuggestion, or went beyond it into authentic telepathy and clairvoyance, or even further into the Tibetan and Yoga fields of alleged occult miracle-working, I never became convinced—for the reason that I've never yet become convinced that power in these latter categories can exist at all. But whatever category Gurdjieff's power may have lain in—in those days he had power.

He had brought with him from Europe a group of forty disciples, and on the evening of January 23 gave a public demonstration at Leslie's Ballroom, 260 West 83rd Street. On February 9, he gave another demonstration to a crowded audience in Carnegie Hall. A number of other demonstrations, some free and some with an admission charge, were given at the Neighborhood Theatre, and elsewhere, and there was a farewell demonstration on March 3, again at Carnegie. These demonstrations consisted, as the programs put it, of "Movement, Music and Production of Phenomena," the latter based chiefly upon "hypnotism and magnetism in the broad sense." There were also "tricks, semi-tricks and real phenomena occurring in religious ceremonies."

The "hypnotic," "magnetic," mindreading, clairvoyant, and telepathic parts of the performances were varied and interesting, but since they were fundamentally no different from those of Houdini, who specifically denied any supernormal power whatsoever and insisted that the audience was being entertained by "stage magic," there is no point in describing them.

What excited and interested me was the amazing, brilliant, automatonlike, inhuman, almost incredible docility and robot-like obedience of the disciples, in the parts of the demonstrations which had to do with "movement." They were like a group of perfectly trained zombis, or like circus animals jumping through hoops ringed with fire, or like the soldiers of Christophe who marched without breaking step off the parapet of the citadel on that sheer mountainside in Haiti. They did things, without suffering any apparent hurt, almost as dangerous as dropping off a cliff, and certainly more dangerous than leaping through fiery hoops.

The group consisted of young and youngish women, most of whom were handsome and some of whom were beautiful; and of men who looked as if they had come, and probably did in most cases, from the best British and continental homes and universities. I met some of these disciples, and they were almost without exception people of culture, breeding, and intelligence. The demonstrations, I imagine, were to show the extent to which the Gurdjieff Institute in Fontainebleau had taught them supernormal powers of physical control, co-ordination, relaxation, etc. And there was no fake about it, regardless of whether it was supernormal or not, because if they hadn't learned supreme co-ordination, they'd have broken their arms and legs, and maybe their necks, in some of the stunts they did. But what I felt the demonstrations showed, even more than their control over themselves, was the terrific domination of Gurdjieff, the Master. At his command, they'd race, spread out, at breakneck speed, from left to right across the stage, and at another low command from him, freeze full flight as if caught by a race-track camera. Once I saw Gurdjieff push a dancer who had been "frozen" by his command in an attitude of difficult equilibrium. The dancer tumbled and rolled over several times, then rolled upright and was back again, apparently without volitionally *assuming* it—in the original frozen position.

Gurdjieff himself, a calm, bull-like man, with muscles in those days hard as steel, in immaculate dinner clothes, his head shaven like a Prussian officer's, with black luxuriant handle-bar mustaches, and generally smoking expensive Egyptian cigarettes, stood casually down in the audience, or off to the side beside the piano, which was not on stage. He never shouted. He was always casual. Yet always in complete command. It was as if he were a slave-master or wild-animal tamer, with an invisible bull whip swishing inaudibly through the air. Among his other qualities, he was a great showman, and a climax came one night which literally had the front rows out of their seats. The troupe was deployed extreme back stage, facing the audience. At his command, they came racing full tilt toward the footlights. We expected to see a wonderful exhibition of arrested motion. But instead, Gurdjieff calmly turned his back, and was lighting a cigarette. In the next split second, an aerial human avalanche was flying through the air, across the orchestra, down among empty chairs, on the floor, bodies pell-mell, piled on top of each other, arms and legs sticking out in weird postures—frozen there, fallen, in complete immobility and silence.

Only after it had happened did Gurdjieff turn and look at them, as they lay there, still immobile. When they presently arose, by his permission, and it was evident that no arms, legs, or necks had been broken—no one seemed to have suffered even so much as a scratch or bruise—there were storms of applause, mingled with a little protest. It had been almost too much.

Audiences which saw some of these fantastic performances

included New York *Times* reporters, an editor from *Collier's*, some of the editors from the *Bookman*, Fannie Hurst, J. Julius Forman, Walter Damrosch, Carl Brandt, Percy Stickney Grant, Christopher Morley, Mrs. Philip Lydig, Walter Kingsley, Arnold Genthe, Rebecca West, and numbers of professors from the universities.

According to Orage, who had abandoned the *New Age* and the single-tax movement to become Gurdjieff's right-hand man; according also to Ouspensky, to Claude Bragdon, and to numbers of other distinguished experts and students of such matters, Gurdjieff was at that time also wielding powers of "white magic" in the field of the occult which were even more extraordinary in their way than any of these sensational exhibitions in New York.

Whatever it was—or whatever its basis—Gurdjieff certainly had power. On the question of what it was and what its basis may have been, I have already defined pretty clearly the limits of my own skepticism. I submit the available facts about Gurdjieff, and let you form your own opinions. Many of these facts I have at first hand. Others I learned from Orage and his associates. A few facts and dates are culled from the library of the New York *Times*.

George Gurdjieff was born, in 1873, of Greek parentage, in the Transcaucasian town of Aleksandropol, which made him a Russian subject. He was christened George S. Gorgiades. He ran away to sea at an early age, and later spent many years in Outer Mongolia and Tibet, where he is said to have been at one time a Tibetan monk, and to have absorbed the mystical practices and teachings of the Sufis, Yogis, Melewi, Rufiah, and Persian dervishes. I can testify of my own knowledge that Gurdjieff knows more about dervish mysticism and magic than any man I have ever met outside a dervish monastery.

During the Russian revolution and the years immediately succeeding it, he was in Constantinople, in London, and finally established himself in Fontainebleau, outside Paris, where he founded the Institute which is said to represent the first organized effort to bring to the Western world the esoteric practices developed in India and Tibet. The disciples in this Institute, which was housed in a fine château with its *dépendances*, on a superb estate, were principally wealthy, cultured, and in a few instances celebrated, people. There were also a limited number of nonpaying students, men and women.

Rhythm, ritual, and physical discipline played a large part in the routine at the château. Classes began their exercise-dances at dusk, and danced for several hours during the night. In the daytime the disciples, including a princess or two, assorted countesses, and a number of wealthy bankers, broke rock, trundled wheelbarrows, tended pigs, pulled weeds, and worked at other heavy manual tasks. A theory was that when they became so tired that collapse was imminent, strength would come from an inner source of reserve power—that they would get their "second wind," as it were, or whatever they call second wind on the top of the Himalayas.

Said Gurdjieff sententiously one day, "Pig-raising and weed-pulling have a tendency to teach people with their heads in the air that their feet must be still on the ground." Thus he taught the countesses humility and obedience—but for different disciples he had different preliminary treatments. Gurdjieff, I keep telling you, was a great man in those days, and I really think he was. For instance, in dealing with pupils who were of the severe, puritanical "New England" type, he prescribed—instead of weed-pulling and rock-breaking—"soft music and perfumed wines!" Said he, "Of course I know intoxication is not always good—but neither is sobriety always good. The lure of music and the kindling of feeling are remedies, however, which do not avail with all my pupils."

For others he prescribed "the rigors of suffering, hardship, torture, even with whips . . . long hours of meditation."

Gurdjieff had learned whatever he learned from esoteric mystics in the East. Gurdjieff was not umpiring parlor games. Gurdjieff was turning on the heat. While French, British, and American journalists were permitted to visit the setup whenever they chose, and frequently did, and while a number of them definitely disliked Mr. Gurdjieff, no scandal or suggestion of scandal was ever connected with him or with the Institute. When Gurdjieff and his Fontainebleau cult are mentioned, the first thing the general public is likely to remember is "Oh, yes, that's where Katherine Mansfield died." So she did, but she was dying of tuberculosis before she ever went there.

A cardinal point in Gurdjieff's teachings was the breaking of habit, and to help accomplish this, many of the dances were wild and eccentric in the extreme. So far as anybody knows sex never "reared its ugly head" in Gurdjieff's *modus operandi*, but apart from that the dances were a cross between a voodoo *bamboche* in the jungle and a temple celebration of the Mysteries of Eleusis. Limbs, heads, muscles, body, just went hither and yon. Our jitterbugs at their best and fanciest are unimaginative earthworms compared to Gurdjieff's disciples when they really got going.

Scores of them—at one time he had almost a hundred—clad in flowing white, gray, and crimson garments, danced. The musicians were hidden. The music was exotic, oriental, sometimes mystical and sensuous, sometimes wild and crashing. Gurdjieff, the Master, remained out of sight behind a curtain, whence he issued his commands. Each individual dancer responded to the commands "as his soul dictated."

A visiting Sunday *World* reporter, describing one of these typical evenings, wrote:

Tired business men, bankers, intellectuals, actresses, barons, countesses, millionaires, gave themselves up to the music. At a command from Gurdjieff they stood perfectly rigid for several minutes, and then began to move their arms in unison; rapid, jerky movements, their joints giving the effect of working on ball bearings. The music quickened its pace, so did the arms. Legs and bodies swayed, heads bobbed frantically from side to side. Arms, legs, hands and heads acted in complete independence of one another, and each dancer seemed to be executing a series of movements different from his neighbor's, yet the total effect of the group was harmonious as it shifted with electrical rapidity from one pattern into another. The music grew louder. At another command from Gurdjieff the music stopped suddenly and the dancers stood as if petrified in bizarre attitudes until released by another command.

Gurdjieff's disciples apparently worked systematically, under his control, to break all their habits, both good and bad, thus freeing their lives from the ordinary man's usual slavery to habits. They lived a communal life. They did not regard their rhythmic exercises as rites or ceremonies. They regarded communal life as necessary for producing in highly concen-

trated form all the friction, all the reaction, pleasant and unpleasant, that are met with in ordinary life. Indifference to
these reactions was one of their goals.

Essence of the teaching seemed to be that through intense
physical labor, fasting, and elaborate exercises, the physical
machine is made perfectly obedient and responsive to the will.
They believed that in doing this the individual becomes possessed of faculties far exceeding those of the average man.
Clairvoyance, ability to see at a distance, power to know what
another is thinking, telepathic capacity, were supposed to be
some of the accomplishments. Also, a larger vision of the
universe.

Gurdjieff said: "If we live calm, monotonous days and
peaceful nights, we stultify. We had better torture our own
spirit than suffer the inanities of calm."

His disciples therefore were wakened at all hours of the
night, suddenly, and had learned to remain "frozen" in whatever positions they had chanced to stand or fall in when
leaping out of bed.

I'd have enjoyed being Gurdjieff in those days. I've got a
whole list of friends including a couple of darling and digni-
field old "River" ladies whom I'd vastly enjoy having in
such a menagerie. But I'm not sure I'd care to be one of
Gurdjieff's disciples. The man had power. But whether he
was able to impart it to others is a different question. It
seemed to me that when disciples entered Gurdjieff's cult,
they sacrificed their wills and personalities, rather than enhanced them. I know, of course, that greater masters than
Gurdjieff (including indeed *The* Master), taught a deep and
similarly paradoxical philosophy. But like nearly everything

in the realm of "white magic," its mystical efficacy in our modern world remains an open question.

One of Job's celebrated sayings, which my friend Gurdjieff had evidently never read, was:

"Would that mine adversary had written a book!"

The more you think that one over, the better it gets—as this episode concerning Gurdjieff may serve to illustrate.

Mr. Gurdjieff came back to New York in January, 1931, rented a number of luxurious apartments at 204 West 59th Street, and telephoned me one day that he had written a book. He knew that I liked him. He had not only written a book, but as amateur authors so frequently do, he craved to have some of it read aloud to a group of people who might be capable of appreciating its beauty and wisdom. He always did things in the grand manner. He asked me to invite as many selected friends as I chose, to his apartments on a certain evening, for the reading, and to enjoy an Arabian Nights collation afterward. I knew the supper would be marvelous, and felt it my duty to choose only *intelligent* friends to hear the reading. I was accused afterward of having chosen individuals whose intelligence was distinctly in the nine-minute-egg category. If I did, it was as a compliment to Mr. Gurdjieff. Among those who came, I recall particularly Behaviorist John Watson of Johns Hopkins, the late Lincoln Steffens, William Pepperell Montague and a couple more of the Columbia Pragmatists, George Seldes (I had also invited Gilbert and it seems to me he dropped in for a while), Carl Helm of the *Sun*, two Harvard psychologists, etc. Among the ladies were Irita Van Doren, Claire Spencer, Virginia Hirsch, and Blair Niles.

The evening—apart from the superb Algerian melons, stuffed eggplant, stuffed grape leaves, great cook pots of stewed goat or whatever it was, all in true Baghdad splendor —was a complete, if always polite and amiable, fiasco.

Disciples and secretaries read us long portions of an opus provisionally entitled "A Criticism of the Life of Man; or Beelzebub's Tale to His Grandson."

Late in the evening, Mr. Steffens and John Watson began whispering. Presently Mr. Watson said,

"Either this is an elaborate and subtle joke whose point is completely over our heads, or it's piffle. In either event, I don't see much that can be gained by hearing more of it. I propose, if Mr. Gurdjieff is agreeable, that we now converse for a while."

So we all relaxed, and conversed, and presently supped, with equal amiability on the part of both host and guests. Mr. Gurdjieff was more brilliant, and more witty, than the manuscript had been. He was so agreeable, so keen, and so affable, that Steffens, Watson, Montague, and all the rest of them took him into their complete confidence and explained unanimously their conviction that—unless he was trying to put over a cosmic joke of some sort whose point had not yet become manifest—his future did not lie in the field of authorship. Gurdjieff suggested that his purport might be too deep for our limited comprehension.

There was a difference of opinion among my friends after we had left, as to whether I had deliberately played a joke on Gurdjieff in selecting his auditors—or whether Gurdjieff and I had been in collusion to make monkeys out of *them* for an amusing evening—or whether Mr. Gurdjieff was spoofing all of us. I'm not quite sure myself. So far as I know, "Beelzebub's Tale" has not yet had a publisher. Gurdjieff is a great man, but I doubt that his field lies in *belles lettres*.

It was through the late Frank Harris that I first met Aleister Crowley, around 1917, in New York. Harris had finished his Shakespeare and Oscar Wilde biographies, had not yet besmirched himself with *My Life and Loves*, and was editing *Pearson's Magazine*. He was living prosperously in one of the verandaed houses on Seventh Avenue, in a Greenwich Village which still had Theodore Dreiser in a step-down on West 12th Street, Edna St. Vincent Millay in the same block, Sinclair Lewis in a duplex studio on Tenth Street, and Eugene O'Neill producing his plays in the Provincetown Playhouse, south of Washington Square. I had served for a while with the French on the Western Front, had been gassed at Verdun, had recovered enough to come home and start writing again. Aleister Crowley, a strange Englishman who had devoted a great part of his life to "white magic" and was accused ignorantly by his many enemies of practicing black magic too, was living at No. 1 University Place, to the utter terror of two conventional ladies from the South who had rented him the ground floor. He was a Cambridge man, a distinguished poet, was in many British anthologies, including the *Oxford Book of English Mystical Verse*. He had been in the Himalayas as a mountain climber, was supposed to have studied Tibetan lore. In 1905, according to the *Manchester Guardian*, he had led an expedition to ascend Kinchinjunga, 100 miles southeast of Mount Everest. The party attacked the southern face of the mountain, above Yalung Glacier, but met with disaster. One climber and several porters were swept away by an avalanche. Crowley was either part Irish or an Irish sympathizer, and was denouncing England during the World War as a "vampire among nations." He was considered to be pro-German, and was for a while associated with George Sylvester Viereck on the *Fatherland* and *International Monthly*. These matters left me indifferent, and I was never then or subsequently concerned in any of them. I was wanting to meet Crowley because he was supposed to be an authority on medieval sorcery, and was pleased when Frank Harris arranged it.

We met at lunch in Mouquin's. Aleister Crowley was a strange, disturbing fellow, with a heavy pontifical manner mixed with a good deal of sly, monkeylike, and occasionally malicious humor. He wore an enormous star sapphire on the forefinger of his right hand, and had his head shaved just then in the manner of Erich von Stroheim. He later sprouted an American Indian warlock which curled slightly and made him somewhat resemble (with his round, smooth-shaven face and big, round eyes) a nursery imp masquerading as Mephistopheles. The talk at that luncheon left me gasping. Frank Harris was one of the greatest conversationalists of this or any other century, and Crowley talked like Pain's Fireworks. No magic, black or white, was mentioned until the end of it, when Crowley said he'd heard I was interested in magic and invited me to call on him.

I telephoned late one morning, caught him at home, and went around before lunch. On entering the spacious living room, I was presented to a young lady by the name of Leah Hersig. At least, as I subsequently learned, that was her name in the phone book, and in the cold world outside. Here in the nice, warm magician's castle, she was naked as a jay bird, and just as unconcerned as one. They were not nudists. It wasn't anything like that. I slowly gathered that Leah was a high priestess, and that she also occasionally turned into Astarte, Ashtoreth, and Isis. Since these are goddesses with a precedent dating back some hundreds of centuries, her lack of embarrassment became more easily understandable.

What remained surprising, however, until my host kindly explained it, was the one thing she did wear. She couldn't very well avoid wearing it, because it had been branded into her fair hide with the red-hot point of a Chinese sword: on her breast she wore a star, pointing to the pickle jar, as did young King William's. The Master Therion (who was Crowley) had done a neat, artistic job of it, and after you got over the first shock, it rather enhanced the charm of the high priestess.

After that first visit, I got to know them both pretty well, and over a long period of time. Crowley had a cult, with followers and disciples. He never tried to make me a member of it. He accepted me as a sort of apprentice fellow-sorcerer, and I attended numbers of their ceremonies. They were Holy Grail stuff, mostly. Some of the invocations were quite beautiful, and Leah made a splendid combination of high priestess and goddess. The ceremonial part of Crowley's A. A. and O. T. O. is neither here nor there for purposes of this book. There are hundreds of such cults, mostly harmless and generally tiresome when you've seen much of them. What interested me in Aleister Crowley was the same thing, finally, that had interested me in the African witch-doctors and later in Gurdjieff. Behind the mumbo jumbo, whether in spite of or because of the mumbo jumbo, Aleister Crowley too had power. Whether it was a kind of power worth having, or a kind that can ever—in anybody's hands—have any profound effect upon the world, or whether he always used it honestly, are questions outside any point I'm trying to make, and which I don't pretend to answer.[4]

I propose instead to recount a number of happenings of which I had close personal knowledge. They will cast some light on my assertion that he had power, and may cast a little light too on why I write good-humoredly about him. During the years in America, he was part pontifical and part monkey, part primate and part primate, if any man ever was. I recall that one summer our Master Therion gathered his followers around him, announced that his planets were in such and such conjunction, and that the time had come for him to go into a forty-day retirement in the "wilderness" for prayer and mystical meditation. It was hot as hell in New York, and my own idea was that he simply wanted to go to the country. He happened to be out of cash at the moment, and fasting for forty days and nights was not included in his program. We decided to stake him to a camping trip, up the Hudson River—got him a canoe, a tent, supplied him with some money and a list of American canned goods, provisions which he was going to buy next day. These, with the canoe and tent, were to go aboard the Albany day boat, and we were going down to see him off next morning. When we got there, he was pleased as Punch, looking very important,

[4] Aleister Crowley himself has written a hundred or more volumes on both points. At least ten books have been written about him, including a literary biography called *Star in the West* by Major General J. F. C. Fuller, who years later became one of the only two Englishmen invited to Hitler's fiftieth birthday dinner. The British press, in particular the *Daily Express*, *Daily Mail*, and *Daily Telegraph*, have published tons of stuff about Crowley and his magic, mostly denunciatory.

supervising the embarkment of the provisions. The "provisions" looked suspicious, and since we'd paid for them, we decided to inspect them. They consisted of fifty gallons of red paint, three big house-painter's brushes, and a heavy coil of rope. We investigated further. He hadn't bought so much as a can of beans or a loaf of bread. He'd blown every cent for the red paint. He had nothing in his pockets except the ticket for the trip up the river.

"What are you going to eat, for crying out loud?" we asked, and he replied, in his heaviest pontifical manner,

"My children, I am going to Esopus Island, and I will be fed as Elijah was fed by the ravens."

"Are you coming back in a chariot of fire, or in a Black Maria?" we yelled as the boat pulled out, and he waved us good-by with a grin.

Upstate New York farmers are a hard bunch for anybody to make monkeys out of, or to play the monkey with—but neighboring farmers fed Aleister Crowley for the whole forty days—and at the end of the forty days all the summer excursionists going up and down the river saw painted on the cliffs south of Kingston two enormous legends:

EVERY MAN AND WOMAN IS A STAR!

DO WHAT THOU WILT
SHALL BE THE WHOLE OF THE LAW.

He had rigged himself a sling, and painted, we were told, from sunrise to sundown. Thereafter he had sat cross-legged, on the ground in front of his tent, while neighbors, whether regarding him as a mighty prophet or a harmless crank, had brought him eggs and milk, occasional sweet corn. Frequently, when they chanced to pass next morning, he would still be sitting like an idol, with the eggs and milk untouched. They said he ate sparingly, once in every twenty-four hours, and that it was a mystery when he slept—unless he slept while sitting like a Buddha in the lotus posture. He never made any effort to commercialize or cash in on, or gain credit for, the two legends painted on the rock. He had wanted to paint them there—and that was that.

A. C. came back to New York in September, sunburned, lean, fit, and in a fine good humor. Acquaintances who were not among his converts said he was crazy as a loon. I thought so, but recalled that the Lord Gautama had sat thus under a tree for eleven years. It was crazy in the age of motor cars and airplanes, I agreed, but it was something.

On the day after he had returned to New York, I invited him to the grillroom of the Plaza, for lunch, where he regaled himself with whitebait, steak tartare, creamcake, topped off with a Napoleon brandy—then lighted a Belinda perfecto.

I said, "What did you get out of it, beyond cleaning out your colon and taking weight off your belly?"

"I have gained greater power."

"What kind of power?" I asked.

"Perhaps," he replied, "I can show you."

"If it's done in the dark," I said, "or behind curtains, or with spooks, I wouldn't believe it."

"It's a bright, sunshiny day," he said, as if dropping the subject (or was he?). "Suppose we stroll in the park in the sunshine."

I said, "I'd like to stop at Brentano's. Suppose we stroll down Fifth Avenue instead."

"Anywhere you like," he replied.

We strolled. The Avenue was crowded. "On a block where it thins out a bit," said he, "I'll show you."

"Show me what?"

He replied majestically, "I will show you."

The crowd looked thinner ahead of us in front of the Public Library, and as we crossed Forty-second Street, A. C. touched me lightly on the elbow and put his fingers to his lips. Ahead of us was strolling a tall, prosperous-looking gentleman of leisure, and Crowley, silent as a cat, fell into step immediately behind him. Their footfalls began to synchronize, and then I observed that Crowley, who generally held himself pompously erect and had a tendency to strut, had dropped his shoulders, thrust his head forward a little, like the man's in front, had begun to swing his arms in perfect synchronization—now so perfect that he was like a moving shadow or astral ghost of the other.

As we neared the end of the block, A. C., in taking a step forward, let both his knees buckle suddenly under him, so that he dropped, caught himself on his haunches, and was immediately erect again, strolling.

The man in front of us fell as if his legs had been shot out from under him . . . and was sprawling. We helped him up, as a crowd gathered. He was unhurt. He thanked us, and looked for the banana peel. There was no banana peel. With his hand on somebody's shoulder, he looked at the soles of his shoes. They were dry. He brushed himself off, regained his hat, tried his legs tentatively, thanked us, and strolled on.

I think I know all the answers. The easiest one is that the gentleman was a stooge. The only trouble with it is that I was the one who had suggested strolling down the Avenue, and I had been at A. C.'s side ever since. The gentleman, if a stooge, however, could have been loitering outside the Plaza, waiting for a signal. Identification of him and affidavits from him wouldn't have helped at all, since he might always have been lying. The hell of all this stuff is that something of that sort is always the easiest answer.

Another answer is that the gentleman, without being conscious of it, *heard* the faint sound of Crowley's catlike footfalls, mingled in perfect synchronization with his own, unconsciously identified the rhythm with his own rhythm, and fell when the rhythm was violently broken. There are a number of variations of that answer, splitting hairs a bit, but still leaving the phenomenon in the field of the sensory. Still another answer is that Crowley possessed supernormal powers, was generating and sending out supernormal and supersensory emanations. I think I know all the answers—but I'm not satisfied with any of them.

One following summer—it was around 1920—I invited A. C. to spend July and August with me on a farm near Atlanta. We got to talking one night about the Trappist monks, about their vows of silence, etc., and he suggested that we try an interesting variant. He proposed that for a week we limit all verbal communication and all conversation to one prearranged monosyllable. We experimented with several, tried various animal monosyllables, including urr, woof, moo, baa, and finally decided upon "wow."

We stuck to this for the whole week. Katie was amused and tolerant, visitors wondered whether we'd gone crazy, while Shep and Vonie, our two Negro servants, were convinced we'd either joined or were founding a branch of some new religion. We learned in the first couple of days, or believed we did, a good deal about the manner in which animals communicate with one another. We were both surprised how much, by mere change in intonation, volume, etc., we could communicate. After we'd become pretty good, or thought we had, in "Pass the butter," "I don't care for any more," "Would you like to take a walk?", "That's a pretty girl!", "It's a fine morning," "yes," "no," "maybe," "I like it," "I don't like it," "the hell with it," "Isn't it wonderful?" and elementary things of that sort—it chanced that one night Shep brought me a gallon of moonshine corn.

A. C. and I sat up that night, drank most of it, and held a long, deep, philosophic conversation, in terms of "wow," until the wee small hours, when Katie finally made us shut up and go to bed. She still insists that we simply got drunk and sat and barked at each other all night, but A. C. and I felt the talk had been profound and illuminating.

It was at any rate profitable, for I later wrote a fantasy on what might happen if human language were abolished, and sold it to H. L. Mencken. It is entitled "Wow," and has appeared in a number of anthologies.

A. C. subsequently went to Sicily, taking his high priestess Leah with him, bought the equivalent of an old monastery and grounds in the hills near Cefalù, outside Palermo, gathered some disciples from England and America, and founded there his College of the Holy Ghost.

I was in Africa again when the unfortunate episode of the young Oxford poet and the cat occurred, but I have closer knowledge of another drama which concerned a moderately well-known American actress who has had roles on Broadway and in Hollywood. The story contains nothing to anybody's discredit—on the contrary!—and she lent me her diary covering the entire Cefalù period, with permission to quote from it, but requested that I leave her name out.

She had been suffering, as our best actresses sometimes do, or did, from the heebie-jeebies; from an unrequited passion for Horace Liveright, Jed Harris, Max Eastman, Max Bodenheim, or some other intellectual *homme fatale* of the speakeasy epoch; from too much bathtub gin, despondency, and a couple of other depressants which I believe included veronal. She had met Aleister Crowley, suffered also from a curiosity about the occult, and as an alternative to suicide had gone over to become one of his disciples for the summer.

What happened after she had matriculated in the College of the Holy Ghost and taken up her residence in the Abbey of Thelema wasn't anything that she'd expected.

On a small isolated promontory within the abbey grounds, and overlooking the sea, the Master Therion set up the Sicilian equivalent of a pup tent—a shepherd's shelter, a thatched lean-to on poles, not much larger than the wardrobe trunk she'd brought across the ocean. Behind it, he dug a small lime pit to serve as a latrine. Her entire wardrobe and camp equipment was to consist of a burnoose to cover her nakedness when she got cold at night, or if it rained. It was a voluminous, coarse woolen robe with a cowl. No bed, no chair, no bunk, no straw, no blanket, no pillow—no toilet articles, no books, no cards, no games. She would have, said the Master Therion, the sun, moon, stars, sky, sea, the universe to read and play with. She was to stay up on that rock alone for a month. No one was to go up except a little boy who would come quietly to deposit a coarse loaf of bread, a bunch of grapes, and a jug of water each night while she was sleeping. She told the Master Therion he was crazy. He told her there was a boat touching next day at Palermo, and that there was her unpacked trunk, and there was the open door, and there was a telephone—but that when the boat sailed north, she'd be sitting up there naked on the rock, watching it disappear.

And for a month!

What an outrageous trick, you say? Let's look at it a minute. Its horrors combined a perfectly balanced frugal diet, a rest cure, sun baths, a fresh air cure, a sojourn by the seaside overlooking one of the most beautiful bays on earth. She undertook to try it, and did. I have neglected to mention that at the end of seven days, pencil and paper were to be sent up to her by the little boy, so that she could begin keeping a diary. The diary was interesting for many reasons. The progressive steps it shows are perhaps the most interesting thing in it:

During the first days, she was nervous, uncomfortable, angry, and resentful, but determined to stick it out. Then, for a while, she was just as nervous, but less uncomfortable, no longer angry and resentful, but beginning to be *bored*.

Then for a number of days, she was "calm, but bored."

It was boredom and not the hardship and discomfort, which she no longer felt, that tempted her when nineteen days had passed to give it up.

She stuck it out, and during the last ten days experienced "perfect calm, deep joy, renewal of strength and courage." As she put it, she had "let go of herself" in New York, and had "gotten hold of herself again," there on the rock. Also, what with the limited diet, self-imposed calisthenics, sun and air, she had "lost sixteen pounds in the right places" which doubtless partially accounted for her "deep joy."

She came down off the rock, remained in the colony for the summer, studied principally self-control and the drawing on her inner resources and reserve force, went back to Broadway, and resumed her career.

The methods of the Master Therion had savored of spectacular boloney, but I doubt whether Bill Brown, the late Muldoon, or their most orthodox and expensive prototypes patronized by wealthy ladies could have done a better job.

Following the death of the young Oxford poet and athlete Raoul (Frederick Charles) Loveday, after he had sacrificed a cat on the altar of the cult at Cefalù and drunk a cup of its blood, the young man's widow, Betty May Loveday, former model, raised a tremendous hullabaloo with the help of the British press, and in the spring of 1923, Aleister Crowley was expelled from Italian territory by the Fascisti. He raised a counter-hullabaloo with libel suits, but was granted no damages. Those who have read the *Daily Mail, Daily Express,* or *Telegraph* may sense a belief on my part that "the devil is not always as black as he is painted," or if not that, a desire on my part to whitewash him a bit.

Rather than use a whitewash brush on the Master Therion, since he has always insisted he was a white magician anyway, I suggest that the old schoolbook adage *de gustibus non disputandum* may have a bearing on the cat. I have eaten cat in Naples and caterpillars on the Ivory Coast. I have also eaten stewed young man. I have drunk the sacrificial blood of goats and bulls at voodoo altars, and have seen my surpliced betters drinking from a cup on the greatest altar of all, a liquid which people wiser and better than I am assure me has been miraculously changed into the blood of a man who once became a god. I have also seen my aunt from Hawkinsville, Georgia, kneeling before one of these same greatest altars and eating a substance which she believed to be a part of the body of the man. The greatest and noblest of the Greeks habitually sacrificed birds, beasts, more rarely their daughters, and consulted the steaming entrails. So that if Aleister Crowley and his disciple Raoul Loveday, founding a new religion, chose to assassinate a stray cat and imbibe its lifeblood, it seems to me that it was nobody's business unless the Italian S.P.C.A. chose to intervene. And if it made Raoul sick afterward, it seems to me, similarly, that it was his own private misfortune.

One can hardly have expected, however, so detached an attitude on the part of his beautiful young model-widow. She was known as the "Tiger-Woman," and so titled the book she wrote about herself in 1929 for Duckworth. As an amateur psychoanalyst, I suspect that Betty May was subconsciously thinking "a tiger is also a cat. Maybe I'd better get out of here while the going's good." At any rate, she ran away, and here's what she tells us in *Tiger-Woman* about the other cat—and about her young husband's untimely demise:

The ceremony opened with the solemn entrance of the Mystic clad in the gorgeous robes of a Grand Master of the order of Freemasons. After he had seated himself on the throne before the brazier with the charcoal fire, around which hung the sacrificial knives and swords, the other members of the cult took their places on the triangular stools at the points of the star. They were dressed as a rule in robes like those in which I first saw Leah, with the cowls drawn down over their faces, and only their eyes visible through the narrow eye-slits. Clouds of incense hung about the room everywhere. When all were assembled, the Mystic rose from his seat, and taking one of the swords from the side of the brazier, held it pointing towards the altar while he intoned an invocation in a language with which I was not familiar. From hearing it every day, however, the sounds remain fixed in my memory.

> *"Artay I was Malcooth—Vegabular,*
> *Vegadura, ee-ar-la—ah moon."*

The last was a high-pitched note in contrast with the rest of the chant. Following this, he walked over to Raoul, rested the point of the sword on his forehead, and uttered a further rigmarole, finishing up with a loud shriek of "Adonis," which was the name by which my husband was known in the abbey. Then he went through the identical performance in front of Leah, except that to begin with he stood silently in front of her for a full minute, breathing deeply the while—breathing in the soul of his priestess, as Raoul explained it to me afterwards.

These preliminary invocations done, the Mystic proceeded to execute a variety of ecstatic dances. This was both impressive and ludicrous. He lashed himself into an absolute frenzy, brandishing his sword, and dancing and leaping about in the magic circle. His eyes blazed. The words he chanted had a compelling monotonous and exotic rhythm, and his eyes were alight with fanatical enthusiasm. Every Friday night there was a special invocation to Pan, in which, as is shown by the hymn for these occasions, the doctrine of the cult became manifest. It was written in English, and I will quote the first few lines,

> *"Thrill with lissom lust of the light,*
> *O Man, my Man;*
> *Come careening out of the night*
> *To me, to me;*
> *Come with Apollo in bridal dress—"*

On the evening of the sacrifice

everybody took their accustomed position, except that for this occasion Raoul, as he was to be the executioner, changed places with
the Mystic. The cat was brought out and placed, still in the sack,
on the altar. The opening of the rite was the same as the [cere-
mony of] Pentagram, which I have already described. The air
was thick with incense. Raoul recited the invocation, and walked
with upraised sword towards Leah and the others and placed its
point on their brows while he uttered the usual formula. I sat outside the magic circle and watched the gruesome performance.

Presently, when much of the ceremony had been gone through,
I saw Raoul take a kukri [Gurkha knife] from its place by the
brazier and approach the altar, on which was the squirming sack.
He untied it, drew forth the struggling and terrified Mischette
by the scruff of the neck, and held her with his left hand at arm's-
length above his head. In his right he held the kukri with its
point towards the brazier. The Mystic stilled Mischette's struggles by applying a dab of ether to her nose. All was now ready
for the sacrificial invocation, which Raoul had written specially for
the occasion, and which he now had to recite in the fatiguing
posture that I have described.

It was a long invocation, and before it was half done I could
see his left arm quiver with the strain. As he approached the
point where the killing was to take place Leah stepped down from
her triangular stool, and taking a bowl from the altar, held it
underneath Mischette to catch the blood, none of which is supposed to be lost. At last the moment had arrived. I saw him lift
back the kukri, and then closed my eyes till it should be over. . . .
Then swaying slightly, he laid the carcass on the altar. This done,
his resources were exhausted, and the Mystic had to take over
the conducting of the ceremony.

Having concluded the invocation, he took the bowl containing
the blood, uttered some consecratory formula over it and handed
it to Leah, who was standing by. Together they approached
Raoul. The Mystic then flung back the cowl from Raoul's face,
and dipping a finger in the blood, traced the sign of the Penta-

gram on his white, glistening forehead, and so to all the others, himself last.

The final rite . . . now alone remained to be performed. . . . The Mystic took a small silver cup, into which he scooped some of the blood from the bowl and handed it to my husband, who drained it to the dregs.

For a time I was convinced that Raoul had been poisoned by the blood of Mischette. But when he got steadily worse and a doctor was summoned I found out that he was suffering from enteric, a not uncommon disease in those parts.

It is quite understandable, if you know the British, that the reported pentagrammed [5] shindigs of these two British gentlemen, one of whom was a Cambridge honor man and the other an Oxonian, were somewhat shocking to the learned judges who heard the libel suits brought by the Master Therion, and who concurred fervidly with the juries which refused to grant Mr. Crowley so much as a farthing in damages.

Quoting from *The Times* (London) of April 14, 1934, "His LORDSHIP, in directing the jury, said that he had never heard such dreadful, horrible, blasphemous, and abominable stuff as that which had been produced by the man who described himself as the greatest living poet."

Said Mr. Justice Swift on the same day, from the bench, "I have been more than forty years engaged in the administration of the law in one capacity or another. I thought I knew of every conceivable form of wickedness. I thought that everything which was vicious and bad had been produced at one time or another before me. I have learned in this case that you can always learn something more if you live long enough."

[5] See Appendix, p. 359.

Mr. Crowley got no satisfaction from the courts, but had the subsequent fun of predicting the present world war, and of suggesting that if the courts and British public had been more sympathetic to him, the catastrophe might have been averted. According to the *Daily Express* of December 23, 1937, portions of a prophetic book of Aleister Crowley's "were read at Cleopatra's Needle, at 6:22 A.M., as the sun entered Capricornus, by an Englishman, a Jew, a Negro and a Malayan. There was a short speech by Crowley as Priest of the Princes. He proclaimed the law of Thelema, and handed copies to the white, red, brown, black and yellow representatives. He stated that he had published three times, and that each time war broke out nine months later; that 'the might of this magick burst out and caused a catastrophe to civilization.' He said that if everybody would do what he told them, the catastrophe could be averted."

He missed it a little on his timing. But it came. War, as Nostradamus knew, is always a safe bet for prophets. Old Nostradamus, who was a great medieval magician in St. Rémy, wrote a book of prophecy, *Centuries*, which has recently been reprinted in a popular edition and has become again a best seller in Paris.[6]

I am possibly too casual, but feel that the British in general, apart from Nina Hamnett's treatment of him in *Laughing Torso*, have been a bit heavy in their attitude toward the Master Therion. If he had been an American, I can't help feeling that we'd have had more fun with him. As a matter of fact we did, while he was over here. I saw him last in Paris in 1933. We lunched, on his invitation, at Foyot's. He was still having a good deal of fun with the world.

[6] See Appendix, p. 365.

IV. Upton Sinclair's "Mental Radio"

OF all the experiments in telepathy outside cold laboratories on the one hand, and outside spook-ridden séance cabinets on the other, the ones which seem to me most worthy of general interest are those conducted, in their own homes in Pasadena, California, by Upton Sinclair and his wife, Mary Craig Sinclair. I visited them several years ago, had many talks with them, and came away deeply impressed. While I remain respectfully dubious concerning the whole subject of extra-sensory perception, I feel that what the Sinclairs have accomplished is more important, perhaps, than anything which has yet occurred at Duke.

Without ever "turning on the heat" in the way my Tripolitan dervishes did, they have operated on the dervish theory that the "blanking" out of the sensory clutter which streams in continually through all our five normal senses, plus the utilization of autosuggestion, are the preliminary essentials to establishing contact with extra-sensory impressions. They have worked on the assumption, as Professor William McDougall said, that "if the faint and unusual telepathic processes are to manifest themselves, the track of the mind must be kept clear of other traffic." And without wishing to be too

insistent in my partisanship for dervish practices as opposed
to casual guessing games, I cannot help feeling that there is a
parallel between the physical condition in which Mary Craig
Sinclair chanced to be when she first became an adept, and
the physical conditions which the dervishes deliberately induce as a preliminary step toward supernormal vision. In the
prime of life, she suffered a long and painful physical illness.
It was, her husband writes, "a story of suffering needless to
go into: suffice it that she had many ills to experiment upon,
and mental control became suddenly a matter of life and
death. . . . If she now believes anything, rest assured that it
is because she has tried it out in the crucibles of pain. . . ."

The heat, in that sense, had been "turned on" by fate during the period when Mary Craig began to learn and employ the technique of detachment which produced the astonishing results told by Mr. Sinclair in *Mental Radio*,[1] with an
introduction by Professor William McDougall, then at Duke
University.

Before going into the phenomena, I want to present, with
Upton Sinclair's permission, and from Mary Craig Sinclair's
own statement, the approach she used and the technique she
employed in the unlocking of the "door" beyond which lies,
perhaps, the answer to a great mystery.

To what extent she was influenced by her wide reading of
the Sufi and Melewi mystics, I do not know, but her concept
of the nature of concentration is identical with theirs. "The
first thing you have to do," she says, "is to learn the trick of
undivided attention." By that, she means what the Melewi
mean, and not at all what *we* mean when we talk ordinarily
of concentrating.

[1] Published by Albert & Charles Boni, 1930. 239 pages, illustrated.

One "concentrates" [in our ordinary sense] on writing a
chapter in a book, or on solving a problem in mathematics; but
this [sort of concentration] is a complicated process of dividing
one's attention, giving it to one detail after another, judging, balancing, making decisions. The kind of concentration I mean is
putting the attention on *one* object, or one *uncomplicated* thought,
. . . and holding it there steadily. It isn't thinking; it is inhibiting
thought, except for one thought, or one object in thought.

You have to inhibit the impulse to think things about the object,
to examine it, or appraise it, or to allow memory-trains to attach
themselves to it. The average person has never heard of such a
form of concentration. . . .

The attention must never stray to the sensations of the
body. To concentrate in this undivided way, you implant in
yourself the "suggestion" that you will relax your mind and
your body, making the body insensitive and the mind a
blank. . . . You must relax completely your mental hold
of, or awareness of, all bodily sensation.[2]

All this, Mrs. Sinclair points out, is hard work, and I
think she is also aware of its dangers when carried too far,
because she explains that you must reserve the power to
"break" the concentration. This involves the seeming paradox
of completely "letting go," yet at the same time "holding
on." Pain, she says, is tension, and pain can be inhibited by
autosuggestion. Drop your body, a dead weight, from your
conscious mind. Make your conscious mind a blank. It is the
mind, conscious or subconscious, which holds the body tense.
And to make the conscious mind a blank, it is necessary to
"let go" of the body. If, after you have practiced letting go
of the body, you find that your mind is not a blank, you have
not succeeded in getting rid of your body. Darkness, either

[2] See Appendix, p. 367.

turning off all the lights, or keeping your eyes closed, or both, are recommended.

Now all this, obviously, is totally different from the casual manner in which card-guessing laboratory games are played. Professor Morton Prince wrote to Mary Craig, after she had learned to "slide" completely through the door, as the dervishes do, "You are playing with powerful and dangerous forces." Of course she was, but being a sane, and above all good,[3] and balanced person, she was able, without sliding too far, to bring back from the other side of the "door" a series of experiences which I believe are the most exciting up to date.

Instead of using ESP cards or any other fixed, set symbols, the Sinclairs experimented in telepathy (mind-reading) with arbitrary pencil drawings. Mr. Sinclair, or one of their close friends, would make, with pen or pencil, a rough sketch of some object, real or imaginary, which might be anything. The one who had drawn it would then sit and concentrate on it, and Mary Craig Sinclair, lying elsewhere in the dark, would try to "see," and then describe, or reproduce with a drawing of her own, what she had "seen."

Some of the results are so astonishing that I find myself "on the spot" in continuing to confess that even these Sinclair phenomena, which I regard as the best yet produced in America, or perhaps anywhere, by reputable and rational people in our own Western world, still leave me bewildered and in doubt. I know of no possible way to interpret them, and can suggest none, other than by accepting it as a fact

[3] I am profoundly convinced that essential goodness is the sole protection against encountering horror and possible destruction on the other side of that dubious and mysterious "door."

that extra-sensory thought transference (and in certain instances clairvoyance too) did actually occur.

Some of the Sinclair phenomena, while simple and dealing with simple things, almost as childish as parlor games, are nevertheless loaded with terrific implications.

As for instance:

On the morning of July 13, 1928, Robert L. Irwin, a young business man, was sitting in a room of his house in Pasadena, at the prearranged hour of half-past eleven. He had agreed to make a drawing of any object he might select, at random, and then to sit gazing at it, concentrating his entire attention upon it, for a period of from fifteen to twenty minutes. With a lead pencil on a sheet of paper, he drew the crude, simple outlines of an ordinary table fork.[4]

At the same agreed hour Mary Craig Sinclair was lying on her couch in a study, in the Sinclairs' seaside house at Long Beach, forty miles away. She was in semidarknes, with her eyes closed; employing the concentration method I have partially described. Having become satisfied, as Mr. Sinclair records, that the image which came to her mind was the correct one—because it persisted, and came back again and again —she sat up and took pencil and paper, and wrote:

"See a table fork. Nothing else."

Two days later, the Sinclairs drove to Pasadena, where the drawing and writing were produced and compared. They were all so excited about it that Mr. Irwin and Mary Craig made affidavits, which are on file. They might as well have been a set of affidavits about the virgin birth of Our Lord

[4] See Appendix, pp. 369-372, for this and other drawings, reproduced by permission of Upton Sinclair.

and Saviour Jesus Christ. Affidavits in this realm are even more absurd than those you sign when you turn in your income tax report. People either believe it, or they don't. I believe this happened, in exactly the way they tell it—or that they think it did—because I know the Sinclairs. He has what are to me fantastic ideas about a lot of things, other than extra-sensory perception. But he never cheats. Nor do any of the people connected with those drawings.

One evening Upton Sinclair sat in his study and made a pencil drawing of a five-pointed star such as children cut out of gilt paper and paste on paper hats. He was alone, with the door closed before the drawing was made, and it was not opened until the test was concluded. He held it before him, and concentrated on it for a period of ten minutes. His wife, who was lying on a couch in a different part of the house, with closed doors and walls between, made five or six drawings, all of which had the geometric essence of the star, or of one of its parts or attributes—and had finally drawn the star.

The cases in which the original drawings were misunderstood and distorted by Mary Craig seem to me more astounding than those in which she clearly identified the fork (or whatever it chanced to be).

The upside-down foot of a boy on roller skates, who had presumably fallen sprawling, which had been drawn deliberately to confuse and puzzle Mary Craig, underwent a weird transformation. She drew the upside-down leg and shoe as the neck and head of a queer animal, with the wheels of the roller skate as eyes! There was a general similarity of outline, as of something "seen through a glass darkly," which is more disturbing to me as a skeptic than a clearer sketch would have been.

In 290 drawings, the total of complete successes was 65 (or around 22 per cent), but the total of partial successes was 155 (or around 53 per cent). The total of complete failures was 70 (or around 24 per cent).

What puzzles and interests me most is the amazing recurrent partial successes.

One day, under circumstances similar to the case of the table fork, Robert Irwin, who was the husband of Mary Craig's younger sister and consequently related to them all by marriage but not by blood, drew a crude, full-face view of his open-faced watch. What Mary Craig drew was the crude, full-face view of a flat flower, like a Japanese chrysanthemum, with crude, separated petals, enclosed in a circle. She was worried about it, and wrote on her drawing, "I think it is not flower but wire (metal, shining). The 'petals' are not petals but wire, and should be *uniform*. . . . I see no flower but shape of one on paper. Then decide it is of wire, but this may be merely because I see drawing, which would have no flower color. However, I see it shining as if it is metal. . . ." She never guessed it was a watch.

Sinclair once drew the head of a comic Bolshevik with wild hair and whiskers. What she drew, after long struggle, was a sunrise or sunset, behind a mountain peak, in which the penciled rays of the sun made lines similar to the Bolshevik's wild hair and whiskers!

Once the pedals on a harp became a pair of feet in slippers, with the outline of the harp mistaken for a woman's flaring skirt above them.

The most disturbing case of all occurred in connection with

an attempt in which Irwin had taken a pair of compasses and drawn a simple circle. It is necessary to explain that Mr. Irwin was physically ill. Some years previous the doctors had given him only a few months to live, on account of tuberculosis. I'd better quote Mr. Sinclair direct in this case. It was "the most sensational of all," he says.

. . . I have to ask your pardon for the medical details involved. So much vital knowledge hangs upon these tests that I have asked my brother-in-law to forget his personal feelings. The reader will please consider himself a medical student or hospital nurse for the moment.

The test occurred July 11, 1928. My wife made her drawing [in which she endeavored by telepathy to reproduce whatever drawing Irwin had made], and then told me about the matter at once. Also she wrote out all the details and the record is now before me. She saw a feather, then a flower spray, and then she heard a scream. Her first thought in case of illness or danger is her aged parents, and she took it for her mother's voice, and this so excited her that she lost interest in the experiment. But soon she concentrated again, and drew a series of concentric circles, with a heavy black spot in the center. Then she saw another and much larger spot, and this began to spread and cover the sheet of paper. At the same time came a feeling of intense depression, and Craig decided that the black spot was blood, and that Bob had had a hemorrhage. . . .

. . . Bob's wife drove him to our home, and in the presence of all four of us he produced the drawing he had made. He had taken a compass and drawn a large circle; making, of course, a hole in the center of the paper. "Is that all you thought of during the time?" asked my wife. "No," said Bob, "but I'd hate to have you get the rest of it." "What was it?" "Well, I discovered that I had a hemorrhoid, and couldn't put my mind on anything else but the thought, 'My God, my lungs—my kidneys—and now this!'"

A hemorrhoid is, of course, apt to be accompanied by a hemorrhage; and it seems clear that my wife got the mood of depression of her brother-in-law, his thoughts of blood and bodily breakdown, as well as the circle and the hole in the paper. . . . I do not see how there could possibly be more conclusive evidence of telepathic influence—unless you suspect all four of us of a series of stupid and senseless falsehoods. . . . The comment written by my wife [on her own drawing at the time she made it] reads: "All this dark like a stain—feel it is blood; that Bob is ill—more than usual."

The experiments conducted with Mr. Irwin were discontinued because it was soon discovered that, in his bad health, they were too much of a strain on him. The Sinclairs kept on experimenting. They never permitted the astonishing results to upset or derange their normal, busy, active outside lives, but when it became generally known that this famous couple were interested in extra-sensory and supernormal phenomena, it naturally attracted to their home numbers of "adepts," practitioners, "mediums," as well as occasional visitors like myself who were interested not only in this field, but in its varied ramifications.

It was there I first met "Bishop" Arthur A. Ford, head of the General Assembly of Spiritualist Churches in America, sometime head of the Organized Spiritualist Churches of the world, and frequently referred to in public print as the "Pope" of the Spiritualists.[5] Ford had had a lot of front-page publicity in connection with his unsuccessful efforts to establish contact with the ghost of the late Houdini. He was now on his way to help reorganize the Spiritualist churches in Australia and, like myself, was visiting in Pasadena, seeing the Sinclairs. The Sinclairs were not spiritualists—and have

[5] See Appendix, p. 369.

241

never been—but were interested in Mr. Ford, and were wondering, as I have often wondered, whether or not some of the phenomena which occur in spiritualist séances and meetings may not be attributable to telepathy among the living rather than to communication with the dead. On any other assumption, the case for the spiritualists, in my opinion, is so completely minus zero and has been so completely shot to pieces in hundreds of investigations that it would be useless to rehash it in this volume. My enthusiasm for the experiments conducted by the Sinclairs, and my needless-to-state conviction of their obvious sincerity, did not include or extend to Bishop Ford and his Spiritualists, a number of whose meetings I attended in Los Angeles.

Nor did my credulity or sympathies extend to a Polish gentleman by the name of Ostaja, whom I met subsequently through the Sinclairs, and who had been for a time a protégé of theirs.

Mr. Sinclair writes with more tolerance than I could command of their earlier association with this extraordinary young man, who had studied for a while in India. He had a habit of having himself buried in yellow silk pajamas, and subsequently dug up, all over California, preferably with the press and newsreels present, and one night, after the Sinclairs had dug him up and invited him to dinner, it seems he had a heavy table, spook-controlled, floating precariously in the air over Upton Sinclair's head. I wouldn't have liked it. The spooks might have dropped it on Sinclair. And if they had, it would have blotted out more and better brains than are possessed by all the fakirs from Tibet to Timbuktu. Here's Mr. Sinclair's kindly account of it:

In our home he gave what appeared to be a demonstration of levitation without contact. I do not say that it really *was* levitation; I merely say that our friends who witnessed it . . . were unable even to suggest a normal method by which the event could have happened. There was no one present who could have been a confederate, and the psychic had been searched for apparatus; it was in our home, where he had no opportunity whatever for preparation. His wrists and ankles were firmly held by persons whom I know well; and there was sufficient light in the room so that I could see the outline of his figure, slumped in a chair. Under these circumstances a 34-pound table rose four feet into the air and moved slowly a distance of eight feet over my head.

Mr. Sinclair gently adds, "We saw this; our friends saw it; yet, in my mind, and likewise in theirs, the worm of doubt would always creep in."

In my mind, that worm of doubt is a full-sized boa constrictor.

According to Mr. Sinclair's narrative, this young man Ostaja, whom he refers to as Jan, "was a peculiar person. Sometimes he would be open and frank, and again he would be mysterious and secretive. At one time he would agree to teach us all he knew, and again he would hold on to his arts, which he had had to go all the way to India to get. Was it that he considered these forces too dangerous for amateurs to play with? Or was it merely that he was considering his means of livelihood?" asks the always kindly Mr. Sinclair. What I can't help wondering unkindly is whether he wasn't afraid the worm of doubt would turn into the boa constrictor right there in that mild and friendly domicile?

Jan, it seems, was among other things a hypnotist, and in this field Mary Craig, who was a bit of an amateur hypnotist herself, and a bit of a "white witch" too in the best connotation of the Tennysonian phrase, took delight occasionally in making a monkey out of him. One day when he was staring at her, making passes with his hands, and trying to hypnotize her, Mary Craig, instead of going docilely to sleep, stared back!

An essential part of Jan's technique, says Mr. Sinclair, as Jan explained it, "was in outstaring the patient and never blinking his eyes. Now suddenly he blinked; then he closed his eyes and kept them closed. 'Do your eyes hurt?' asked his patient, in pretended innocence. 'No,' he replied. 'Are you tired?' she asked. 'No, thank you,' said he. 'What was I thinking?' she asked. 'To hypnotize me,' he replied, sleepily." Now she closed her own eyes and willed that Jan should get up and go to the telephone. Jan opened his a little, and seeing hers closed, said, "Shall I go on treating you?" "Yes, please," she replied. But Jan hesitated, and then said, "Excuse me, I have to telephone a friend!"

However Mary Craig may have done it, the hypnotist was hoist on his own petard. Mr. Sinclair writes of these adventures in *Mental Radio*. He protects himself by saying "these stories of Jan . . . are the strangest, and the least capable of proof," and then generously recounts a good many which indicate that the young man did possess extraordinary powers. Those I naturally like best, however, are accounts of the numerous duels which took place between this Master of the Esoteric from the East and his sometime "apprentice sorceress."

Says Mr. Sinclair:

Jan goes into one of his deep states—a cataleptic trance, he calls it—in which his body is rigid and cold. He has the power to fix in advance the time when he will come out of the trance, and his subconscious mind apparently possesses the power to keep track of time—days, hours, minutes, even seconds. I have seen him amaze a group of scientists by coming out on the second, while they held stop-watches on him.

But now my wife thinks she will vary this procedure. Jan goes into the trance in our home and Craig sits and silently wills, "Your right leg will come out; you will lift it; you will put it down again. You will sit erect"—and so on. Without speaking a word, she can make him do whatever she pleases.

Jan is a "continental male," and Craig sometimes makes "fierce feminist war upon him." It is the fashion among young ladies from the South to tease the men, and Craig has a lot of fun from time to time, "tormenting her psychic instructor." The Sinclairs were kinder to Mr. Ostaja than I have made it appear. They were wonderful to him. But I like to think, and am inclined to think, that they were never completely "sold" on him—any more than they were completely sold on Bishop Ford and the spiritualists.

Indeed, they had enough—and maybe too much—which was astounding and disturbing in the seemingly supernormal powers with which Mary Craig was gifted.

I can't help doubting that any complete, controllable, and revolutionary power lies beyond that "door in the wall" but *something* lies behind it, and whatever it is can sometimes get out of hand, and be dangerous. Upton Sinclair is touching lightly on that, I think, despite the surface humor of his phrases, when he calls Mary Craig his "witch-wife." She is a pure "white witch" who has never radiated anything except kindness—but an evil woman, endowed with powers like herself, whatever they may be, could have radiated ruin and destruction just as surely as ever did the witch of Africa. Mr. Sinclair has a marvelously illuminating paragraph on this point, in which he says, "She has never tried these experiments with or in the presence of a stranger. . . . She learned from her experiments with her sick brother-in-law that the agent can send you pain and fear, as well as chairs and table-forks, and she would certainly not enter lightly into a condition of *rapport* with those whom she did not know and trust."

The Sinclairs would believe that in my doll duel with the notorious Abbé Penhoël, I had *sent* pain and fear to him through similar mysterious channels. I cannot quite believe it.

V. W. E. Woodward with a Hatpin
Driven through His Jaws

BILL WOODWARD looked like a portly Cupid, shot through the head with one of his own darts, and was saying, with pleased conviction,

"Ii u-u uu a aa! Ii o-i uu a i-ou o-i i a u-i ow. I a ee ou aa a aa, aa, ii a ou-a."

His wife, Helen Rosen, scared and nervous, but giggling in spite of it, said, "I used to understand baby talk. I guess he can't pronounce his consonants. I think he's saying it doesn't hurt him at all. He says it only hurt a little, going in and coming out. He says he can't seem to talk at all, and that that is a nuisance."

"A i o!" agreed the famous author, biographer of George Washington, General Grant, and Lafayette, lighting a cigarette, which added another star point projecting from his jaws like the spokes of a Fourth of July pin wheel—and went over to admire himself in the mirror. . . .

In those days before the depression, the old Grosvenor was—and pretty nearly still is, I'm told—the most ornately dignified and old-fashionedly impressive apartment house on lower Fifth Avenue. And normally, Mr. W. E. Woodward was as dignified as was his domicile. No such shenanigan had ever occurred under that old roof before, or probably ever will again. But you'll recall, perhaps, that before Woodward became a biographer, he had won considerable celebrity with a book entitled *Bunk*. Deflating stuffed horses and stuffed shirts, though generally in a kindly way, has always been one of his hobbies. He'd invited a handful of us there that evening, including the Upton Sinclairs, Joseph Cragmore, Katie Seabrook, and myself. We had been invited to meet the Polish gentleman named Ostaja who had studied in India, among the fakirs, and had produced, or so it was said, some extraordinary phenomena in California whose climate, as the late Cardinal Gibbons once charmingly remarked, seems "peculiarly conducive to miracles."

There's something, on the other hand, about the rough climate of our North Atlantic seaboard, particularly in its metropolitan areas, which seems on the whole less conducive than is California to these subtle phenomena, and on this warm autumn evening the Woodwards had the windows open, with a fine, salty breeze blowing in from the ocean.

Mr. Ostaja had been striving to please, and the Sinclairs, with their deep, friendly, intelligent interest in these matters, were inclined to believe he possessed strong, supernormal, psychic powers. They may have been right about it. I have a profound respect as well as a sincere affection for the Sinclairs, and I'm not sure they weren't right. But whether because of the unconducive climate, or for other reasons, the demonstrations, on the whole, had been inconclusive. That doesn't mean, however, that some of it hadn't been fascinating. Professor Cragmore, for instance, while totally indifferent so far as I know to mediums and swamis, is passionately fond of anything that smacks of old-fashioned "parlor games." And we'd had some good ones—swami variants of button, button, who's got the button . . . blind man's buff . . . puss in the corner . . . with Mr. Ostaja always in the star role—or in the corner. And on a couple of occasions, even before the hatpin episode, the corner had been a pretty tight one.

One of the games was played like this:

With Mr. Ostaja present, and with his knowledge, we agreed on the object to be hidden. We chose, at random, a pencil stub which chanced to be lying on Bill's desk. Mr. Ostaja picked it up and held it fondly for a moment. Then he went out of the room, and went down to the other end of the hall, so there could be no keyhole peeking or listening to our movements. We hid the pencil, in a small table drawer, in the southeast corner of the room. Mr. Ostaja came back. We all sat around and did what we pleased. He stood in the middle of the room, and was going to find the pencil. Extra-sensory perception, manifested as clairvoyance or telepathy, or both, was going to enable him to find the pencil. Since we all knew *where* it was, he might be guided by our thought waves. That would be telepathy. Since he knew *what* it was, he might be able to *see* it, unaided by our thought waves. That would be clairvoyance. Maybe both would be operative.

Mr. Ostaja's performance was brilliant. He moved slowly around the room, approaching localities, objects—approaching us too where we sat. He would stand rapt in trance-thought or whatever it was, studying a vase, or studying one of us. That seemed quite proper. The object might, of course, be hidden on one of our persons. We talked of other matters, or kept silent as we chose. Inside of ten minutes—which is a long time under such circumstances—Mr. Ostaja was concentrating on the corner of the room where the pencil was hidden. At the end of about ten minutes more, he opened the drawer and took out the pencil. We made admiring noises. But Mr. Woodward, and some of the rest of us too, were unconvinced that any extra-sensory hypothesis was necessary. After the polite comments were over, Bill began whittling it down, with Occam's celebrated razor. It was superbrilliant, he agreed, but even though Mr. Ostaja might be sincere in imagining he'd done it by telepathy or clairvoyance, we had all known when he was getting warm or getting hot or getting cold, and he could have been guided to the goal by subtle indications, picked up subtly, unconscious perhaps on his part and on ours, but nevertheless through the medium of the normal senses. "Furthermore, technically," said Bill, "any one of us could have been in cahoots with you, and could have guided you by prearranged signals. I don't believe it for an instant. I know it's not true. But it technically could be."

Mr. Ostaja was not miffed or ungracious. He could do the same thing, he assured us, blindfolded and with his ears stuffed with cotton, stripped over with adhesive tape. Helen led him down the corridor and left him, with distance, space, heavy walls, and two closed doors between him and the studio. We took a little ivory elephant from the mantel and stuffed it down behind the cushions of a sofa. Helen was in the room when we did this.

Ostaja was brought back to the center of the room, looking like the bandaged victim of a bombing raid, and we didn't see how he could possibly find the elephant—unless by an extra-sensory miracle. It developed, however, that somebody must hold his hand. He liked his hand held when he was in the dark. Someone must stay beside him, must be with him as he moved about, must keep contact with him. "H'm," whispered Bill, "I could never do it, and none of you could either. I think perhaps I know how it's done, but you've got to be good to do it."

So Helen held his hand, and we were all silent this time, as they began to wander slowly around the room, "like Pelléas and Mélisande," whispered somebody.

It was very brilliant. There was nothing spectacular about it. Ostaja wandered about, apparently leading Helen. Helen knew the possibilities, with their implications, and was obviously making a definite effort to let herself be led with complete passivity. She was as passive, I think, as anybody could be. But when they were approaching something Ostaja might bump into or stumble over, she seemed, almost unconsciously, to hesitate, ever so little. She let him bump into the object or stumble, but just prior to it, it would seem to me, she gave the impression of drawing back, if ever so slightly. There was almost nothing to see or hear. It went very slowly, but it was a brilliant thing, for presently he found the elephant.

We were almost sorry, all of us, when Woodward said: "I'm sorry. It's wonderful. I am not impugning Mr. Ostaja's sincerity, but I've seen John Mulholland do it, at the Dutch Treat Club. Houdini used to do it. Ostaja's done it, and I congratulate him. Maybe there aren't a dozen people in the world who could do it. And on that basis, Mr. Ostaja is wonderful, but no matter how passive Helen tried to make herself, she was probably having neuromotor reactions all the time, as he got 'warmer' or 'colder,' as they used to say in button, button, and Mr. Ostaja, consciously or unconsciously, was registering these, by his *sensory* contact with her. It's marvelous, but if we're asked to accept it as evidence of anything outside the normal senses, it leaves me still in doubt."

Mr. Ostaja, this time, was obviously miffed. The Upton Sinclairs, no sponsors of credulity, and the gentlest, kindest people I have ever known, were a little miffed too, as among good friends, when good friends disagree. Mr. Woodward was saying,

"I guess some of us are unreasonably skeptical in our refusal to accept the supernormal. But that's the way I am. I suggest that we call it an interesting evening and all adjourn to the basement of the Brevoort."

"No! Stop!" said Mr. Ostaja, now furious. "You scoff at me, you have no faith, you disbelieve! Will you believe, perhaps, if I drive a dagger through my head?"

"I beg you not to," replied our startled host. "I did not know that your sense of honor was so Japanese. Over here, we don't feel it necessary to go so far as that. And besides, I don't keep daggers in the house."

"I have a samurai's sword," said Professor Cragmore hopefully. "My apartment's only half a block away. I'll be glad to run over and get it. . . ."

The Sinclairs explained hastily that we had misunderstood their protégé. Mr. Ostaja was not threatening suicide.

Mr. Ostaja happily possessed, it seemed, among his other supernormal gifts, that of rendering his body immune to pain. Wild horses could romp and stomp harmlessly upon his chest while he lay supinely rigid and cataleptic. For a motion-picture film, he had lain in a trance, like a plank or planked shad, as rigid and cold as one, with his head on one chair and his heels on another while a rock from Alcatraz weighing 150 pounds had been broken on his tummy with a sledge hammer. He could also be screwed in a coffin and buried underground, while a ball game, including home runs and cheering ad lib., could be played over his grave.

Unfortunately, Mr. Woodward had no wild horses handy, and the Grosvenor kept no stable. There happened to be no rocks or sledge hammers handy, either, in the apartment at the moment. Cragmore, always helpful, recalled there was an Italian undertaker on Bleecker Street who stayed open all night, and sold coffins as cheaply as $25. "Lined with gray cheesecloth and with stainless nickel-plated handles." Professor Cragmore offered to contribute the twenty-five dollars, and suggested cheerfully that we might plant Mr. Ostaja in Washington Square. He was on excellent terms with some of the bootblacks, so we might even organize the ball game, with cheering, next morning.

Mr. Ostaja, however, now completely furious, was bent on vindicating himself then and there, by driving something long and sharp and pointed through his jowls.

It was in the days when ladies still wore hats, and one of them delightedly proffered an extra-long and murderous hatpin, adorned with a gold-plated Prussian eagle. It was a war souvenir—had been part of an officer's insignia—and had been welded to the hatpin, for a head. The other ladies shivered and said "oo!" Mr. Ostaja was steamed up, and really going to do it. He was wiping it, as one might a duelist's rapier, on an immaculate silk handkerchief.

Mr. Woodward had been quiet, but I'd noticed him poking gingerly with a finger at one of his own healthy, beefy clean-shaven jowls. Suddenly he arose and said,

253

"Now, wait a minute. I apologize to Mr. Ostaja. He has been very kind, and I haven't been very gracious about it, so I apologize. I think the evening has gone far enough. I think we should thank him, and all adjourn to the Brevoort for a friendly drink."

It's when Bill Woodward is being most suave and self-deprecatory that his friends, and some other people too, have learned from experience to lay off. But Mr. Ostaja had met Mr. Woodward only that evening, had not become awfully fond of him, and had probably never heard of Mr. Woodward's major opus, entitled *BUNK*.

So Mr. Ostaja replied heroically, "But I insist. You have doubted me, and I insist on showing you."

"Showing us what?" said Bill. "If you must insist, I may as well tell you, I don't believe it would hurt much anyway. And I don't believe it would bleed if anybody did it. So why bother to do it?"

Mr. Ostaja then made his slip. Neither he nor any of us knew it was a slip. But he said, with a polite, personal, Polish sneer,

"I suppose you think *anybody* could do it. . . ."

"I think *I* could," replied Bill mildly as a lamb. "At any rate, I'm going to try."

"You are not," said Mrs. Woodward hastily. But her wifely protest was nothing compared to that of Mr. Ostaja. He was hopping. After about a minute of Alphonse and Gaston farce, in reverse English, in which both he and Bill were insisting on having the honor, Cragmore said,

"Why don't you get another hatpin and both do it?"

Bill said, "Sit down, all of you." He took the hatpin, puffed his cheeks, opened his mouth like a dying fish, and began pushing the hatpin slowly into the flesh. After about five inches of it had disappeared laterally, traversing the buccal cavity, the cheek on the other side began to bulge slightly outward. The hatpin point came through. He kept pushing until it was sticking out several inches on both sides of his head. He smiled, or tried to, and began talking baby talk.

Mr. Ostaja had meanwhile been looking for his hat and walking stick, and presently slipped unobtrusively out of the door.

I've included this frivolous anecdote on a more or less serious subject to show that, while psychic anesthesia may be an authentic phenomenon, it isn't necessarily always occurring when it seems to be. Saints, mystics, dervish adepts, possess it, I believe, but seldom demonstrate their power to audiences, and never demonstrate it merely for the sake of proving they possess it. For all I know, Mr. Ostaja may have possessed it. I am not denying that he did. But he wasn't proposing to uncork it that night. It's easier, and often more theatrically impressive, to simulate this phenomenon—as in the case of the hatpin driven through the jaws, which involves no concentration strain at all and very slight pain or discomfort—than it is to invoke or induce the self-hypnotized state in which Saint Lawrence can smile ecstatically while his body—which has become merely *a* body to him—fries and sizzles on the gridiron.

It's easier—and more spectacular—to lie comfortably or even a little uncomfortably on a bed of spikes than it is to kneel for twenty-four hours as frequently did the great Saint

255

Theresa of Ávila, or to dangle all night by one wrist as do the Moslem saints in Tripoli.

I tried a fakir's bed of nails, in Turkestan, and it's even more of a phony than the hatpin driven through the jaws. The latter takes a little nerve, and hurts a little—but the bed of spikes, though it looks terrific, is only slightly more uncomfortable than the lumpy bed in my aunt from Hawkinsville's spare room, or the top of the billiard table in the saloon around the corner from her house where I used to sleep off my juvenile corn-liquor jags in Georgia. You can try it yourself, if they let you—the bed of spikes, I mean—the next time you see one in a freak show. You'll be surprised. I was, when I tried it, on the road to Kashgar. To obtain the honor, I paid the owner twenty rubles, and to save the fakir's face let him proclaim to the not-at-all-interested onlookers that I was a visiting fakir.

What the bed of spikes adds up to is a supersimple sum in arithmetic. If you count the number of nails, and guess the weight of the fakir, you'll find there are generally several nails to each pound avoirdupois of fakir. The nails or spikes are never needle-pointed. They're no more sharply pointed than those you buy at any hardware store. Now you can take four hardware store nails—or three for that matter—and drive them through a shingle, and then poise on their points a pound of beans wrapped in tissue paper. The nails won't pierce or tear the tissue paper—unless you've used Mexican jumping beans or push the bag around. It's as simple as that. And that was probably the reason why honest fakirs originally invented the bed of spikes as an aid to mystical contemplation in the privacy of their own bedrooms, before it began to appear in Coney Island side shows and oriental marketplaces. The sharp differentiation between a bed of nails and a Simmons mattress is—that you must lie still on it.

This was the secret of the celebrated Fakir Blakaman who starred in the Cirque Médrano in Montmartre, in the late twenties. He lay on his back on a pile of broken beer bottles, while heavy weights were laid upon his chest and while he balanced tables with his feet. Tourists imagined the broken beer bottles were phony, but they were jagged and real. Blakaman, who was a great performer, had learned to keep his back and all its muscles motionless. Despite that, his back was often pierced with slivers. If he'd moved, shifted, or twitched his muscles, his back would have been cut into bleeding cat meat. If the fakir's bed of nails is an easier stunt than the hatpin driven through your jaws, the bed of broken beer bottles is an infinitely more dangerous and difficult one.

In recalling the details of the evening years ago at Mr. Woodward's, I dropped him a line the other day, and here's what he wrote me:

Dear Willie:

According to my diary the young man's name was Ostaja (at least it sounded like that and so I have it spelled) and he was a Pole. He was a protégé of Upton Sinclair.

I had never thrust a hatpin through my cheeks before, and I did it then just to see if I could. I remember that it made Mr. Ostaja furious. He thought I was stealing his show, which was not at all my intention.

Since then, I have thrust hatpins through my cheeks numbers of times. There's nothing to it; anybody can do it. Just get a *clean* hatpin, which must be very sharp. There's a slight pricking pain as it goes in through the skin of the right cheek, and when it comes out through the skin of the left cheek, but the slight pain stops immediately. While the pin is in place, you can't move your tongue, or talk, and that is a nuisance.

Best wishes,

W. E. W.

PS. The date was Sunday—Oct. 21st—1928.

The debunking of parlor tricks, whether in New York or on the road to Samarkand, doesn't abrogate the possibility that self-induced anesthesia to bodily pain, stress, and fatigue may lead into a fascinating and perhaps important field. The intrinsic control by this method of pain as pain is of doubtful importance, except in rare cases where ordinary sedatives or anesthetics are unavailable. Eastern adepts, indeed, consider its only importance to be that of providing one of the "doors" through which the mind (or soul), wrenched free from sensory concerns, whether painful or pleasant, can "pass through" into other realms of contemplation and experience. I propose to examine some of those supposed experiences in my concluding chapters.

VI. Justine Dervish Dangling

WHAT Professor Rhine calls "precognition," the glimpsing of events to come, the glimpsing of future events through the current "slit" or nick of time, is perhaps the most disturbing and exciting of all seemingly extra-sensory phenomena.

The young lady I am going to call Justine seemed on rare occasions to possess this power, but could apparently evoke it only when prolonged fatigue and strain of some sort had brought about the separation and detachment of her subjective "self" from the sensory envelope of the objective body.

What happened on these occasions seemed essentially similar to what had happened to me, under the fortuitous strain of fatigue and prolonged loss of sleep, when I succeeded in detaching my inner "self" from the robot body which had sat meanwhile like a zombi at the wheel of Hal Smith's yawl and steered it all night through a storm. Except that where my supposed astral "self" had merely lain unconscious, Justine's seemed, in detaching itself from her wearied robot body, to move backward and forward in time-space, to strange and sometimes beautiful adventures. The technique I had used on the yawl had been taught me by the Melewi dervishes, and the technique which I employed habitually with Justine for several years is one which the Rufiah, an allied dervish sect in Tripoli, has been employing for many centuries.

We had tried all sorts of fantastic methods, and had finally hit on "dervish dangling" as the best and least dangerous. In Tripoli, in the dervish convents and monasteries of Arabia, it's as normal and respectable as our flagpole sitting at county fairs, fasting on Fridays, or kneeling in long meditation in a church or chapel. If it seems here to transgress the bounds of the bizarre, it's only because we were doing it in New York City. I never covered it up—everybody always knows everything anyway—and friends who occasionally did walk in on it were violently perturbed on a number of absurd occasions. But we both knew what we were about, and we both liked it. We were in love with each other, and if we hadn't enjoyed the games we played—we'd certainly never have gone to all that unselfish trouble for the dubious advancement of general knowledge (un-laboratory-controlled, in our case, and consequently doubly worthless), in so doubtful a new scientific field as extra-sensory perception.

Our games sometimes risked getting out of hand. But it is often when things in this category are on the edge of getting out of hand—on the edge of going too far—that they produce the most interesting results.

I shall tell here at the beginning, instead of saving it for a later climax, the result of what happened one night when the dervish dangling got out of hand, through my carelessness, and catapulted Justine through what seemed to be the "slit" in time to a seeming experience in precognition whose denouement came many months later in a place three thousand miles away.

Justine was on tiptoe that night. I had arranged everything with unusual care, because we'd begun early and had a chance to let it run, if it ran, for seven or eight hours—even longer. We hadn't got round to inventing the mask yet, so I had turned out all the lights, as she preferred, had drawn the velvet curtains of the big studio window, so that the room was almost in complete darkness. A soft light, less than the softest moonlight, came from the street outside through the thinner curtains of a smaller window. We had tried it on former occasions with one arm, as the Rufiah do—passing one wrist through the loop of a soft, heavy rope dangling from a ring in the ceiling and then revolving until the rope tightens to give the right tension—but she had found it worked better and left her mind more free when she was fastened up by both wrists and "stayed put." This left her helpless as a modern Andromeda—too helpless, in fact, because she didn't like being fussed over, or eased, or interfered with. So we had worked out an arrangement with the telephone books. On that night, all three of them—the Manhattan, the Brooklyn, and the Classified—were solidly under her feet when it began, so that as she stood with her wrists fastened above her head, she was slightly on tiptoe, but with her toes firmly on the phone books. If the rope sagged, as it sometimes did, or the soft straps round her wrists slipped a little, she could push one or more of the books out from under, with her toes, without my interference, to restore the tension.

Sometimes, in a long evening, nothing at all would happen, and we'd give it up. On other evenings when she went through the "door," she would sometimes tell what was happening in that other world in time-space, beyond our three-dimensional horizon . . . if there is any such other world. Just as often she'd be silent the whole time, and tell me about it only afterward, if at all. In the near-darkness, it frequently took a lot of patient waiting. I've sometimes gone out and left her alone for a whole evening. I might as well have gone out during the early part of this evening, for nothing happened until close on toward ten o'clock, and then I heard her shuffling the phone books with her toes, pushing one of them out from under, as I imagined, to increase the tension a little.

Soon she began to talk . . . dreamily at first. She was through the "door," and was having a lovely time. She seldom went through that door into any horror or violence. She was not like Nastatia Filipovna. In her trances, or whatever they were, she nearly always encountered things that were good and beautiful. If there is any such other world, beyond our normal ken, there's at least one moral-weighted aphorism true there as here. Wherever you go, you have to take yourself with you. It's only if you have the soul of a werewolf here that you will turn into a werewolf, or encounter werewolves, on the other side of the "door." The things Justine encountered, in addition to being beautiful, were also sometimes surprising and amusing. She had never been in Europe then, but she was wandering along a quai, overlooking a river, and behind the quai was an enormous castle or palace. There were crowds, streetcars, shops, motorcars, people on bicycles. I thought it might be London, as she described with delight the things she was glimpsing. She was walking. She stopped to look at little boats that passed in the stream. I wanted to ask her what language the street signs were in, what language the people in the streets were speaking—but we'd learned that such interruptions often short-circuited the contact. As she talked on, describing, and exclaiming at the quaintness or beauty of the buildings, I got the impression that it wasn't London. I wondered if it might be Budapest, or possibly a part of old Florence. It was on a big river, and it was lovely as she described it. But I wasn't very excited about it. Whatever specific city it turned out to be, she could easily have seen it in newsreels, in photos in the *National Geographic,* or in any casual, forgotten magazine—or perhaps in some old book she'd seen as a little girl and long since forgotten with her conscious memory. That's why supposed "clairvoyance" of this or any other sort is difficult to prove or make stand up.

She turned into a side street, leading away from the quai and the river, attracted by the sound of music, and presently came to a carnival, with merry-go-rounds, confetti, clowns, Ferris wheels, booths, tents. It wasn't exactly a carnival either. There was a menagerie, she said; there were animal cages, there was a dancing bear with a pointed hat on its head; there were clowns. It was like a circus, only the clowns and animal wagons weren't under the tents. It puzzled her, but she was enjoying it. She was seeing one of the big street fairs on the continent—perhaps the *Foire de Neuilly.* But what if she was? She could have seen it first (and consciously forgotten about it while it stuck in her subconscious) in a topical news-reel—or for that matter in a screen play made in Hollywood. She went into one of the tents presently to see the trained lions. There was a woman lion-tamer, on an elevated stage, behind bars, putting a lion through its tricks. Justine presently chuckled a little. It was a funny lion. It was an *old,* tired lion, and it looked as if it had been kept in moth balls.

The lion-tamer was "cute," in her boots and red jacket. She was pretty. She was pretty, even if she did have blondined hair and too much red paint on her cheeks. Now she was going to put her head in the lion's mouth. Yes, she was lying down with the lion. Oo, yes she did! She'd put her head right inside the lion's enormous mouth. And afterward the lion had got up and yawned. It had come to the front of the cage and yawned. "If that was *my* lion," Justine giggled, "I'd teach it to *roar*."

Justine was silent now, in the semidarkness, for a couple of minutes, and then let out a gasp and giggle, and said, "I don't believe it! It didn't happen!" I was wondering what she didn't believe, what didn't happen, when she burst into gales of laughter, and cried,

"Yes, it did happen! It really did happen! The others thought it was a joke first, a part of the show. And I did too. But it really happened. That woman in the front row with the baby was simply too funny!"

Justine had presently left the street fair and was going back to her hotel, or wherever she was going in the trance, and had taken a taxi. She was still calm, apparently still enjoying herself. Her voice was calm, smooth, pleased. I had forgotten, almost as completely as she had, the other Justine who had been standing all that time with her wrists drawn up above her head, there on her tiptoes, on the phone books. And now, in a period of silence, I didn't like the sound of that other Justine's breathing. And I switched on the light.

It was now nearly two o'clock in the morning, and the last shuffling of the phone books, or any other movement, had been before 10 P.M. What she had done had been to push or kick all three of the thick phone books aside. For more than four hours, she had dangled there clear of the floor, suspended by the wrists, her whole weight hanging by her wrists, with her toes swinging nearly two inches clear of the floor. The lips from which that always calm, tranquil, amused, and at times gay and laughing, talk had been streaming, were bitten and bruised by her own teeth, and her face was contorted as that of a girl who weeps when no tears flow. Her eyes were glassy, clear, ecstatic, wide open in the light. The light bewildered her, but she was still far away. When I lifted her and loosed the straps around her wrists, she said, "Don't! Don't! I'm seeing. . . ."

I carried her to a couch, made her drink a little brandy, and began chafing her wrists. We never quarreled—but that night she was so angry that she threatened never to come back.

I said, "Look at your wrists! They'll be black and blue tomorrow, and your thumbs will be numb for a week."

She said, "My thumbs! I thought you were so brave and daring, and you tell me my wrists will be black and blue! They're *my* wrists and my thumbs. Something wonderful was happening to me. It was different from anything that has ever happened before."

I said, "You played a dirty trick on me there in the dark. I wouldn't have done that to you—for four hours. And I wouldn't have let you do it to yourself. . . ."

She said, "You lost your nerve and I'm ashamed of you. I tell you this was different."

How different, how on the edge of something possibly tremendous if it could ever be controlled—how perhaps actually *over* the edge, Justine had been that night, I didn't know, and I still didn't know the following summer, when more than six months had passed, and she was on her first visit to Europe, and we were spending a week together in the south of France.

One afternoon we drove to Avignon, and were walking along the quai toward the old bridge, with the Papal Palace on our left, when she said:

"But this is it! This is where I was that night, the night we quarreled because you brought me back too soon. There's the man on the bicycle, with a derby hat, those three girls with shawls, that priest on a bicycle. I remember how funny the priest was, in robes, with a beard, on a bicycle. . . ."

I was a little bit scared, and still skeptical. I thought, "She can have seen Avignon without ever being in Europe before. The Papal Palace, the quai, the famous bridge, are travelogue stock subjects." And I thought of another point too, which I maliciously made.

"You never mentioned any priest on a bicycle, or a man with a derby hat on a bicycle either."

"Didn't I, Willie?" she asked. "I don't know what I said that night. Did I tell you about the street fair? Listen, you can almost hear the music now. The merry-go-round will be up that second corner, round another turn, with the tents and clowns."

We made the first turn, and I began to hear the merry-go-round, and it gave me goose flesh. The back of my neck felt cold. I was goose pimples all over, and we were holding each other's hands pretty tightly when we walked into that street fair. I tried to get a grip on myself, I kept thinking, "No, it can't be. There's a fair here every summer, same fair, same clowns, same animals, same dancing bear, same lion-tamer. She must have seen it in a film somewhere." I kept telling myself she must have seen it in a film somewhere, when we came to the lion-tamer's tent, and went in and sat down. I kept telling myself that the lion-tamer is always a little woman in boots, red jacket, with blondined hair, and too much rouge on her cheeks. It was always an elderly lion, and she always lay down and put her head in its mouth. But did it always yawn, as it was now doing? It must have yawned, in whatever film or travelogue Justine had seen and forgotten. For it was yawning now. It was surely a part of the act. Justine said, and I began to have goose pimples again, "If it was *my* lion, I'd teach it to roar."

Then as we sat there, she said, excitedly, "It's going to turn now! It's going to come to the front of the cage and turn its back! Yes, it's going to do it!"

"Do what?" I asked, and she whispered, *"It's going to wet those people down there in the front row."*

The front row benches were six feet away from the barred stage, and on a lower level. The great cat lumbered, sidling to the front bars, turned its back, half squatted, and loosed a mighty stream of amber liquid, that arced through the air and splashed on the clothes and faces of the people in the middle of the row down yonder.

The audience was amazed, then giggling, then shouting with joy, and Justine burst into gales of laughter. She clutched me and said, "Watch that woman with the baby! She's going to get up now. . . ."

The woman, a bareheaded peasant in a black shawl, holding aloft a wailing brat whose face she was wiping, arose, climbed on the bench, and screamed furiously in the Marseillais dialect:

"You saw it! I call you to witness! In the face! In the eyes

267

of my darling innocent! In the face, it pissed! In the face of my little Poupoune! For this I paid two francs and fifty centimes!"

The audience howled and egged her on. I said to Justine, "Could you understand what she said?"

Justine said, "No, I couldn't understand a word of it, *either time*. But it was simply too funny, wasn't it? I'm glad you've seen it too."

I was more disturbed, perhaps, than I have ever been about anything. I was thinking of the "slit" in time, of the Einstein corollaries, of a phrase written by Columbia University's greatest mathematician, Dr. Cassius Jackson Keyser, "Simultaneity of events is relative, not absolute; the sense of time is only an imperfect sense of a fourth dimension in space." Yet I was unconvinced. There's a tenet in philosophic logic known as "Occam's Razor." It says, *"Essentia non sunt multiplicanda praeter necessitatem."* I thought, "It *can* be that this whole thing has happened before. It can be a part of the act . . . just as the yawning might be a part of the act . . . and it *can* have been caught in a film—or Justine can have read it."

Next morning I went and tried to shave the little liontamer with Occam's Razor. She thought I was a lawyer, or making a complaint, and said I'd better talk with her husband, who was the manager of the show. I convinced them that I was a journalist, and that all I wanted to know was whether the thing had been part of the act—or if not part of the act, whether by chance it had ever happened before.

"But *mon dieu!*" they protested, of course it had never happened before! They had only bought the old lion in

January. They had bought it because it was an old "trouper" born in a cage, born in the show business.

Had they ever heard of such a thing happening before with *any* lion? They laughed. "Not through the bars of the cage! Not on the audience! It had been funny, if one hadn't been splashed. Impossible, unexpected things animals did were always the funniest. One night with those three performing bears at the Médrano . . ." the woman was saying, and I asked,

"Did you work at the Médrano?"

"All my life," she said proudly. *"This is the first season I have ever worked in a street fair."*

Justine and I had long talks about it, and felt that perhaps we were on the edge of something tremendous. We both knew that if we could control, even to some slight extent, and then *focus* these glimpses through the slit of time, if that was what they really were, we'd soon be having rings on our fingers and bells on our toes and elephants to ride on, if we preferred elephants to Rolls-Royces. That's the hell of this whole business—that if anybody possessed and could control any phase of clairvoyance, he could become more powerful than J. P. Morgan or the Pope. The fact that nobody ever has used clairvoyance or precognition with practical effectiveness, whether in Duke University or on a mountaintop in Tibet,[1] is the strongest evidence to me that extra-sensory perception, if any, has never yet been controlled or focused to a degree worth getting excited about.

If Justine, for instance, could ever see and read *next year's* stock-market page in the *Herald Tribune*, or *next week's* or

[1] See Appendix, p. 379.

tomorrow morning's for that matter, she could be richer than a maharaja's maharani before the next sun went down.

But whatever fleeting power she possessed, though it came flitting back at times, we could never control to the slightest extent. And as for *focusing* it—the only practical thing it ever brought us was a barrel of iced fish, once, from Canada. It was just like talking with the ghost of Euclid, at a mediumistic séance, and having the ghost of that great genius tell you that a straight line is the shortest distance between two points. It was tremendously exciting, but it got you nowhere.

VII. Justine in the Mask

IT is common knowledge that when certain of the five normal senses are dulled or blanked out, whether temporarily or permanently, other senses in the normal group may tend to become more highly sensitive.[1]

Look around you at any audience in Carnegie Hall, or at any group listening to chamber music. Numbers of people will be listening raptly with their eyes shut. This isn't always a pose, though it lends itself easily to posturing. Many people actually hear better with closed eyes, or in the dark.

It is equally common knowledge among people who have, for any purpose whatsoever, experimented in such things outside laboratories, that steps taken in the direction of soothing to somnolence, lulling, dulling, blunting, or blanking all five of the normal senses to whatever extent may be devised is a first step toward inducing extra-sensory receptivity.

The most commonly known phenomenon in the realm of the five ordinary senses is the case of the blind, whose sense

[1] The one exception to this rule lies in the close relationship between the two allied senses of smell and taste. Apparently these two senses are so closely interlocked that when one is dulled, both are. But no other two of the five senses are thus interrelated.

of touch is nearly always abnormally acute, and whose sense of hearing is frequently so. The increased touch sensitivity in the blind seems in some cases to extend far beyond the actual physical contact with any object, with the fingers or with the skin.

Paul Donahoo, blind attorney, was coroner of Richmond County (Atlanta), Georgia. He could tell, could "sense" in some way, indoors and outdoors, whenever he approached to within about four feet of any solid object or obstruction. It didn't have to be a massive wall, or an extensive surface, like the side of a house, though such heavy and large-surfaced obstructions were the easiest. He could always tell when he was approaching a wall. He could similarly always tell, when approaching a door, whether it was closed or open. He could nearly always tell, but not infallibly, when he was approaching or passing within four feet or so of a telegraph pole or lamppost.

Paul wasn't interested in clairvoyance or any aspect of the supernormal, and didn't attribute his sensitivity to anything mysterious. He was willing to talk about it, however, and I learned that while he couldn't be certain how he did it, he believed it could be explained in terms of hypersensitivity of touch, hypersensitivity of hearing—perhaps a combination of both. He couldn't be sure, but believed that he felt, perhaps on the skin of his cheeks or hands, perhaps with his whole body, some subtle difference in the density of the air, on approaching large, solid objects; or some difference perhaps in air vibrations or air currents. That would be the normal sense of touch, subtly hypersensitized—but as definitely sensory as when you feel a breeze on your cheek—or are hit by a cyclone. With reference to his possible hypersensitivity of hearing, he thought that perhaps any sounds, even the faintest, which happened to be in the air, made waves which were interrupted, diverted a little, thrown back distorted a little, by their contacts with the solid objects. If this was true, it would have been the normal sense of hearing, abnormally sensitized—but just as definitely sensory as when you go out behind Johnnie Mack's barn, and shout, and hear the echo. Dog whistles which no normal human ear can hear hadn't yet been invented. If they had, I'd have liked to try one on Paul.

Justine was a wide-awake sort of girl, acute, sensitive, and active as a kitten, in full possession of all five of her physical senses, and as much a slave to them and their habits as anybody. She was inclined, indeed, to be a flibbertigibbet. And in our experiments, if they can be dignified with that appellation, in the "games" we played and fantasies we indulged, she soon discovered that when temporarily deprived of this or that sense and its attendant habits, it made the senses which were left free more receptive and more interesting. There were days, for instance, on which we played the game that she was not permitted to use her hands. She was not permitted to *touch* anything whatsoever. If she forgot, and picked up something, or smoothed her dress, or pushed back her hair, or scratched the tip of her nose, I'd tie her hands behind her back for a couple of days. We didn't do it solemnly, in hushed silence, or in hiding. We never flaunted it, but we never bothered to cover it up much either. With Justine in a loose cape, we walked and sat in the park, took taxis, went to cafés and theaters. We were never exhibitionistic about it. But we went places instead of staying shut up together in the studio. People never gave us more than a second glance, didn't give a hoot in hell. Justine was pretty as a picture in those days, poised and happy as a child. Nobody interferes with a girl who's poised and happy, not even if the boy friend is jabbing pins in her. People figure that it's the girl's own affair. Nobody, not even the waiter or the couple at the next table, ever gave more than two glances, even if I was holding a glass or spoon to her lips, or brushing back her hair. They saw a girl who wasn't mutilated, crippled, or deformed, but who couldn't use her hands. They were correct about that. She couldn't. They figured that if there had been anything criminal about it, we wouldn't have been there in the tearoom of the St. Regis enjoying ourselves. They were correct about that too. We enjoyed it. We were a couple of cuckoos, tired of monotony, and making our own little play worlds to live in. I confided all of it, back in the days we were doing it, to my friend Dr. A. A. Brill, dean of the Freudians in America. He listened with surprised but unshocked amusement . . . told me the Greeks had a name for it. We needed no dean of the Freudians to tell us that. The erotic fun we got out of it was strictly our own business and is of no importance in connection with certain adventures in the field which this book attempts to cover. If I mention that angle at all, it's not in the nature of apology, but simply to clear the fact that I'm not an ostrich, and am not writing for ostriches . . . or for innocents either. There are erotic overtones, perverse in their different and more familiar ways, in every other page of the daily newspapers, in the Socratic dialogues, in Holy Writ, in the Sapphic odes and the Shakespearean sonnets. Such overtones are neither here nor there so long as they're not suffocatingly emphasized and harped on. If harped on, they are of no interest to anybody but another hippopotamus.[2]

One thing which came out of the business with the hands, and which may be of general interest, was our discovery of the casual, almost unconscious, and generally unnecessary tactile contacts the normal person makes with the hands in the course of an ordinary day. Without being aware of it, you and ninety-nine per cent of everyone you know will be, for instance, touching lightly your chin, cheek, forehead, hair, as if brushing away imaginary cobwebs, or as if your own face were a kitten which you stroked, ever so lightly and absent-mindedly at odd moments. You will be doing this, unless your hands are otherwise continually occupied, as in knitting or rapidly typing, or tightening bolts on the Ford conveyer, on an average of at least 150 times a day. You will be patting your knee, or fondling your elbow, unnecessarily adjusting a detail or fold of your garments, touching or tapping the chair arm or table, etc., many hundreds of times in the course of the same eighteen hours. All these involve slight, generally unconscious sensory impressions—unless you absent-mindedly pat a red-hot stove or cake of ice by mistake—and this fact helps to explain why the oriental adepts and yogis remain motionless and numb, like wooden images or plaster statues,

[2] Sacher-Masoch's *Venus in Furs*, parts of D. H. Lawrence's *Lady Chatterley's Lover*, Alfred de Musset's (?) *Gamiani*, André Gide's *Corydon*, are interesting only to other hippopotami. *Women in Love*, the Shakespearean sonnets, Gide's *Counterfeiters*, and Thomas Mann's *Death in Venice*, in which the cerebral eroticism is not overemphasized or harped on, are of lasting interest to everybody. I've known some quite attractive hippopotami, but this narrative is not for them.

when endeavoring to induce the detachment from the senses which may let extra-sensory perception come in.

In this game of trying to lull, anesthetize, or "blank out" the myriad sensory things which impact unconsciously at the rate of perhaps several thousand per second through the sum total of the five ordinary senses, we tried some experiments with sound and hearing, but never got very far with them. Paul Morand had given me a box of pink pellets made with wax and cotton—then recently invented—to make sleep easier when fire engines pass in the street or your apartment-house neighbors are making whoopee after midnight . . . but they merely lulled sound. And besides, your own ears buzz inside. The elder Pulitzer spent thousands of dollars to have a room cork lined and wound with silk, cocooned (walls packed too, they say, with mineral wool), but he still heard, or imagined he heard, church bells ringing. And even if he didn't hear *outside* sounds, it was still a noisy place. His pen sounded like cats scratching, and when he dropped a pencil on the rug it sounded like a depth bomb with a retarded explosion. A vacuum is the only thing that will blank sound completely, and you can't live in a vacuum.

In the field of light waves, sight, and seeing, Justine and I made better progress, and got a lot of interesting results. If my way of defining that field seems tautological, it's because, as we soon found out, the field itself is complicated, tricky. Any pressure on the closed eyelids makes you see tiny shooting stars and rainbows. If you press hard on your eyelids with the balls of your thumbs, you see the Aurora Borealis and the San Francisco fire. And any slight pressure, such as being blindfolded for a length of time or wearing the satin "sleeping mask" which has since become popular and is sold in all fashionable stores; or merely holding your eyes squinted tight shut, produces tiny recurrent darts and spots of light, or their illusion. We tried it in those various ways, indoors and out, and discovered that though only comparative darkness was induced, Justine's other faculties already became keener. Her sense of smell, her sense of sound, her sense of touch, would tell her more than she supposed they normally could.

She could sit on a bench in Central Park, with her eyes squinted shut, on a summer morning, and tell whether it was a big dog or a little dog; when it was one man, two men, or a man and a woman passing; when it was a baby carriage, and when (by smell from a distance of thirty feet if the wind wasn't in the wrong direction) it was the popcorn wagon which ran on rubber wheels and made—she said—identically the same sound as the baby carriage.

Indoors, we tried a lot of blindfold tricks, but blindfolding is tricky, annoying to the subject, bothersome, frequently inconclusive.

Justine sometimes kept her eyes closed—was on other occasions blindfolded—in the dervish-dangling experiments, and in others with clairvoyance of some sort or another as their objective. But she worked best with her eyes unclosed, in darkness or near-darkness. What we were after, by now, was not merely the blanking of one sense to increase the acuteness of the other senses, but a blanking, or lulling, of all five normal senses, to prevent them from interfering with her adventures in that other world which was purely subjective, and perhaps extra-sensory.

The mask we finally devised was partly my idea, and

partly hers. When I later, living in France, permitted the French Museum of Natural History to publish, in one of its official bulletins, a photograph of Justine wearing it—with a scholarly essay concerning its psycho-erotic aspects, written by Michel Leiris—people who saw the photo but misunderstood the essay thought the devil had invented it.

After we'd planned it, made a couple of sketches, and decided what we wanted, we went to see the best glove-and-leather expert I happened to know—at Abercrombie and Fitch's.

They were a bit British about it, lifted their eyebrows since it had no precedent, but not too highly, since I'd once bought a lot of African equipment—and thought it might be done. The cost, however, if they did it, what with a mold of the young lady's head to work from, what with trial and probably error—might be pretty steep. They weren't passionately desirous of undertaking it at any price, and suggested that some less expensive leather-worker who specialized in theatrical costuming might be found who could do it just as well, and at a lower figure. I took their always excellent advice, and we were given the address of an elderly Italian named Sinatra, who limped a little and had a shop of his own with a half dozen workmen in a converted brownstone house on West 47th Street, east of Broadway. He was interested, precisely because it involved the making of something which had never been made before, and in a week or so turned out a beautiful, skilled, craftsman-artist's job.

It was made, on his advice, of soft, smooth, glacé kid. We experimented first with suède, but (believe it or not) any suède which was soft and light enough proved not to be completely lightproof. The smooth leather, on the contrary, was as lightproof as a sheet of lead.

The mask covered Justine's entire head, following all the contours of her face, and, when laced tight in the back, fitted smoothly and tightly as her own skin. The only opening was a slit for the mouth, which followed the lines of her lips, and through which she soon learned to breathe, deeply and steadily.

But now that it was done, and she began to wear it, she went through periods of hating and fearing it, because it accomplished, as she said, *too completely*, the things we'd hoped it would.

Instead of producing the ordinary effect of blindfolding, or of closing the eyes, her eyes, wide open inside it, stared in utter blackness. Sense of smell was blanked, since there were no holes for the nostrils. Sense of hearing was dulled, and the tactile sensitivity of her cheeks (normally feeling warmth, coolness, air currents, when a window was opened or closed, when she was merely blindfolded) was likewise blanked. It shut her off—as completly as a conscious mind can ever be shut off—from everything outside. Often, in what came close to panic, she could not tell whether I or anybody was in the room at all, whether I might be close beside her, or whether I had gone away and left her there totally alone. It was like being back, she said, "in the womb of time." And it was more than she had bargained for. There were times when she hated and feared it, and would have torn it off if I hadn't kept her hands always tied or chained, well away from her face and head. Eventually she became accustomed to it, gave up "fighting" it, let it "take her," as she said—and ended by liking it. She wanted to be in it whenever she could, even when I might have to go away and leave her all day alone, as I occasionally did.

We now began trying, not very scentifically, but certainly with "the heat turned on," a series of experiments in the supposed extra-sensory. Rhine's ESP cards, which Farrar & Rinehart have popularized as a parlor game with rules, handbook, scoring pad, etc., hadn't yet become generally available, and we worked often with an ordinary poker deck. I had been told by Montague of Columbia, then president of the American Philosophical Association, who had served on some of the old Eusapia Palladino committees, that if any person ever succeeded in making extra-sensory perception work with accuracy and *controlled certainty*, it would revise the whole present aspect of the universe and rank in importance with the discoveries of Kepler, Galileo, Copernicus, and Einstein. I kept such records as I could, but their sum totals and percentages were no more impressive than Rhine's, or than those which the sardonic John Mulholland produced with *inanimate* equipment borrowed from the International Business Machines Corporation.[3]

Most of the time, it seemed to me that what Justine was doing was the equivalent of pure guessing. And it seems to me that this is what the scores, whether high or low, made by Rhine's subjects, always seem to be. There were other rare occasions when Justine seemed to "slide over," as she called it, into flashing moments of what seemed actual illumination, when she seemed to be on sure ground. In those impatient moments, she'd name the cards, insisting that she *saw* them. What did she mean by *seeing?* It was, she said, like closing

[3] See Appendix, p. 327.

your eyes in memory, and *seeing* a familiar face or object. In doing that, in thinking of a face, or doorway, or landscape, there is no vision in the sense of light impacting on the eye, but nevertheless the cerebral image you have is *visual*. She said that when she "slid over" and it "happened," it was like that. And it was an eerie, emotionally if not scientifically convincing, experience when she'd sometimes say, "But I see it plainly . . . it's the nine of spades, and you're holding it sideways."

As to whether it was telepathy, clairvoyance, sheer accident, I don't yet know. She wasn't interested in card experiments anyway, and was always impatient with them. I'm not sure she wasn't right in being impatient.

What Justine enjoyed was the adventures that came spontaneously, the subjective experiences, trance visions, or whatever they were, when her mind, shut away from impacts with the sensory world and consequently freed from it, wandered into that other world—which is perhaps really another world in some fourth-dimensional region of time and space—or perhaps merely a dreamworld of cloud fantasy built with nothing more than the released imagination.

Three or four times, in the course of a number of years, she slid over again into what seemed to be the field of precognition—the field which had most excited and interested us, since the night she had first slid into it and seen the streetfair lion. Her glimpses into the future, however, if that is what they really were, never brought back anything of serious importance or intrinsic value. She never foresaw the armistice, or the boom, or the depression, or the death of the Pope. It was always something intrinsically trivial, usually fantastic, pucklike, poltergeistlike, verging on the edge of the unexpected comic—as in the case of the absurd micturating lion.

The other time Justine strolled into fourth-dimensional time-space, as it were, the only thing she brought back was a barrel of fish. She'd been sitting in the mask all day, crouched, in a posture we'd borrowed from Peter Freuchen's Eskimo seers and wizards,[4] with her wrists fastened to her ankles. When she began to talk that evening—it was in January—she seemed to be shopping in Saks Fifth Avenue, in the summertime, with her cousin Lucy. They bought some summer clothes. She was talking with Lucy about the heat, and about whether they'd walk home or take a taxi. She bought some dresses and gewgaws, seemed to be enjoying herself. They were going to have an ice-cream soda presently. . . .

This cousin of hers, Lucy, lived in the East Sixties, in a small but la-di-da apartment, with a tiny kitchenette and colored maid who came only in the late afternoon. I'd been there a couple of times to tea. That was where they were going now, as I gathered from Justine's chatter with Lucy. They were walking a few blocks. It had become cooler, so they walked the whole way. Justine was chattering along, with the silences filled in, as I imagined, by Lucy, when they reached the apartment and were let in by the maid.

"*What?*" Justine was saying. "What did she say had come? *A barrel of fish!* The expressman brought it, and it's in the kitchenette? It must be a joke! I don't believe it!"

There was a spot of silence, and then Justine was shrieking with laughter. There was a barrel of fish in the kitchenette—it seemed—a small barrel, but a barrel. "Fresh . . . fish!

[4] See Appendix, p. 381.

. . . Perishable!" shrieked Justine, still almost inarticulate with laughter.

There was now a prolonged period of silence. Then Justine stirred, struggled a little, groaned, whimpered like a baby. She had come "out of it" or had "come back" or whatever you want to call it. The thread of whatever it was had been broken.

She said, "Willie . . . are you there? My wrists hurt, and my shoulders ache. What time is it? Please let me go now."

Late one evening in June, Justine was on the telephone, after having tried to reach me repeatedly since six o'clock, and said:

"I'm at Lucy's, and the fish are here! They came from Canada, and Lucy thinks she can guess who sent them. We've had the janitor up to open the barrel. It was mostly full of salt and ice. He says they're lake trout and landlocked salmon."

"Hey," I said, "I'm coming around right now."

I went and saw the barrel of fish. Lucy heard next day from the returned vacationing friend who had sent them. He was back in New York. I had never met him, but went to see him. He couldn't understand why I had come to see him.

He had known Lucy longer than I had; Lucy was *his* girl, and what business was it of mine anyway? Why had he sent them?

Why did anybody ever do anything? He'd sent them, he said, "partly on impulse, and partly as a joke."

Had he ever promised Lucy, or any of her friends, that some day he'd send Lucy a barrel of fish?

Say, what was this? He hadn't thought of it until after he'd caught them, and then he only thought of it because the guide had told him it could be done. He wanted to know, finally, if the fish had spoiled.

The fish hadn't spoiled. I ate some of the salmon, but lovely as it was, it didn't sit well on my stomach—nor does it, to this day, sit any better on my mind. I am fully aware that, whereas in the case of the lion, there hadn't been one chance in quadrillions of ordinary predictability, or of collusion, this barrel of fish was a different kettle of them. If Justine, the blondined lion-tamer, and the angry mother with her brat, had been mysteriously in transatlantic cahoots, it still left the whole episode up in the air—*because the lion would have had to be in on it too.* But in this latter case of apparent precognition, since we had, of course, told Lucy about it, nothing would have been easier than for Lucy and her boy friend to have played an elaborate joke. They hadn't, as a matter of fact, but neither I nor anybody nor they themselves on oath can prove a negative of that sort, in terms of what the laboratories properly demand as proof. There was no presumption of control in this case, and I have made no attempt to imply any. It's as wide open as any other—fish story. It was unfortunately the same on the couple of other occasions when she seemed again to pass through "the door in the wall" to step forward in fourth-dimensional time-space. We never again got anything as good as the lion.

These precognition experiences of hers were of extremely rare occurrence. They occurred four times in all, in a period of more than five years. She had soon begun habitually, and seeming to prefer it so, to slide *backward* instead of forward —to slide into the past, in trances which, if authentic, were in the field of what Professor Rhine has labeled retrocognition. It was in these that Justine reveled, but in these excursions *backward*, as Rhine so ably points out in *New Frontiers of the Mind*, there is almost never any possibility of control. If you'll follow Dr. Rhine's reasoning, closely and tightly, you'll see why this is so:

If it is something out of the past that is *known*, even though it dates back to before the building of the pyramids, there is always the possibility that the entranced excursionist, no matter how sincere, may have heard it or read it or seen it (in pictured illustration, in museums, or on the screen), and retained it in the deep well of the unconscious mind.

If it is something out of the past which is *unknown*, there is almost never any way of proving that what he seems to see in retrospect ever happened originally. The only way to establish control in a case of this latter sort would be, for instance, for the excursionist to dig up the lost chest of gold, or the old family plate, which, in the vision, he had seen his great-grandfather secretly burying. Since neither Justine nor anybody else has ever put retrocognition to any practical and profitable use of that sort, the whole field is still shrouded in thick fog and foxfire.

It was in these uncontrolled fields and vistas of fog and foxfire that Justine generally now wandered when she went through the door in the wall. It was there that she liked best to wander. It seemed to me that she suffered less strain . . . that she was less torn . . . experienced less subsequent prostration and fatigue . . . in these excursions *backward*, than she had on the rare, violent occasions when she seemed projected into the *future*.

Wandering in the past, Justine had long adventures—sometimes commonplace as cooking on an open fire or drawing water from a well, sometimes gorgeous and fantastic as anything in the Thousand and One Nights, but there can be no point, in this context, in relating or embroidering them. For reasons Rhine has given, they have no clinical value, and their only real value, which lies in the field of art, when they're intrinsically good enough—a field which has nothing to do with the general purpose of this present book—is a value which has already been amply demonstrated by more than one great master. Kipling wrote "The Brushwood Boy," Du Maurier wrote *Peter Ibbetson*, Arthur Machen wrote *The Hill of Dreams*, Viola Hunt wrote "The Coach," H. G. Wells wrote "The Door in the Wall," and ninety-seven other great ones, including our own Poe, Ambrose Bierce, Jack London, Mary Austin, have contributed their classic and near-classic tales, more than often based on what they believed to be authentic experiences. They are all, as a matter of fact, "door in the wall" stories, and the wall is always the same wall—the wall which imprisons all us normal humans in the three-dimensional sensory here and now, which bars us from the fourth-dimensional field of space-time, familiar to saints, geniuses, and mystics long before Einstein gave it a potential scientific basis in his Theory of Relativity.[5]

Justine had more joy wandering in that realm than any other, but so many have wandered there, and have brought

[5] "One of the most beautiful things we can experience is the mysterious. It is the source of all true science and art. He who can no longer pause to wonder is as good as dead."—ALBERT EINSTEIN.

back such rich treasures, shared afterward with the world, that if she and I tried to recount all her adventures, it would be merely bringing more coals to a Newcastle where many of the coals have been already polished to the radiance of diamonds.

Are they really diamonds, or are they merely polished carbon? Some people think they know the answer, but I am not sure of anything in this realm of the supernormal. I am not even sure—I can't be after Justine's adventure with the lion—of the validity of my own doubts.

Part Four

APPENDIX: SUPPLEMENTARY NOTES, ANECDOTES AND ILLUSTRATIONS

Notes on Foreword

1. WE HAVE A BENEVOLENT WHITE WITCH in Rhinebeck. She is a crippled lady who knows what suffering is, and uses her "white magic" to help others. A couple of weeks ago our Rhinebeck *Gazette* told about a kindly "miracle" that left the recipient puzzled, grateful, and amazed. One day delivering bread he told the dear lady he was suffering from pains in his head.

When he came back early the following morning she said, "Well, how's your head now?"

He said, "It still hurts."

She said, "That will be all right. At exactly ten o'clock this morning, it will stop hurting you entirely."

He went his rounds. The pain stopped completely. He looked at his watch. It was exactly ten o'clock. The delivery man says, "I don't know what happened, but I tell you, it makes you think."

It probably makes *you* think that I've picked up a small town coincidence that doesn't prove anything. Maybe you won't be so sure when I tell you some facts recently presented by one of America's leading scientific authors, George W. Gray, author of *The Advancing Front of Science* and *New*

World Picture. In *Harper's Magazine,* May, 1939, and condensed in the *Reader's Digest* of June, he tells of some startling cures accomplished in ordinary clinic routine by the employment of "white magic" in cases where the patients, as it were, had "hexed" themselves.

A man came into the hospital one day whose arms were pimpled with a bothersome skin disease. He told them it always broke out worse on Monday mornings. "What do you do on Sundays?" asked the doctor. Usually, said the patient, he visited a young lady. It developed that for some years the couple had been engaged, but the girl repeatedly postponed naming the wedding day. Each Sunday, says Dr. Gray, the man pressed for a decision; each Monday was the day after a frustration. And almost every Monday his skin protested his anxious state by breaking into eczema.

To the same big Eastern hospital came a man critically ill with asthma. After weeks of treatment he was relieved, and a day set for his discharge. Suddenly, on the night before his scheduled departure, all his former dangerous symptoms returned. Treatment was resumed; again his breathing became free; again arrangements were made for the journey and again asthma returned in full force. He was a college teacher who had become embroiled in a faculty fight and feared for his job. Subconsciously he felt it safer to be in the protective walls of a hospital than go back and face possible dismissal.

"In these cases," says the author, "there was more than the physical condition. There was a mental or emotional disturbance which had its counterpart in the physical mechanism."

Dr. Erwin Moos reported the case of a man with a systolic blood pressure of 280 who was also afflicted with a lung disorder and whose urine showed traces of albumin. Rest and drugs brought no help, but one day the patient remarked that he had done a great wrong to his estranged wife. The doctor immediately arranged a meeting, and after a reconciliation between the two, the man's blood pressure fell to 150, his lung symptoms abated, and the albumin disappeared. Several years later the patient was in good health, with a blood pressure of only 130.

And mind you, the gentlemen who recount these things are neither faith healers nor cranks. These facts are based on hospital records. I am bringing them in to make it easier for you to believe in my dolls.

Gray tells of a businesswoman who had been highly capable in a minor capacity and who was unexpectedly promoted to an executive job. Three months later she developed a severe physical ailment. The doctor presently guessed that her increased responsibilities were a source of apprehension. When she was persuaded to resign the executive job for which she was unfitted, and resume her old place as an assistant, for which she was admirably fitted, the physical ailment disappeared.

A key to the way black magic and the doll can kill you (i.e., by *deliberately implanted* anxiety and fear) is given, I think, in the following scientific analysis in which Gray, in the article I have identified above, expresses his conviction that anxiety can actually become a biochemical factor as dangerous as bacteria:

The whole physiology of anxiety is bound up with the idea of protection, and has its origins far back in human history. How to save one's skin was a supreme problem of primitive man. Every day there was the necessity of taking strong action either in fighting or fleeing. These demands gradually built into the body an automatic scheme of swift adjustment for action.

In time of fear or anger powerful changes go on within the body: the heart muscles are stimulated to more rapid pulsations, circulation is shifted from the stomach and intestines to the heart, brain, lungs, and skeletal muscles—all resources are mobilized for most effective fight or flight. The mechanisms of these automatic reactions are largely chemical—caused by powerful substances secreted by the glands and the nerve endings. And every impression from the outside world that threatens the security of the individual, that provokes him to anger or inspires him to fear, automatically calls into play this complicated biochemical mechanism to prepare the body for action.

Now the man who has just lost his fortune in a bank failure suffers a fear just as real as was the fear of a cave man confronted by a wild beast. However, whether the cave man ran, or stood and fought, he needed the stronger heartbeat, the change in blood distribution. But to the victim of the bankruptcy these adjustments are superfluous. They prepare him for action which does not take place. They glut his system with powerful substances he does not need, and which cause internal conflict. Such conflicts tend to be suppressed, but the fact that they are unconscious does not mean they are innocuous. Quite the opposite. The poisoning effect of a source of anxiety seems to increase in inverse ratio to the victim's awareness of its identity.

It seems likely that the stresses of life affect one individual differently from another because of differences in constitution, in relative weakness of certain organs which ordains which shall give way rather than others, and in the conditioning experiences of early childhood. Dr. Leon J. Saul of the Chicago Institute for Psychoanalysis observes: "One child may be allowed to express his rages quite freely, as compared to another. Later in life he will allow himself to become very angry, while the other gets a headache. Again, a person who has been overprotected in childhood will more readily feel the stress of a highly competitive society which demands extreme aggressiveness and independence, and such a person will more readily develop symptoms." The aggressive business man who has repressed longings for a retreat to love, care and protection, often has a tendency to express his hidden conflicts in a gastric ulcer. Beneath the surface of a gentle, considerate personality, on the other hand, may be hidden a state of chronic rage—a repression that frequently expresses itself in high blood pressure.

The wise physician takes into account all the circumstances. He may use drugs, surgery, suggestion, social readjustment, anything that will get at the root of the anxiety. He does not treat only hearts, lungs, intestines or kidneys. He treats not only that which is sick but also him or her who is sick. Dr. Stanley Cobb has said that the criterion for calling one disease organic and another functional is artificial, and that the line between physical and mental is fictitious.

We have seen that changes in the "structure" of the blood are wrought by minute quantities of added substance—adrenalin, for instance. Blood may be regarded as a fluid organ. As this circulating organ is changed by slight alterations of its chemical content, so are the other organs changed as they are bathed by these altered fluids.

Anxiety thus becomes a biochemical factor. Through automatic stimulation of secretions it may release materials as upsetting to the system as bacteria.

A. J. Cronin, author of *Hatter's Castle* and *The Citadel*, gives an account in the *Cosmopolitan*, July, 1939, of a case that will give you even more to think about. He presents it in the guise of fiction, but I'm guessing it to be based on his own or some colleague's actual experience. It concerns a little cockney barber's assistant whom Dr. Cronin calls Jamie in the story, an obliging, kindly, competent little fellow but "shy, mild, timid." Jamie fell in love with a pretty girl named Nancy. One evening, some months later, Jamie went to see a patron of his, an old-fashioned doctor, a general practitioner. Jamie was desperately unhappy because he couldn't get up his nerve to ask Nancy to marry him.

He had tried whiskey to "stiffen his nerve," but it hadn't helped any. The doctor gave Jamie thirty drops of what Jamie believed was a mysterious and terrifically powerful drug. Jamie rushed out and won the girl. Five years later Jamie returned to his old doctor-friend, in desperation. A big bruiser had moved in on him and Nancy, and he didn't dare to throw the man out. Same dose. Jamie rushed home strong as ten tigers, and mopped up the bigger man. Ingredients of the terrific drug had been water, a drop or two of burnt sugar to color it—and Jamie's faith.

It's the same in reverse with the incantations and spells of the black, evil witch and her foul dolls. Perhaps they can't hurt you if you don't believe in them, but if you *believe* in them, they can destroy you.

Sir Baldwin Spencer, K.C.M.G., F.R.S., Professor Emeritus of Biology in the University of Melbourne, sometime Special Commissioner for the Government of Australia and Chief Protector of Aborigines in the Northern Territory, records a case in which these same mysterious forces operated, to kill—and to cure. It concerns an Arunta native who was hit by a boomerang—who would have surely died if left to the care of modern science—but who recovered under treatment of the witch-doctors. It is a common thing for these aborigines to "charm" a weapon by "singing" over it. I have never heard them sing, but Sir Baldwin has heard them, and says it's the same old Mother Goose stuff. In muttered tones, the witch-doctor hisses out the following incantations, endlessly repeated:

"*I-ta pukalana purtulinja appinia-a*" ("May your heart be rent asunder").

"*Purtulinja appinaa aintaapa inkirilia quin appani intarpakala-a*" ("May your backbone be split open and your ribs torn asunder").

"*Okinchincha quin appinaa ilcha ilchaa-a*" ("May your head and throat be split open").[1]

Next, and here is something interesting, if the owner of the weapon foresees no immediate chance of meeting his enemy and socking him with it, or sticking it into him, but knows in what camp his enemy resides, he stealthily approaches that camp until the features of his victim are clearly discernible by the firelight. He now sits out there in the darkness, points the weapon toward his enemy, and repeats the incantations. Within a short time—a month at most—the victim is supposed to sicken and die, unless his life be saved by the magic of another medicine man or witch-doctor.

When they get into battle, or into whatever their equivalent is of a barroom fight, any spear, club, or boomerang which has been "sung" over is supposed to be endowed with *Arungquilta*—that is, magical poisonous properties—and any native who believes that he has been struck by, say, a "charmed" spear, is almost sure to die, whether the wound be slight or severe, unless he be saved by counter-magic. Says Sir Baldwin, with a lifetime of scholarly responsibility, "*There is no doubt whatever that a native will die after the infliction of even a most superficial wound if . . . he believes the weapon which inflicted the wound had been 'sung' over.*"

If the victim has merely been scratched by a "sung" spear

[1] Sir Baldwin Spencer and the late F. J. Gillen, *The Arunta: a Study of a Stone Age People*, Macmillan & Co., London, 1927. 2 vols.

or bumped by a "sung" boomerang, he simply lies down, refuses food, and pines away. Sir Baldwin said in 1927:

Not long ago a man from Barrow Creek received a slight wound in the groin. Though there was apparently nothing serious the matter with him, still he persisted in saying that the spear had been charmed and that he must die, which accordingly he did in the course of a few days. Another man coming down to the Alice Springs from the Tennant Creek contracted a slight cold, but the local men told him that the members of a group about twelve miles away to the east had taken his heart out, and believing this to be so, he simply laid himself down and wasted away. In a similar way a man at Charlotte Waters came to us with a slight spear wound in his back. He was assured that the wound was not serious, and it was dressed in the usual way, but he persisted in saying that the spear had been "sung," and that though it could not be seen, yet in reality it had broken his back and he was going to die, which accordingly he did.

It is impossible to prove that death would not have followed under any circumstances—that is, whether the native had or had not imagined the weapon to have been "sung"— yet with a knowledge of what wounds and injuries he would normally survive if he did not suspect the intervention of magic, it is impossible to explain death under such circumstances except as associated directly with the firm belief of the victim that magic has entered his body, and that therefore he must die.

Boomerang brawls like those in Alice Springs occur frequently here in northern Dutchess County. Any which start in Lafayetteville, Mrs. Lena Grosenbeck is always ready to calm with the sawed-off baseball bat she keeps behind the bottles on the bar. Lena taps them, and they're carried out cold to their cars by the state police, and wake up feeling not too badly next morning, since Mrs. Grosenbeck is not a witch, and they have no superstitious worries. The Arunta boy friend, steeped in superstitions, who would have died unless saved by counter-magic, was smacked by a boomerang which inflicted a wound no worse than Lena's kindly tap. The "wound" was merely a bump on the back of the head, valid only for a headache or hang-over such as we survive here after drinking Lena's excellent Scotch, and being smacked maternally by her sawed-off baseball bat.

The trouble was that the chap at Alice Springs was convinced that the boomerang that had laid him low was fatal. When he woke up next morning he declared that the weapon had been sent down by the Ilpirra tribe which lives away to the north of Arunta, and that it had been "sung" by an Ilpirra witch-man. An Arunta medicine man was of no use, but fortunately there was an Ilpirra witch-doctor available. He was found, hired, paid, and consented to "sing" the counter-magic. He made passes, sucking and muttering over the wound. As the witch-doctor belonged to the same locality as the man who had originally "sung" the boomerang, the Arunta native had *faith, confidence, belief* in the efficacy of the counter-magic. Instead of dying, he got well because he *knew* he would get well.

Instances of such occurrences, in modern hospital clinics in New York, Chicago, London, as well as in the Australian bush, could be multiplied to a point which would make this intended-to-be-readable appendix an encyclopedic treatise.

Notes on Part One

1. APROPOS OF SHOOTING 'EM, the *Herald Tribune* boxed this recent AP tidbit on its front page:

Londoners Can Shoot 'Hitler' for a Dime

LONDON, Oct. 10 (*AP*).—For a sixpence (about a dime) Britishers now can obey that impulse to work off hate against a prominent Nazi. Shooting galleries around London have introduced targets that are figures of Adolf Hitler, Hermann Wilhelm Goering, Paul Joseph Goebbels, Joachim von Ribbentrop and other German leaders.

The faces show the Nazis looking over their shoulders at the marksman and howling with pain.

In the early days of the other world war, the British, who surpass us Americans in vulgarity, exploited a chamber pot in whose bottom was the face of the Kaiser. In December, 1939, *Time* carried the letter of a gentleman who had been sticking pins in a picture of Stalin. In 1925, when I was in Arabia, young Prince Fuad, son of Amir Nuri Shalin of the Roualla, bought the photo of an enemy in Damascus, took it out in the desert, and peppered it with bullets.

CHAPTER II

1. CURRENT AMERICAN WITCHCRAFT CASES occur with steady frequency and in pleasing variety at the rate of several dozens a year. Here, to begin with, are a few more from the 1939 and 1940 crop:

December 11, 1939, *World-Telegram* tells how Salvatore Petruzzella poured salt in the form of a cross before the home of his Coney Island neighbor, Alex Colona. It's one of the oldest and supposedly most deadly of the Italian equivalents for the witch's doll. Colona went in terror to the police who had sense enough to arrest the sorcerer. Magistrate Joseph C. H. Flynn found him guilty of disorderly conduct. It was testified that many Italians believe death will come to a house cursed with salt. Petruzzella had been apparently planning a neighborhood "witchcraft" massacre since he had put salt crosses in front of the houses of several enemies. "That kind of stuff doesn't go in this country," the Magistrate said to the complainants. "Don't be afraid, I'll take the curse away."

November 15, 1939, San Jose, California, *Mercury Herald* tells how witchcraft entered the jury trial in a $17,000 will contest over the estate of Joseph Botelho before Superior Judge Warren Tryon. It was testified that Botelho's daugh-

PHILADELPHIA, PA.
Evening Public Ledger

Fortune Tellers Gave
Father of 4 'Medi-
cine' for Spouse,
Says

20,000 Came to

Bolber Tells
As Witch Do

SAN JOSE, CALIF.
MERCURY-HERALD
NOV 15 1935

Loved Wife, Poison Suspect Sobs,
Blaming Death on Witchcraft

Bolber Tells Story of His 'Witchcraft Knife'

Arsenic Defendant Taught
'steries of 'Power'
Sorceress

WITCH DOCTOR JAILED
WHEN MAGIC FAILS

THIS CLIPPING FROM
NEWARK, N. J.
LEDGER

Charged with practicing witchcraft,
33 Lewis st., found his magic powers unavailing last
held for the grand jury in $500 bail.

Witchcraft'
Row Revived

ead Spectres in 'Hex' Murders

Laferla Replies to
Letters of Critics

'evil eye'

Counter Curses, Still Sou
Magic Potions to Halt Hexes,

iggist asserts fightin
hopeless a...

Witchcraft Superstitions
Feature Will Fight Tes

For Alles
Fraudult

POISON DEAL BAF

'WITCH' WOMAN

RIVERHEAD, N. Y.
WEEKLY NEW-
JUL 28 1939

HELD IN VOODOO CASE

Huntington Colored Man Used Drastic
Methods to Break Spell

Baffling Injuries
of Woman Laid
to Indian Ghost

POLICE INVOKE
THE 'EVIL EYE'

STATE BEGINS
FIGHT TO SEND
WITCH TO CHAIR

'love slave'
s evil-eye lure

By EMORY A. MALLOWAN

Witch
Has a New Case Lifer
Baby

Witchcraft in Phil,

TRIAL STARTS TODAY

Salty Curse
Kicks Back
At Hexer

"WORLD-TELEGRA
DEC 11 1939

ter, Mary, was believed by the old man to be "a devil on a cross," which is the Portuguese designation for witch. It was testified that the daughter had used her witchcraft to terrorize and influence her father.

August 13, 1939, Buffalo *Courier-Express* tells of a druggist who had been besieged by people who believed spells had been cast on them by witches and begged him to sell them countercharms. A well-dressed woman had come in a new car, had asked to see the druggist in private, and had talked to him with tears streaming down her face. A woman had put a witch's curse on her, she was getting sicker and sicker, and begged for a charm to break the spell. The druggist, who knew something about mental suggestion, sold her for twenty cents a packet of quassia chips, or bitterwood. He told her to brew and drink it, and that when she did, the curse would be lifted. The druggist explained to the reporter that though he believed his action had been slightly nonethical, it was nevertheless good psychology. He must have been right, because the woman, who had been on the verge of complete collapse and nervous breakdown, came back cured. Another woman, a mother, wanted a love charm to save her son from the clutches of a "bad girl," and threatened suicide unless the druggist supplied it. He gave her some sugar of milk in solution, and again the charm worked. Frequently he has calls for mandrake or mandragora, but refuses to sell it, although it's a harmless root, if he suspects the customer is superstitious. He knows that mandragora is used in the concocting of death spells.

July 29, 1939, Newark, New Jersey, *Ledger* tells how a Negro, John Baptistalk, accused of witchcraft, was held in bail under grand jury indictment. He had been giving credulous people "magical baths" and had sent James Elijah to a cemetery at midnight to bring back earth from a freshly dug grave.

July 28, 1939, Riverhead, New York, *Weekly News* tells how Edward Smith, of Huntington, used a milk bottle to break the spell cast over him by Melinda Carman, whom he believed to be a witch. He tried to break the spell by breaking a bottle over Melinda's head—which was as good a way as any.

May 11, 1939, Detroit *Free Press* revives the famous case of Mrs. Laura Pichette, who is serving a life term in the House of Correction for killing a young witch by the name of Marian Doyle. Mrs. Pichette, the "witch killer," got into the news again by having a baby.

March 9, 1939, Detroit *Free Press* tells how Mrs. Jacqueline Thomas awakens every once in a while in the morning to find her body covered with deep painful scratches supposed to be inflicted by the spirit of an Indian medicine man. Mrs. Thomas married a full-blooded Indian from the Six Nations' Reserve at Branford. The husband's grandfather, a mighty powwow man, had forbidden him to marry into the white race, and the husband is convinced that the grandfather's magic is punishing his wife. Doctors have seen the marks and don't know what causes them. Mrs. Thomas sleeps alone in a locked room, yet the scratches occur. Spiritualist mediums have tried to lay the ghost, and local hospitals have interested themselves in the mystery, which may have a similarity to the stigmata cases which still occur in Europe.

January 1, 1940, New York *Times* (AP) has a tale of witchcraft and hexing from a northern New Mexico moun-

tain village, Mora, about twenty-six miles north of Las
Vegas.

R. E. Cooper, assistant District Attorney, returned from Mora
and said that a preliminary hearing was conducted in Justice
Court there for a man charged with mayhem and accused by
townsfolk of "turning himself into a frog" and "hexing people."

The defendant, Evelion Espinosa, was charged with mutilating
his wife and cousin, Mrs. Amadeo Sisneros, as they slept on
Christmas night. Mrs. Espinosa's fingers were injured and Mrs.
Sisneros lost two teeth.

"They testified Espinosa acted queerly Christmas night and
that he made signs on the floor near their beds," Mr. Cooper
said. "They said when he left the house they became frightened
and locked the door."

Mr. Cooper quoted Mrs. Espinosa as saying that the next morning "there was a frog in the room but it disappeared when I called
my husband and he entered another door."

Mrs. Espinosa testified that "If the frog did it, my husband
couldn't have."

Mr. Cooper said that the mountain folk had long accused Espinosa of being "the man who turns into a frog." A large crowd
milled around the courthouse during the hearing.

Espinosa put up $1,000 bond pending District Court hearing.

January 11, 1940, Denver *Post* has the following story
from Pretoria, South Africa.

Fighting witchcraft will be part of the task of L. F. W. Trollope, who has just been appointed magistrate and native commissioner of the eastern Caprivi Zipfel by the native affairs department of the South African government.

The duties of Trollope and his assistants are thus described
in an official statement issued by D. L. Smit, department minister.

"Administer the territory, making full use where possible of
native institutions, to combat the evil of witchcraft."

January 31, 1940, New York *Herald Tribune* reports that the Rev. Josephine Carbone, pastor of the Chapel of Miracles, a Pentecostal church at 1558 Sixty-ninth Street, Brooklyn, was found guilty of grand larceny in the first degree by a jury in Kings County Court. Angelo Nicosia, a fifty-nine-year widower, said he had paid her $557 on October 25, 1938, to work a miracle and get him a new wife. The miracle had not come to pass. The jury recommended mercy and Judge Edwin L. Garvin remanded her to the Women's House of Detention for sentence on February 14.

On February 20, 1940, in the New York *Herald Tribune*, a United Press item from Palm Springs, California, tells how a young mother, member of a voodoo cult that allegedly believes in human sacrifice, confessed that she killed her five-year-old daughter, Geraldine, because the child was "too good to live."

March 21, 1940, New York *Sun*, under the heading "Jersey Extortion Laid to Witchery," says:

The police of three New Jersey cities were unraveling today the fantastic story of a former Ridgefield Park patrolman who, Police Capt. August F. Winklemann of Elizabeth said, bewitched a nineteen-year-old girl into aiding him to extort money from her employers.

Winklemann said George Barning had "hypnotized" the girl into thinking the lives of the Whites were in danger.

More than half the population of the United States believes in witchcraft, and every year scores of cases reach the courts and newspapers. Here are a few scattering recent ones during the last two decades:

October 2, 1936, in Woodbridge, New Jersey, Mrs. Terese Czinkota was accused by neighbors of being a witch and a werewolf. The case was heard in Magistrate's Court before Recorder Arthur Brown. The complainants were Mrs. Harry Rottenhoffer, Mrs. Gertrude Mutter, Mrs. Rose Czepeter. Mrs. Rottenhoffer told how they had looked through a window and seen Mrs. Czinkota making magic brews and performing witchcraft rituals. One of the women testified "her body changed, horns appeared on her head, and she went on all fours like an animal." Another witness swore that the witch had merely been dressed in the skin of an animal and that the horns were merely streams of light. Another said, "I saw her bend down and change into something like a dog." Another said, "She was on all fours, dressed in the skin of an animal and there was a blazing stream of fire over her head." When another witness testified also that Mrs. Czinkota changed into a horse and walked on her hind legs, Recorder Brown threw the case—and the dear ladies—out of court.

February 26, 1935, in Williamsport, Pennsylvania, a young boy named John Fritz started carving his baby brother with a butcher knife. A gray-bearded hex-doctor, named Dave Snyder, 84 years old, was accused of having hexed the boy and making him do it. The hex-doctor's family said he couldn't read and write and consequently couldn't be familiar with *The Long Lost Friend* or *The Seventh Book of Moses*, which is also known in Pennsylvania as the "Black Art Bible." *The Long Lost Friend*, first published in German in 1820, is Johann George Hohman's *Der Lange Verborgene Freund*. It has run to more than fifty editions and enjoys an enormous sale in America.

April 10, 1931, in Wilkes-Barre, Mrs. Carl Thomsen, aged 29, a graduate of Wellesley, killed an alleged witch,

Miss Minnie Dilley, aged 76, with a knife and a ginger-ale bottle. The habit of attacking witches with bottles seems peculiarly American. Said Mrs. Thomsen, "She had cast a spell over me and my husband, and it was her life or mine."

February 25, 1929, Brooklyn *Daily Eagle* tells how Nathaniel Conway killed his wife "because she was a witch and had put a death curse on me." He killed her with a knife and subsequently "strangled" her, because no matter how dead a witch looks from knife or gun, you can never be sure unless she is strangled or burned.

May 17, 1929, a locally famous "witch" in Rome, Georgia, was found murdered in her house. The police said she had practiced witchcraft for many years and that one of her clients or victims had murdered her.

In 1927, in Bluefields, Nicaragua, a lady by the name of Doreth Fox, married to a Wisconsin man named John Bolton, became a high priestess of local black magic. She was ambushed and killed on Pearl Lagoon by three men who feared her magic. They were sure they were right when dogs dug up her grave.

In Mobile, Alabama, a few years ago (I can't locate the exact date), King William Carpenter and four high priests of his local voodoo temple were arrested because an aged man had died while they were trying to exorcise an evil spirit that was supposed to have entered his body. One of the methods of exorcism was to fasten the patient to a post with a trace chain and beat him with whips.

I have the record of about twenty other homicide cases among Negroes in America within the last five years, in which voodoo and witchcraft were the motivating causes.

308

Since cases of this sort, whether white or black, never become public knowledge unless somebody gets arrested, it is anybody's guess how much larger the number of cases may be which we never hear about.

2. APROPOS OF THE YORK HEX MURDER, and its "happy ending" for the two comparatively innocent young participants who left prison last year with that one bad nightmare spot in their past lives wiped out, John M. McCullough wrote in the Philadelphia *Inquirer,* August 6, 1939:

It is difficult to describe "hex" or "hexerai" (to give it its full name) in words that mean anything to the average person, for it is a combination of superstition, witchcraft, medieval demonology and primitive religion.

Under its alleged influence, murders have been committed, innocent children have died in agony without benefit of medical attention, and men and women have gone to their graves haunted by the grim bogies against which they struggled with counterrites to no avail. . . .

It is the grossest error to assume that all or even a measurable number of hexerai's adherents and believers are of feeble mind. They are not. Many a stout barn, resting amid its lush acres in Lancaster, York, Berks, Lehigh and Lebanon counties, has on its gable, the curious cabalism, roughly shaped in the form of a Lorraine Cross, which wards off evil spirits.

In fact, during the trial, a minor county official told this writer:

"Of course I don't believe in hex, but it is a fact that a carbuncle which none of the physicians could cure when I was a boy disappeared immediately after a hex doctor prescribed for me."

Contemptuous and half-ashamedly defiant in the same breath!

The "prescription" had been an amulet of frog's leg, chicken liver, and other oddments, prayed over at a rotten stump in a certain requisite phase of the moon!

The terrible power of belief in hex has demonstrated its capacity for tragedy again and again in the history of dozens of States of the United States.

Physicians appreciate that it is a problem for youth education and, in its most aggravated phase in the adult, for the most careful, sympathetic and painstaking practice of the science of psychiatry. Belief in the power of a curse, spawned by family environment, can be as horrible in the mind which it infects as knowledge of hereditary insanity can be in the mind of an otherwise normal and unaffected member of a family. . . .

It is easy to be contemptuous about such imaginings . . . and yet:

Have you ever noticed a person of substance and intelligence, whom you know, make an elaborate though apparently nonchalant detour to avoid walking under a ladder? Have you ever been all but catapulted through a windshield by a highly intelligent motorist, slamming on the brakes to avoid crossing the path of a black cat? Have you ever been lectured by a friend for daring to take the third "light" from a match?

CHAPTER III

2. IN MOTHER GOOSE, EDITH SITWELL, GERTRUDE STEIN (as in all African mumbo jumbo, and as in all medieval magical word rhythms, cantrips, spells, incantations), words are used for their piled-up, tom-tom impact on the emotions, plus the impact of the words' intrinsic emotional content, as distinguished from the other set of values and contents contained in words when they are connected logically to express cold, logical statements and meanings.

"Pigeons on the grass alas" and "a rose is a rose is a rose is a rose" have deep tom-tom and emotion-contact impact—which is the reason they have become world-famous and familiar even to people who deride them.

310

Mother Goose has survived over a century and will continue to survive because it is similarly laden.

> Hickory, Dickory, Dock

makes the eternal clock tick whether a mouse subsequently runs up it or not.

> A diller a dollar,
> A ten o'clock scholar

survives in memory no matter what happens when he arrives at the little red schoolhouse.

> Diddle, diddle, dumpling, my son John,
> He went to bed with his trousers on;
> One shoe off, the other shoe on,
> Diddle, diddle, dumpling, my son John.

John will live as long as the band of revelers on Keats's Grecian urn, not because of what he wore to bed, but because of

> Diddle, diddle dumpling.

> Therefore ye sweet pipes, play on!

Edith Sitwell added the sweet pipes when she made a set of Decca Records (25632 A et seq.), chanting her "Façade" to music. They are hot with the heat of tom-tom impact and superheated with the emotion impact of words strung together solely for the value of their emotion content, as cunningly chosen as if by any black African witch:

> Man must say farewell
> To parents now
> And to William Tell
> And Mrs. Cow—
> Man must say farewell.

Gertrude Stein is a sorceress, but also an intellectual, and she sometimes gets her roles mixed. As a sorceress, I think she can do more with words in weaving spells and incantations than any other living writer. I give this opinion not as a literary critic but as an apprentice African witch-doctor. My name is Willie, and as Willie, I think some of her "Lily Lucy" lines in *Four Saints in Three Acts* will last as long as Shakespeare and Joyce.

In a recent children's book, she writes:

> My name is Willie I am not like Rose
> I would be Willie whatever arose.
> I would be Willie if Henry was my name
> I would be Willie always Willie all the same.
>
> My
> What a sky
> And then the glass pen
> Rose did have a glass pen
> When oh When
> Little glass pen
> Say when
> Will there not be that little rabbit
> When
> Then
> Pen.

It's nonsense, and so is Mother Goose, and my witch-doctor's guess is that Gertrude Stein's little glass pen is less fragile than it seems. Whether I'm right or wrong about it, a lot that she writes (even when not infected by her deep learning) impacts with the power of jungle doggerel on me —and I take more delight in it because she is on the side of

the children and angels, instead of on that of the demons
and darkness and death:

> Bring me bread
> Bring me butter
> Bring me cheese
> And bring me jam
> Bring me milk
> And bring me chicken
> Bring me eggs
> And a little ham.
>
> Once upon a time something can
> Once upon a time nobody sees
> But I I do as I please
> Run around the world just as I please
> I Willie.

I, Willie too, think it's so goddamned beautiful that I just
wish it was true—of I Willie.

CHAPTER VII

1. THE MAGICAL PROPERTIES OF SALT AND
METALS are believed in by all primitives. Salt is a potent
factor in casting spells, and if you are already under evil enchantment, salt becomes poison. I mentioned this in my account of zombis in *Magic Island*, and last year Dr. Rolph
Reiseman commented further on it in *Kölnische Zeitung:*

One Easter Sunday a woman was left on a plantation to look
after the zombis. She was extremely anxious to go to the neighboring village and see the Easter Parade, and decided to take the
zombis with her. These creatures sat down in the market place
and watched the procession with unseeing dispassionate eyes. In
view of the general festivity of the occasion the woman bought a

few sugar buns for the zombis, after assuring herself they contained no salt. But unfortunately, she forgot to notice one thing—the pistachio nuts with which they were topped had been rolled in salt.

After eating them the zombis marched back to their native villages, many miles away.

Metal similarly is powerful in casting or warding off spells, but dangerous to touch if you are already under enchantment. Frank Gervasi had an article in *Collier's*, November 25, 1939, about King Alfonso and the Evil Eye, in which he told how the superstitious Italians always clung to the keys in their pockets when the former King of Spain came to Rome. He tells about a doorman, named Pietro, at the Grand Hotel, when Alfonso, who was stopping there, had greeted him. When he had ascertained that His Majesty was not looking

Pietro reached under his tail coat and withdrew a long, shiny iron key. He removed his white cotton gloves deftly. In his bare hands, he rubbed the polished key and, as he did so, muttered what seemed an Italian incantation. Pietro replaced the key with the air of a man who has just purchased a large quantity of life insurance.

Pietro rubbed the iron key because he, like all other Italians from Benito Mussolini down to the lowliest peasant, implicitly believes that Alfonso is a "*jettatore*," literally a "thrower" of bad luck.

Alfonso, Pietro would explain, has the Evil Eye. One almost foolproof safeguard against the disastrous effects of the evil glance is to make immediate and intimate contact with a bit of iron—key, horseshoe, spike, or whatever is handy.

The superstition concerning the jettatore is as old as Italy herself. Pliny wrote of laws passed for the ostracism of those suspected or proved to possess the Evil Eye. A Pope, during the intellectual sterility of the Middle Ages, ordered with a papal bull the prosecution of "male and female witches" who cast their spells with the eye.

On another occasion, in Naples, Gervasi tells that:

Mothers in the throngs on the docks along the water front spat three times against the breasts of their babies, according to the ancient advice of Theocritus, to protect the children from the blighting blink of the bewildered Alfonso. Fathers wore amulets of iron, carried iron spikes and jingled iron keys. The clatter of hardware rose above the cheers and was something to hear.

Either salt or metal is a protection if you are not already under a spell—but if the curse is already on you, you must wear Paris garters, no metal must touch you—and you don't dare eat salt. You must eat unseasoned food out of a wooden bowl with a wooden spoon.

Notes on Part Two

CHAPTER IV

1. PANTHER SOCIETIES IN LONDON are among the weird cults recently investigated by Elliot O'Donnell. More than once I've told incredulous friends that I've encountered more horror, mystery, black superstition, mystical evil, and weird abomination in the shadows of New York's skyscrapers, London's towers, and Paris's cathedrals (particularly St. Sulpice) than I ever did in the African jungle. It is a pleasure to quote Mr. O'Donnell in confirmation of this, with reference to London. I quote from his *Strange Cults and Secret Societies in London,* with permission of E. P. Dutton & Co., his American publishers. I hope Mr. O'Donnell will favor us with subsequent, similar volumes on New York, Paris, and Berlin.

Concerning suitable playmates in modern London for my bloody little playmates in the Ivory Coast, Mr. O'Donnell says:

If you were to tell any of your friends that there are human panthers and leopards in London, they would not, of course, believe you. Nevertheless, I believe it to be a fact. There certainly is a secret Cult in London that imitates, as far as it dares, the tenets and practices of the Leopard and Panther People of Africa. . . .

One evening, an acquaintance of mine, who is an Irish writer of some repute, having drunk rather more than was good for him, . . . in attempting to stagger home from his club, by some means he could never quite explain, got into a strange house instead of his own, and found himself in a semi-dark room full of queer-looking people, male and female, clad in leopard skins. Being given a skin by a dark, foreign-looking girl, he . . . put it on. . . . Probably no one paid any heed to him, everyone's attention being centered on a woman, who was standing in the middle of the room, haranguing them. My friend could not see her very distinctly owing to the lights being turned down, but he judged her to be colored, she looked so dark, and not a British subject, as she spoke with a decided foreign accent. The cool night air, blowing into the room, through an open window near at hand, gradually sobered him, and his brain became quite clear. He realized then that the people around him belonged to some strange exotic cult, and finally the amazing fact that they were Leopard and Panther People dawned on him.

The woman who was haranguing them was a witch-doctor. She was expatiating on the various qualities of the leopard and panther; extolling their beauty, their cunning, and their courage, and bidding her audience take these animals as their models, copying them as nearly as they could, without actually getting themselves into serious trouble. When she had finished this exhortation, a stuffed leopard was fetched and placed in their midst, and everyone kneeling down in front of it, repeated, in low, monotonous tones, a kind of prayer or incantation, during which, at intervals, the witch-doctor clapped her hands, and everyone touched the ground with their foreheads. The incantation over, one of the company, a very tall man, beat several times on a tom-tom, whereupon all present, forming themselves into a circle, linked hands and danced round and round the witch-doctor and leopard, tossing their heads backwards and forwards, and howling and growling, in imitation, my friend supposed, of the noises made by a leopard. This performance continued until some of the participants obviously getting exhausted, the witch-doctor clapped her hands as a signal, and it ceased. After that everyone sat on the floor, with legs crossed, Turkish fashion, whilst the leopard was removed and the dummy of a woman put in its place. The witch-doctor then, demonstrating the leopards' and panthers' method of seizing their prey, sprang on the back of the dummy, dug the claws of the skin she was wearing into it, and pretended to bury her teeth in its throat.

The spectacle might have struck some people as horrible and revolting, but my friend thought it merely ludicrous. The witch-doctor was decidedly plump, and to see her performing such antics was very funny. The members of the Cult, however, did not think so; they were in dead earnest, and when the witch-doctor had finished her demonstration, several of those present got up, and one after the other, imitated her to the best of their ability, going through the same performance. Eventually, after more beating on the tom-tom and singing, a girl produced a huge bowl, full of raw meat, and proceeded to hand it round. This was the last straw as far as my friend was concerned. . . . He could not stand it, so he decided to beat a retreat. The member who had gone out of the room to fetch the meat had left the door slightly open, and my friend slipped out unobserved. He was reminded of his adventure, some weeks later, when he read in one of the London papers that a girl had been found dead in a lonely suburban thoroughfare, with curious wounds, like scratches made by some large animal, on her back and chest. . . .

Many people will probably recall the case that happened a few years ago, either in London or one of the suburbs, of a youth, who, for no other apparent reason than blood lust or the love of cruelty, killed a boy much younger than himself. He lured the boy into some lonely spot and then, springing on his back after the manner of a wild beast, mauled and killed him. Though no hint was made of such a thing in court during the trial, it was rumored in the locality where the crime had been committed that the murderer might belong to a Panther Society, because men clad in panther skins had been seen, from time to time, in the garden of one of the houses there. . . . A curious story about the same cult was told me by Madame Bessier, who, some years ago, was living in the Faubourg St. Antoine, Paris. She said that she was walking along a quiet road, late one summer evening, when a private automobile passed her and stopped outside a house, on the same side of the road, about twenty yards ahead of her. Two men got out of the car, and then, reluctantly, so it seemed to Madame Bessier, a lady wearing an opera cloak. The men each took an arm of the lady and almost dragged her into the house. There being something about the men Madame Bessier did not like, she paused outside the house, debating in her mind whether one ought to call a policeman or not. She was still standing there, unable to decide, when two other cars drove up and several men and women got out of them and approached the house. As they did so, the front door opened (apparently they were expected) and Madame Bessier saw something that startled her very considerably. It looked like a leopard on its hind legs. However, before she could make up her mind what it was, the door slammed to, rather violently. Fascinated by what she had seen, she remained in front of the house for some time. Presently she moved on, but she had not gone far when she heard a cry, a cry of pain. It seemed to come from the house, and it was followed by intense silence. . . .

She did not pass the house again for nearly two years, and when she did, she noticed it was empty and for sale. Curiosity prompting her, she got permission from the agent, and accompanied by one of his clerks, went to look it over. Directly she got inside the front door she was conscious of a curious smell. It was strangely familiar to her, but at first she could not identify it. Then, suddenly, she recognized it. It was the smell of the big cats of the jungle, the smell she had grown quite used to when living in the Dutch East Indies. She asked the clerk if he could explain the smell, how it got there, whence it came. . . .

After much coaxing on her part, and many assurances that, if he told her, she would not say a word about it to the house agent, . . . he said it was rumored that a queer society, who used to dress up in leopard and panther skins and indulge in all kinds of orgies, once inhabited it, and that after they left, people who looked over it complained of the smell she had spoken about, the smell of wild beasts. . . .

The Panther and Leopard People are said to have had quarters in Blackheath some time ago, somewhere in the neighborhood of Shooter's Hill Road.

O'Donnell, in the Dutton book, goes to town on no less than seventeen strange cults and secret societies which flourish today in what seems on the surface the world's most conventional, circumspect great city. What he has to say about the Gorgons and Mummy Worshipers will perhaps partially explain why the witch's "doll de luxe" which I uncovered in London was less anachronistic than it seemed:

Somewhere on the banks of the Thames, between Richmond and Maidenhead, the Gorgons, a secret society of women, who . . . have no liking for men, have their headquarters.

Their High Priestess . . . is called Medusa. She has been described to me as of middle age, tall and of a masculine build and leonine appearance that is absolutely uncanny. . . .

The Gorgons believe only in Nature and Nature worship. Every night in the week they meet, either in or out of doors, and worship Nature, either in some animate or inanimate form. The nature objects they select for worship are usually either those that were venerated by the Ancients, or those that have been deified by the Cult's High Priestess, Medusa; and they are invariably said by the Cult to be of feminine gender. The sun, the moon, the stars, river, woods and pools, all are deified objects, and strange, indeed, are the tributes these Thameside worshippers pay them. I can, however, furnish my readers with a reliable account of some of the Gorgon ceremonies, since they were described to me by an ex-member of the Cult, who participated in them.

Miss Biggs, my informant, attended her first ceremony, at which homage would be paid to the Thames, soon after she had passed through her final stage of initiations. Her written summons to it was virtually a command. . . .

Her [Medusa's] white dress, like that of her followers, was sleeveless; she wore many and various massive gold bangles on her arms; her bare feet were encased in sandals, and her toe-nails, no less than her finger-nails, were covered with red varnish. . . .

This first stage, Miss Biggs explained, was a somewhat embarrassing and trying affair. The initiate, in order to prove her agility and strength, had to run so many yards in so many seconds, to jump no mean height, pull herself up several times on a horizontal bar, and wrestle with one of the most physically formidable members. But that was not all; in order to prove her willingness to submit and obey Medusa in all things, she had to kneel before her, imprint a kiss upon both of her feet, and take from her three strokes, and pretty hard strokes too, inflicted by a stick cut from an ash tree. . . .

The sacrifice followed, with more ceremonial. Every member had brought an offering either of food or wine, or some article of apparel, and when all these gifts had been placed in tubs, moored alongside the shore, the tubs were set on fire and pushed off, into midstream, to the accompaniment of the Cult song of triumph.

With regard to secret Mummy Cults, there is at least one in London, O'Donnell says, with headquarters in Upper Norward. He describes one of their ceremonies which a friend of his attended.

The members of the Society gathered in the courtyard of the headquarters, around a tomb in which the mummy of a Peruvian princess was laid. After a brief ceremony of worship, four members of the Society, dressed in black, came out of the house carrying a kind of stretcher on which another mummy sat upon a low stool. The mummy was wrapped in a llama skin, the only uncovered parts of her being her hands and feet. The stretcher was set down in the midst of the worshipers. By the side of the wooden stool were several pieces of brightly colored Peruvian pottery; and painted in brilliant red, on what looked like a piece of calico, attached to the llama skin above the mummy's breast, was a flaming device depicting the sun. After the recital of several long prayers by the President, during which the members knelt in silence, the mummy was taken slowly into the *chulpa* (tomb), and there deposited. Then incense was burned, more prayers read, and everyone sat on the ground, legs crossed, and eyes on the door of the *chulpa*. Minutes passed, then slowly the door of the tomb opened and the mummy appeared on the threshold. This time it moved of its own will, passing among the members, her features covered by a veil, her hands and feet free. She even bent and kissed one of the members. Then she faced them all, stretched out her arms, uttered three cries, and glided back into the tomb. The President said a few prayers, shut and bolted the door of the *chulpa* and announced the meeting at an end.

CHAPTER V

1. TORTURE TO DRIVE OUT DEVILS bids fair to be reinstated by science. Most ancient and medieval methods of treating the "possessed" and insane were based on theories identical with those held by early Christian and African witch-doctors. Just as Einstein, Carrel, and the late Steinmetz returned to a theory of the universe which the African witch-doctors and a few late Christians clung to in the face of materialism, so medicine may now be in process of returning scientifically to torture as a therapeutic method and psy-

chological cathartic. They call it "convulsive therapy," and here is part of what *Time* said about it, November 20, 1939:

Today psychiatrists again apply with scientific refinements something very like medieval shock treatment to victims of schizophrenia (dementia praecox). Most common form of insanity, schizophrenia packs 200,000 patients in U. S. mental hospitals. . . .

Metrazol is a powerful stimulant of the centres which regulate blood pressure, heart action and respiration. . . . about five cubic centimeters of the drug are injected into his [the patient's] veins. In about half-a-minute he coughs, casts terrified glances around the room, twitches violently, utters a hoarse wail, freezes into rigidity with his mouth wide open, arms and legs stiff as boards. Then he goes into convulsions. In one or two minutes the convulsion is over, and he gradually passes into a coma, which lasts about an hour. After a series of shocks, his mind may be swept clean of delusions.

. . . So horrible are the artificial epileptic fits forced by metrazol that practically no patients ever willingly submit. Common symptoms are a "flash of blinding light," an "aura of terror." One patient described the treatment as death "by the electric chair." Another asked piteously: "Doctor, is there any cure for this treatment?"

More serious than this subjective terror are dislocations of the jaw, tiny compression fractures of the spine, which occurred to metrazol patients in over 40% of one series of cases. During their violent convulsions, patients arch their backs with such force that sometimes they literally crush their vertebrae.

So although metrazol is widely used, a large number of psychiatrists condemn it as a "very dangerous drug." . . . Most experts now agree that, despite a few spectacular cures, metrazol is far less effective than insulin. A few laboratory workers are experimenting with kindred drugs, trying to concoct a less dangerous substitute.

Notes on Part Three

1. THE UNIVERSE OUTSIDE SENSORY PERCEP-TION, outside our three dimensions and the conventional concept of time-space, was perhaps first glimpsed by Plato. If his majestic ghost could return after more than two thousand years of pendulum-swinging in which the materialism of the nineteenth century became as ridiculous as its earlier antithesis, the majestic ghost might smile to learn that Einstein, Steinmetz, Carrel, Dunne, Haldane & Co., had returned to a concept not unlike that which he had put in the mouth of Socrates. Here's what he has Socrates saying to dear Glaucon:

Behold! human beings living in an underground den, which has a mouth open towards the light and reaching all along the den; here they have been from their childhood, and have their legs and necks chained so that they cannot move, and can only see before them, being prevented by the chains from turning round their heads. Above and behind them a fire is blazing at a distance, and between the fire and the prisoners there is a raised way; and you will see, if you look, a low wall built along the way, like the screen which marionette players have in front of them, over which they show their puppets.

324

I see.

And do you see, I said, men passing along the wall carrying all sorts of vessels, and statues and figures of animals made of wood and stone and various materials, which appear over the wall? Some of them are talking, others are silent.

You have shown me a strange image, and they are strange prisoners.

Like ourselves, I replied; and they see only their own shadows, or the shadows of one another, which the fire throws on the opposite wall of the cave?

True, he said; how could they see anything but the shadows if they were never allowed to move their heads?

And of the objects which are being carried in like manner they would only see the shadows?

Yes, he said.

And if they were able to converse with one another would they not suppose they were naming what was actually before them?

Very true.

And suppose further that the prison had an echo which came from the other side, would they not be sure to fancy when one of the passers-by spoke that the voice which they heard came from the passing shadow?

No question, he replied.

To them, I said, the truth would be literally nothing but the shadows of the images.

It's going to be fun, after quoting from Greek classics, to quote briefly next a "short" from the *Reader's Digest*, January, 1940. They give us this from Lady Eleanor Smith's *Life's a Circus* (Longmans):

It was about three o'clock in the morning, and five of us sat in the dark, empty auditorium watching the final rehearsal of the "Snowbird" Ballet of *Ballerina*, a play based on one of my books. I had been inspired to write the book after I had watched Pavlova dance The Swan a few months before her death, years earlier. Directly or indirectly, Pavlova had inspired us all.

325

The stage revolved to show a woodland glade, and a slight figure, snow-white in a fluffy *tutu*, its head bound with swan's plumage, entered, paused and crossed itself. It seemed to me that the star, Frances Doble, had grown much smaller. Then, as she glided into the spotlight, I caught my breath.

The figure was not that of Frances. It had assumed the form of Anna Pavlova.

Pat Dolin, co-star with Frances, gripped my hand until I thought he would break it. I looked at him; he was ice-pale. He muttered:

"This is uncanny . . . what have we done? Oh, God—why did we ever bring up the past?"

The white form on the stage stood effortlessly upon one *pointe;* it pirouetted three times—a thing Frances could not do— and drifted like swansdown into its dancing partner's arms, as the curtain fell. I looked at my companions—Pat; Charles Landstone, our level-headed business manager; Henry Harrison, composer of the score; and his manager. They were white and dazed. Somebody mumbled: "We're all very tired . . . don't let's imagine things . . ." Somebody else said: "We can't *all* have seen—what we saw. . . ."

Pat and I ran to the pass-door. We were afraid. Frances stood on the stage. She said in a perplexed, mechanical voice:

"Pat, I'm sorry . . . let's take it again. I couldn't dance. I must be awfully tired. My mind suddenly seemed to go blank."

Pat gave me a warning look, and we said nothing at the time. Later he affirmed: "We can't deny it. For a moment that particular spirit from the past had taken possession of Frances' mind and body."

Justine's micturating lion and barrel of fish, which occur in my concluding chapters, are perhaps less absurd in the firelight of Plato's cave and the gasoline flares of Lady Eleanor's circus tent than they seemed to me when I was writing in the sunshine, and perhaps less absurd than they may seem

to you, if you bother to read that far by the light of your
Mazda lamp.

4. RHINE'S FIGURES impress me (as a black magician)
and John Mulholland (as a stage magician) even less than
they do that holy terror of all American psychologists, James
McKeen Cattell, and the skeptical university professors who
combine skill in mathematics and an interest in advanced
psychology.

I have a warm and friendly admiration for Rhine's painstaking care, his scrupulous scientific honesty, and am not involving myself in any controversy concerning the mathematical soundness of the theory from which he derives his
percentages and averages. It is simply that in my opinion and
Mulholland's, *the slight pluses Rhine's figures show are not
enough*.

I think pure mathematicians have complicated their own
negative criticisms so much that they don't prove anything
either. I think Rhine's own figures almost stand up in the
light of their attacks, but I don't believe they stand up against
what all gamblers know. There are not only such things as
"runs," there are also such things as "slides." Take guessing
an ace out of the deck. Your chances are one in thirteen. Or
take matching pennies, where your chances are even. There
are always "runs" and there are frequently "slides." Same
thing in the red and black of roulette. Of course, it always
balances out in time, but there are only given moments in
which it balances. "Runs" and "slides" start occurring again.
The "slide" would seldom be necessary to explain Rhine's
pluses. A series of "runs" could account for most of it. At all
times except the moment when it balances, even if you carry

it to astronomical numbers, there's always a positive or negative "run" one way or the other. If you try to guess the ace googol times, you'll get an average in certain spots of exactly 1 in 13. You'll get that exact average once every several million guesses, but on the millions of times in between, you'll always be having "runs" and sometimes fantastically prolonged "slides."

Here's what Mulholland did with it. He writes in *Beware Familiar Spirits:*

Professor Pitkin and I were interested in seeing what true chance might bring. We therefore asked aid from the International Business Machines Corporation. We not only asked aid from the company but dropped our problem into their lap. While we knew what we wanted, we were most anxious not to have anything to do with getting it, so as to eliminate any possible chance of psychic cause. Jointly we wrote the following letter to the company:

"The interesting experiments of Professor Rhine, of Duke University, in 'parapsychology' seem to show that some people are, in a sense, clairvoyant, while others are televisual. The entire country has been following the card-naming tests which Rhine and his many friends have been conducting. A few scientists still suspect that something in the method or in the interpretations of results requires clarifying. We happen to be of this opinion.

"In recent discussions we have advanced two lines of thought, both so closely interrelated that we have decided to invite your company to conduct one or more fairly simple tests on your machines by way of clearing up a fundamental issue.

"This issue has to do with the structure of long runs of presumed chance events. The so-called 'laws of probability' in their purely mathematical form assert nothing as to specific sequences in the space-time order that we call the real world. All that is asserted is that, out of a given number of events, presumably determined by an indefinitely large number of variables, certain relative frequencies tend to occur. When any particular frequency arises is not known; nor is any unusual frequency regarded as evidence that a 'special cause' is at work.

"In common thinking, however, another practice is followed. People regularly assume that any striking series of similar repeating events implies the 'probability' of a special 'cause.' 'The rule of common sense' or 'the lesson of experience' is invoked here. It seems to us that the parapsychologists have not given due consideration to certain logical weaknesses in this practical type of inference.

"For instance, we should like to compare minutely a very long Rhine sequence with a correspondingly long one made by a method which is incontrovertibly 'pure chance' in the mathematical sense.

"Such runs would be strictly comparable to the total of tests made by all the parapsychologists. The important question would then be directly answerable; it is this:

"Do the right answers recorded by the parapsychologists' subjects relate to the total answers in a manner significantly different from similar coincidences of events mechanically produced?

"Our doubt would then be solved one way or another. We feel that the parapsychologists, by casting out all the persons who answer according to the 'law of probability' and by talking solely about the rare cases who show abnormal correctness in answering to the card draws, distort the picture gravely. Here we agree thoroughly and would like to see a full intercorrelation worked out between total guesses, right and wrong, in the Rhine experiments, and a large series made mechanically."

The International Business Machines Corporation, under the direction of their skilled operators, ran two hundred thousand numbered cards. The first hundred thousand cards were white, and each card carried digits from 1 through 5. There was an even distribution of those digits. Twenty thousand cards carried 1; twenty thousand 2; and so on. The white cards were mechanically shuffled and run through a machine which printed the numbers on paper in the order in which they happened to come.

The second hundred thousand cards were red, and these also had an equal distribution of the first five digits. These, too, were mechanically shuffled, and their numbers were printed on the paper. The finished job, as sent to Professor Pitkin and myself, consisted of page after page with printed columns of numbers—one column from the white cards and one from the red. Just as with Doctor Rhine's test there was one chance in five of the pair of digits in any given line being the same—that is, matching. But, with our test, there was no possible chance of mind-reading or clairvoyance as a factor. In getting a true picture of pure chance, a run of 100,000 is a small number, but it is a large number to work with; for instance, there are not that many words in this book. Of course, as we expected, we got what seemed to be most exceptional runs and lack of runs. When mathematicians say that an event is likely to happen but once in so many times, they do not mean that it has to happen, or that it can't happen more than once in any given series. No segment and no particular time are referred to in the mathematician's statement. If we knew how to state the possibilities of special events, they would cease to be possibilities and would become certainties.

We got some amazingly amusing results. For instance, there were as many as thirty-two lines of figures in sequence without one matching pair. Of course, by chance we might expect to get six matched pairs. Again, there would be runs of matching pairs. Professor Pitkin made a most astonishing discovery about these runs. Runs of five matching pairs in sequence fell 25 per cent below theoretical frequency, while runs of six rose to 25 per cent above theoretical frequency. Runs of seven jumped still higher to 59 per cent above chance expectancy, and with runs of eight we went to 78 per cent above theoretical frequency. Now, if we were to use our short-test run illogically, we might infer that in any long run the tendency is for the striking coincidences to occur oftener than called for by the mathematical formula. And the longer the coincidental run, the higher its frequency as compared with mathematical requirements. Obviously, this ends in pure absurdity. Another amusing freak deviation from theoretical distri-

330

bution was that in the first forty thousand pairs there were almost three times as many runs of five as there were in the next sixty thousand, while with the runs of six it was just the reverse. And neither of these series of runs was to be expected.

We also found that when we arbitrarily selected segments for their high frequency of matching pairs, we would find twenty-five and twice twenty-five with half the pairs matching. These runs were above chance expectancy in 100,000; but in an infinite number they were to be expected. All that we had was a series of numbers in which these matched pairs happened to come.

Totaling the number of "correct guesses" in each thousand of our pure-chance run, we found that twenty-four thousand came within 2 per cent of mathematical expectancy; thirty thousand went above and forty-six thousand went below theoretical chance. The total number of pairs in the entire one hundred thousand was less than 2 per cent away from what was to be expected. The total, by the way, was under mathematical expectancy.

Perhaps Doctor Rhine has proved that a certain few people have mind-reading or clairvoyant powers, but so far the tests do not seem to me to be conclusive. I know that he will agree with me fully in stating that, even granting that there are people who have extra-sensory perception, it is a most uncertain and undependable ability.

Fallacious isolation is so easy in dealing with psychological studies. My mother has been amused for years because of a book in which the author pointed out my extremely youthful identification of music. The author based his opinion on personal observation and on the answers my mother gave to his questions. He saw me get quite excited in a dining room in a hotel when the orchestra began to play a march by Sousa. I was but a baby in a high chair, and he was quite astonished to hear me call out "Sousa!" He came over to the table and asked my mother if I had actually said "Sousa" when the orchestra began to play, and she replied that I had. He then asked for my name and age, and both were given him. It so happened that my baby name for music was "Sousa." The professor had merely failed to ask the right question.

So far, nothing has convinced me of any one's ability to read minds, but then many other people do believe. My mother not only does believe mind-reading possible but bases her proof on the number of times I have read her mind. I think the probability is that on a few occasions I have outguessed her, and mother-like, she has unconsciously multiplied the number many times.

5. POSSIBILITY OF PRECOGNITION is accepted and partially explained by the British military inventor and scientist, J. W. Dunne, in various volumes including *The Serial Universe* and *An Experiment with Time*. Commenting on Dunne's theories, in the New York *Times Book Review*, December 3, 1939, Henry James Forman says:

. . . Mr. Dunne, however popular he tries to be in his manner of presenting his theory, is still and always the engineer, the scientist and the mathematician.

. . . one may state with boldness that if any theory of the present confused age has a chance of surviving and growing Mr. Dunne's theory of "serialism" is the likeliest. For all of us today, from the most intelligent to the least intelligent, are weary of the materialist pummeling we have received during the last seventy or eighty years. To such a degree has the universe been mechanized for us that scientists themselves can no longer bear it. And now we hear from the greatest of them that the universe consists of pure thought. Intuitively we have always felt that to be the case. We have always known somehow that Reality is hidden by the veil of so-called matter and that matter itself does not matter much. It is the poets, saints and prophets to whom we turn to enlarge our spirits, not to theses upon the Diesel engine, however brilliant, nor to techniques of nerve-splicing or operable cancer. . . .

. . . in his first book Mr. Dunne showed, much to his own

surprise, that dreams have certain startling attributes; that actually they reveal the future quite as often as they deal with the past. That the time in and by which we live is very far from the whole story, and that *there is a "Now" of which our past and future are merely small artificial compartments.* Being a scientist, he pursued the experimental method and arrived at some amazing results.

. . . The "self" which we cannot visualize, he shows, but of which we are vaguely aware, is a traveling field altering entropy—a traveling intersection point. "All states which the self at the traveling field regards as 'future' are just as real in the sense of 'existing now' as are those states which the same restricted individual regards as past. All," he adds, "are equally present in the real 'now' . . . But the self can interfere at the place where the traveling field happens to be. . . ."

Thus Mr. Dunne arrives by mathematics and physics to the point where those saints and prophets referred to by Mr. Priestley were when they told us such things as, "Before Abraham was, I am"; or, in the words of the Buddhist sutra, "all sentient beings are identical in essence with the true nature; . . . the nature in itself neither departs nor comes". . . .

This "slit in time" business is just now exciting a lot of practical and hard-boiled people. Lowell Thomas, at Mulholland's request, tells, in *Beware Familiar Spirits,* of a girl who had precognition of his residence in Dutchess County. Lowell says:

Back in my school days I had a girl chum, a young lady who vanished from my life when I grew up. I had entirely lost track of her. After the World War, upon returning from ten years of wandering around the globe, I was walking along a street in the Broadway night life district and to my surprise saw the name of my school friend, Beula Bondi, featured in electric lights in a theatre marquee. I went back stage with the hope that it was

333

the same girl. It was, and there was a reunion, with memories of gay college days.

Said Miss Bondi: "Tommy, although I have not heard from you in years and years, you have not been entirely out of my thoughts. For several summers, I have lived in the foothills of the Berkshires, and every time I passed a certain house, I had a strange feeling that you were there living in that house!"

At that time I had never been in the Berkshires and knew nothing about Dutchess County, and had never heard of lovely Quaker Hill. But two years after meeting Miss Bondi, who is now a celebrated character actress of the screen, I decided I wanted a place in the country, and it must be within one hundred miles of Manhattan Island. Whereupon I began a systematic search of everything within that distance. My dream was to find a perfect all-year-round climate, plus scenic beauty, plus good neighbors. For one reason or another I eliminated Long Island, Northern New Jersey, and both the West and East shores of the Hudson. Eventually my travels brought me to Dutchess County, and to historic Quaker Hill, a ten-mile-long ridge in the Southeastern corner of the county, which is one of the loveliest spots on earth—not as spectacular as the Vale of Kashmir—but in its own way just as beautiful.

And, there on one spur of Quaker Hill I saw just the Colonial House I wanted. The dowager who owned the estate at that time had not thought of selling. But, at last, a deal was made. And that, as you have guessed by now, is the same which Beula Bondi had for many years associated with her college friend, the house in which she, with her prophetic eye, saw me living.

This I discovered later after I had moved into the neighborhood.

Fulton Oursler, as quoted by Mulholland, says:

The riddle of time and space has always seemed to me much more important than the question of personal survival; and I have had actually hundreds of experiences that seemed to indicate the validity of the "slit in time" theory advanced in the last few years by the great Freudian apostate, Jung. I came to the same theory independently. I do not know if I formulated it before Jung did, but I certainly formulated it before Jung announced it.

CHAPTER III

1. A FINE NEW CROP OF WHITE MAGICIANS is coming up in 1940 as this book goes to press. They get photos in picture papers, space in newspapers, including the *Herald Tribune* and the *Times*.

At Oakdale, Long Island, James B. Schafer has founded the Royal Fraternity of Master Metaphysicians, and has adopted a red-haired six-months-old girl baby by the name of Jean Gauntt. The baby is to be subjected to intensive white magic as a candidate for immortality.

At West Hempstead, Long Island, a Russian named Gleb Botkin, son of the physician to the late Czar, has founded and incorporated the Long Island Church of Aphrodite, for the worship of Venus.

In Los Angeles, California, Edwin J. Dingle, F.R.G.S., has expanded the Institute of Mentalphysics, which hopes to regenerate the Western world by Yoga. Mr. Dingle, of course, "lived in a Tibetan monastery," where the priests taught him "secret methods closely guarded for many centuries."

Great white magicians go out of fashion, or come croppers, but my bet is that these will be around for quite a while. The field offers as good opportunity for success as medicine or law, but is almost as crowded. There are thousands of little ones, male and female, who never get further than talking to the ghost of your grandmother through an "Indian

guide"; reading your palm or horoscope for twenty-five
cents; or reading your future in tea leaves at the same price
—with the tea and toast thrown in. The great rewards are
only for the great successes, but if you feel you're in communication with my late aunt from Hawkinsville, Georgia, or
her deceased equivalent in your own family—or with Tibetan
monks or their esoteric equivalent in the great human family,
you might take a flier at it. Maybe it will make you more
money and give more aid and comfort to your fellow-man
than delivering groceries, working in a garage, cooking,
sweeping, or dishwashing. Maybe it will require posterity to
decide whether you're a third Saint Theresa (it was a servant
girl who recently became a second one) or whether you're
merely a deluded servant girl trying to get on in the world—
whether you're another Saint Francis of Assisi or merely the
village idiot. If you're sincere and care more about helping
your fellow-man than you do about making a nickel, you
may go a long way. So many new mechanical gadgets have
been invented and need to be mended, that the human soul,
which perhaps needs the most mending of all, is at a discount.
The soul is the only gadget, so far as I know, that the International Correspondence School doesn't teach you how to
mend. That may be why so many incompetent and unskilled
people try to do it.

Every once in a while a great one, or potential great one,
comes along. They usually emerge from obscurity. The most
promising one in recent years was Krishnamurti,[1] but he got
tired of being a "World Savior" and blew up. The most
interesting one who hasn't blown up is Father Divine (great
white magician among the blacks). I'm paying him the com-

[1] See p. 345.

pliment of leaving him out of this book because he puts honesty, industry, and the cardinal virtues ahead of magic.

At the moment, Jean Gauntt, the baby being coached by metaphysicians for immortality, is getting more publicity than any other candidate in this field. The *Herald Tribune* launched her on November 27, 1939, with a baby picture and a piece by a staff correspondent. *Time* has mentioned the baby several times and on December 4, 1939, she occurred as follows in *Time's* column entitled "Milestones":

ADOPTED. Jean, five-month-old girl; by James Bernard Schafer, Messenger (headman) of the Royal Fraternity of Master Metaphysicians; in Oakdale, L. I. Jean's home will be the 100-room Oakdale mansion (formerly William K. Vanderbilt's) acquired by the R.F.M.M. last year (*Time*, July 11, 1938), who changed its name from Idle Hour to Peace Haven. A religious cult dedicated to Peace and practicing a mixture of Rosicrucianism, Christian Science, Christianity, Supermind Science and faith healing, the Fraternity will attempt to make Jean immortal, by bringing her up in an environment where death and disease (called the products of destructive thinking) are not mentioned or thought about. She will attend metaphysics classes from the start, will be a vegetarian as soon as she can be taken off her special formula.

The *Herald Tribune's* staff correspondent wrote on November 26:

Mr. Schafer, a calm, soft-spoken metaphysician, believes that the child's education can be so shaped that destructive thoughts will never enter her mind, and as a result she will be preserved from destruction—even destruction of the body.

Mr. Schafer quoted the Bible, "The last enemy to be destroyed is death," and Mary Baker G. Eddy, founder of Christian Science, "Death must be overcome, not submitted to." While churches have taught immortality of the soul, he said, schools of truth, such as his fraternity, teach that immortality of the body is attainable as well.

"It isn't a dream," he said. "All of us work from the stand-point of immortality of the body, but most students by the time they come to us have dissipated and ruined their lives. They have so much mental baggage that has to be unloaded.

"A baby has an empty brain. We'll keep impressing on it the beauty of life and the side of life that we are trying to live. If the child doesn't think anything that's bad or destructive it can't be torn down."

As evidence of the possibilities of metaphysics, Mr. Schafer told of his own teacher, who, he said, "is 'way over 100 years old, though to look at him you wouldn't think he was more than forty or fifty." Mr. Schafer would not disclose the name of his teacher.

He also told of a man who broke his leg last week, and an hour later was cured and walking. "There isn't a school of truth in existence that hasn't hundreds of seemingly miraculous cures in its files," he said, "but what would be the use of talking about them? People wouldn't believe it."

Mr. Schafer has started proceedings for the formal adoption of baby Jean, and although he will be the legal foster-parent, all of the students who come to Peace Haven will take part in her education. The infant is a daughter of a couple who, according to Mr. Schafer, were starving themselves to feed her and were glad to have her brought up in the luxurious atmosphere of Peace Haven.

This Long Island Shangri La is the 110-room mansion built in 1901 by the late W. K. Vanderbilt at a cost of $2,500,000. Its great rooms are opulently furnished, there are tennis courts, a swimming pool, a squash court, saddle horses, archery ranges, a gymnasium and other recreational facilities. Students, adepts and master metaphysicians use the estate, Mr. Schafer said, "as an auxiliary home," and there are always from fifty to 100 in residence.

It is in this atmosphere that baby Jean will grow up. She now has a trained nurse who also has had long experience in metaphysics. When she is a little older she will go on a vegetarian diet. She attends classes now, as Mr. Schafer says, "to get the atmosphere." Later she will be fortified against destructive influences by education.

She will learn that there are such things as meat and alcoholic beverages and cigarettes, but she also will learn why they are to be avoided as destructive. She will learn that there is such a thing as death, but will be told that it is an unnecessary evil. "She must be educated to understand everything," Mr. Schafer said. "Where there's ignorance there's fear. Where there's fear there's destruction."

Whether it was Dr. Schafer's own idea or a suggestion from the *Daily Mirror*, I don't know, but in December the "immortal" baby was driven to the Ziegfeld Theatre in her own car, with her own chauffeur and private nurse, where the *Mirror* took pictures of her. The baby sat and behaved herself very well while Dr. Schafer lectured to 1,500 people. Afterward he took Jean before the footlights, recited, "Where do you come from, baby dear?" Jean cooed in response and posed again for the photographers. "See," said Dr. Schafer. "She isn't afraid of the flash bulbs. She will go on forever."

The *New Yorker* has suggested that if she does, she'll probably end by being a bore to her great-great-great-grandchildren.

Another gentleman who feels that we don't need to die is Preceptor Emeritus Edwin J. Dingle, F.R.G.S., of the Institute of Mentalphysics in Los Angeles. I dropped him a postcard and had a letter in return. It was from his private office at 213 South Hobart Boulevard, and contained a pamphlet with a picture of administration offices and audi-

torium at Los Angeles; also a woodcut of a Tibetan lama-
sery in the Himalayas. Or was it a pagoda? The letter was
nice. Mr. Dingle addressed me as his dear friend and assured me that when he had heard from me he felt immediately that I "belonged." He told me not only that God is
within me, but that I, myself, little Willie Seabrook *am* God
in human form. He said this would amaze me, and it did.
He goes on to tell me that I will be further amazed at the
might of my power when I have learned more about it. He
tells me that as I become skilled in my strange new power
my own family (which consists of Marjorie, a Scottie, and
three cats) and also my friends and acquaintances will be
fascinated by the change in me. He's got something there.
I think Marjorie would be pleased to see *any* change. He
says they will be astonished at the radiance of my counte-
nance and the greater strength in my body. Maybe I'll be
able to drive over two hundred yards after I've tapped the
reservoir of power. He tells me I'm like a giant in the hands
of a hypnotist. He says the giant in me is made helpless,
hypnotized by false ideas of my own weakness and by traditional notions of my own limitations. I'm a giant, but a sick
giant. Mr. Dingle tells me that he is a "De-hypnotist." He
is a persuasive letter writer. I got the impression that he was
sincere, that he believed these things (or that somebody
backing him did), and that he also believes he can teach
them. So did Dr. Coué. So did Buddha, Confucius, Mohammed, and Jesus Christ. If Mr. Dingle's approach to the public is a bit more modern and more high-powered-salesman-
ship-mail-order style than theirs—well, this is a modern
age, and mimeographed letters hadn't been invented in the

time of Confucius. If they had, Confucius might have used them.

The pamphlet explains that he's the author of a number of books including *Across China on Foot, China's Revolution, Your Mind and Its Mysteries;* that he is also editor of *Dingle's New Atlas and Commercial Gazetteer of China, Bilingual Map of China, Far Eastern Products Manual.* I can't find him in the British *Who's Who,* or in the American *Who's Who,* but by faith we shall know him.

This field is infested by quacks, crooks, and petty racketeers. So also are the fields of science, law, and medicine. But it's by no means automatically true that all fakirs are fakers. Nor are all founders of new religions necessarily so ridiculous as at first they sometimes seem.

The newspapers were inclined to poke mild fun at Gleb Botkin, when he and his wife put a statue of the Venus de' Medici on their bureau and started worshiping it. But when the *World-Telegram* sent its staff writer, Douglas Gilbert, out to West Hempstead, he refrained from doing any burlesquing. The *World-Telegram* (November 15, 1939) gave his piece the following headline:

APHRODITE GODDESS OF CHURCH
THAT GIVES LOVE A BIG BREAK

Russian Gets License from State to Worship "Sweetly-Smelling,
Laughter-Loving" Beauty

This is what he wrote:

Gleb Botkin, 38, a learned Russian, author of numerous books in English and son of the physician to the Czar—his father was murdered with the Emperor in the Red revolt—has founded a new religion. It is the Long Island Church of Aphrodite.

It was incorporated Oct. 21 when Mr. Botkin received his charter from the State Department of the State of New York and was established May 6, 1938. He made its existence known today.

He already has some 35 followers and about 15 more are "borderline." They meet at his home, 55 Ivy St., West Hempstead, L. I., Fridays—Friday being Aphrodite's day.

There they discuss the new religion with its founder, who is the priest, and those who are earnest in their prophet's belief adjourn later to a rear bedroom in his home and worship before Aphrodite's altar which he has erected on a bureau.

The altar is a figure of the goddess, the post-Praxiteles art work known as The Venus of the Medici. It stands before a purple scarf or tapestry and before it burn nine candles and incense. It is beautiful to look at and impressive in an eerie way.

The members who thus assemble before the altar then recite their credo and chant a psalm, both written by Mr. Botkin. The creed begins:

I believe in Aphrodite, the flower-faced, sweetly-smelling, laughter-loving goddess of Love and Beauty; the self-existent, eternal and only Supreme Deity; creator and mother of the Cosmos; the Universal Cause; the Universal Mind; the source of all life and all positive creative forces of nature; the Fountain Head of all happiness and joy. . . .

The psalm concludes:

Blessed thou art, O beautiful goddess; and our love for Thee is like the sky which has no bounds; like eternity which has no ending; like thy beauty itself that no words could describe. For we love Thee with every atom of our souls and bodies, O Aphrodite: holiest, sweetest, loveliest, most blessed, most glorious, most beautiful Goddess of Beauty.

It is one of Mr. Botkin's cherished dreams some day to have a chapel. Hs religion, he says, is modishly ecclesiastical and he will establish a consecrated clergy.

As a priest Mr. Botkin will wear mainly the Aphrodisian headdress (it is shaped like a mitre), and already he has designed the

Church of Aphrodite symbol. It is a cross, surmounted by a circle. The cross is significant of the love meeting of man and woman; the circle symbolizes eternity.

Sex enters into the new religion of Mr. Botkin but only as an ideal, "divine and wonderful." It is no part of the ritual. He puts a halo on the expression, and in its discussion makes it sound like the necking of angels.

Mr. Botkin's followers are no collection of orgiastic nudist nuts with vine leaves in their hair. Most of them are intellectual friends, he says, of broadminded inquiry and tolerant acceptance. Some live in West Hempstead, some in New York, and a few believers are in Europe with whom he has correspondence. He has had no inquiries from Los Angeles, yet.

Nor is Mr. Botkin a prophet in a nightgown with a shepherd's crook. He is a highly agreeable, well-spoken gentleman, giving every evidence of earnestness and faith. His face is lean and handsome, often wrinkled in smiles, and a half-Hughesian beard enhances his saintly, Messianic aspect.

His wife is a pleasant lady in face and manner with prematurely whitish hair. They have five children, three sons and two daughters. All are absolutely uninhibited and it is a lovely thing to break bread with them.

This reporter, informed of the charter grant to his church in Albany, called upon him unheralded. The Botkins have no telephone. He received us in his study, an alcove off the living-room containing a bookcase, a desk, a typewriter, a deep lounge chair, and a cot.

He was apologetically reluctant to release information about his new church.

"I am afraid of its presentation," he said, "lest it attract neurotics and those emotionally unstable. But I shall some day have to do it and I suppose it may as well be now."

He said that he had long been familiar with the Aphrodisian qualities that are found in most religions and that he had nursed his own ideas about it while a novitiate for the priesthood in the Greek Catholic Church of Russia.

He said this was the basis of his religion of Aphrodite:

"To seek and develop Love, Beauty and Harmony, and to suppress ugliness and discord."

He said that his religion follows precisely the natural instincts of man and that Christianity often denies them.

"The Christian principle," said Mr. Botkin, "is to suppress desires and to develop spirit. The religion of Aphrodite, with minor qualifications, is the antithesis of this.

"Sex, for example, is a divine function. But listen to this: In the Lambeth Conference in 1930 the Episcopal bishops stated, 'sexual relations are a regrettable necessity even when children are desired.' And in reply to this the late Pope Pius XI deplored 'the laxity of the Episcopal bishops.'

"Marriage, within the Christian principle, . . . is a compromise which is permissible when men can no longer stand celibacy. In the religion of Aphrodite the sex expression limits itself within the virtue of its sacredness."

When he is not involved in his Aphrodisian theories and faith, Mr. Gotkin works upon a book he is writing that is to interpret Russia since the fall of the Czar. Russia, not Nazi Germany, which is certain to be defeated, is the coming world problem, he says. But love will find a way.

Hate, he says, is evil, and evil, in the Aphrodisian faith, is only the absence of good. Hate, selfishness, jealousy, are unnatural, he says. He put it quite poetically: "A good gardener pulls up weeds not because he hates weeds but because he loves flowers."

The worship of Venus, Isis, and Astarte was not ridiculous in Greece and ancient Egypt. It is perhaps a bit ridiculous within the shadow of Manhattan's skyscrapers in 1940. If it is slightly ridiculous (i.e., a legitimate butt for slight ridicule), the ridiculousness is not intrinsic or inherent, but derives from the fact that Gleb Botkin's worshiped statue is not merely an anachronism in time and space, but is also archaic. Our Lady of the Immaculate Conception at Lourdes seems equally anachronistic in a 1940 time-space spanned on our little globe by radio and transatlantic airlines—but she is not archaic. She is a living sacred symbol to millions now alive.

Fashions change in gods and goddesses, just as they do in white magicians; just as they did in the hats worn on earth by my aunt from Hawkinsville, Georgia, who now wears a halo, I hope. The Venus Cult has gone the way of my late aunt's hats. But the fashion for worshiping Mary and her Son has scarcely changed in two thousand years—and perhaps the world will be better if it never changes.

1a. KRISHNAMURTI BLEW UP AS A WORLD-SAVIOR when Mrs. Annie Besant and the Theosophists, after grooming him for years to be Lord Jesus Christ's and Lord Gautama Buddha's successor, brought him, not for the first time, to New York on October 19, 1931. Ship news reporters swarmed him. In his first authorized interview, carried on the morning of October 20, in the *Herald Tribune*, *Times*, and by the Associated Press, he renounced Theosophy and repudiated Mrs. Besant.

Behind that unhappy landing lies a tangled story. I am not sure any of it disproves the possibility that Krishnamurti may have been a world savior who might not have blown up. Here are all the known facts, in a sequence not always chronological, but pointing always backward and forward in time to the perhaps inevitable blowup:

On December 29, 1925, Mrs. Annie Besant, then president of the Theosophical Society of the World, had announced at Adyar, Madras Province (Adyar being the home of the Society), that a "world-teacher" had been reincarnated and would appear soon in the person of Jiddu Krishnamurti. Krishnamurti was a young Hindu, then about twenty-nine years old, who had been a protégé of hers and of Bishop Charles W. Leadbeater's since the age of twelve.

I don't need to tell you about Mrs. Besant, on whose shoulders the great Blavatsky's mantle had fallen. I can't tell you much about Bishop Leadbeater, who died a couple of years ago. He was an Englishman whose past became interesting to the *Herald Tribune* in August, 1926, when Krishnamurti first came to America. According to the *Herald Tribune* of August 25, efforts had been made by "unknown persons" to bar Krishnamurti's landing on the grounds that he was guilty of "moral turpitude." The basis was that his former tutor, Bishop Charles W. Leadbeater, "had often been accused and had confessed to immoralities." The *Herald Tribune* declared: "Bishop Leadbeater's exploits, trials and reinstatements have convulsed the Theosophist order since 1906. Now, at the age of eighty [1926], the Bishop lives in Sydney, Australia, surrounded by adepts and novitiates in mystic orders."

The *Herald Tribune* quoted London *Truth:*

Many readers of "Truth" will doubtless remember what was said here at the time as to the disreputable antecedents of one or two of these worthies. That they are not unfair samples of the crowd of disciples which Mrs. Besant has gathered about her may be guessed from a scandalous affair that has just occurred in Holland.

I don't know what the "scandalous affair" in Holland was. The *Herald Tribune* dropped the hot potato. The only additional knowledge I have of Bishop Leadbeater is that he was a cultured, supposedly homosexual gentleman, first and only

Bishop of the Liberal Catholic Church, which was an affiliate of the Theosophist movement, and had nothing remotely to do with the Holy Roman Catholic Church. Bishop Leadbeater and the Liberal Catholic Church disappear quickly from this picture, which has been a headache to all orthodox Theosophists since it started to be painted.

So far as anybody knows, Mrs. Besant met Krishnamurti in India, when Krishnamurti was about twelve years old and was attending a Theosophic gathering with his widowed father and a younger brother. This was in 1908. Krishnamurti's father was a magistrate's clerk in India. Mrs. Besant accepted the guardianship of the boy and his younger brother from their father, and promised to be responsible for their education, "provided I was given entire control over the boys. The father gladly welcomed my offer and gave over the two to my care. From that year until 1925, I remained their guardian, although they were, of course, legally free on their coming of age."

Mrs. Besant apparently felt that the "world-teacher" who had already manifested himself through the bodies of Jesus Christ, Buddha, and others, displacing their souls temporarily or permanently, would reveal himself again through Krishnamurti, to an anxious and waiting world, particularly to Americans, Australians, and other "white Pacific people."

In 1911, Mrs. Besant founded the Order of the Star of the East, to further the work of preparing for the coming of the world-teacher through the person of Krishnamurti. The brothers were brought to England and educated there. It was frequently published that Krishnamurti was educated at Oxford, but Mrs. Besant declared that he went to Cambridge. In 1917, Krishnamurti was an ambulance driver with the British forces in France.

Previously, in 1912, the boys' father, J. Narayaniah, had sued both Mrs. Besant and Bishop Leadbeater for recovery of his sons' custody. Leadbeater's part in the *cause célèbre* in India is scarcely mentioned in newspaper reports later, since Mrs. Besant at the time held the spotlight.

The father's petition charged that Krishnamurti was being made the object of adoration by Theosophists because of Mrs. Besant's belief in his so-called mission. The petition also denounced Leadbeater for alleged immoralities. The highest courts in India ruled that the boys be restored to their father, after a lengthy trial, but the case was brought to the Privy Council, which reversed the previous decision and directed that Krishnamurti and his brother be kept in Mrs. Besant's custody, *but hers alone.*

While resident in England, an income was provided for Krishnamurti by a wealthy Englishman, for about ten years (1915-25). Authority for this was Fritz Kunz, of Hollywood, American head of the Order of the Star of the East, with headquarters in Hollywood, in a 1926 newspaper interview.

Although most papers give 1926 as the date of Krishnamurti's first arrival in this country, he was here at least once previously, and possibly twice. The New York *Journal* carried his photo prior to 1926 under a San Francisco date line, as en route to Bombay from there. Also, he is supposed to have visited this country in 1922.

The December, 1925, announcement of Mrs. Besant's endorsement of Krishnamurti caused a terrific backfire in London and Czechoslovak Theosophic circles. These groups broke away from the world body. Colonel C. L. Peacocke, president of the London Lodge, said: "The disgraceful use being made of the Society by its present president, Mrs. Annie Besant, for booming and advertising her own private beliefs and superstitions is driving out of the Society most of those who are genuine students and searchers for real theosophy."

It was shortly after the December, 1925, announcement, that Krishnamurti began his travels. He was in Paris in June of 1926, where he created a sensation. He then went on to London and was accepted as "world-teacher" by a vote (undoubtedly packed by Mrs. Besant, since the London Lodge numbered but 40 members) of 600 to 3.

On June 17, 1926, James Montgomery Flagg drew a picture and wrote an article for I.N.S. on his meeting with Krishnamurti (carried in the New York *Journal*), in which he waxed lyrical over the young Hindu.

In July, 1926, the first of a series of annual camps took place at Ommen, Holland, attended by two thousand pilgrims and delegates. While they heard him speak, Krishnamurti was said to have been possessed by another who spoke in a different voice, in old English, for four or five minutes. Also, a huge star over Krishnamurti's head was said to have burst into fragments which came raining down. Others were said to have seen elves, fairies, etc., during the camp.

It was also declared that Krishnamurti's body was being possessed more and more frequently by the "world-teacher," and according to Mrs. Besant, the Christ, Buddha, etc., spirit would soon take permanent possession.

Forrest Davis, writing for the *Herald Tribune*, August 15, 1926, said of Krishnamurti:

. . . while always speaking well of the poor, [he] feels more comfortable in the presence of safely invested wealth. He preaches a "spiritual aristocracy," but it may be surmised that a suggestion of regard for yet another sort of aristocracy underlies the phrase. This is no advent to the ragtag and bobtail. The street crowds may not shout Hosanna and spread palms before his motor car, but many a drawing room will be opened to Krishnaji in New York and elsewhere. Here, as in London, people of consequence already are enlisted in the new faith. Women whose names adorn the Social Register, artists and bankers, joined to herald the coming of the Messiah a long while since.

On Krishnamurti's arrival here, August 17, 1926, Mrs. Besant declared that he had covered a total of 30,000 years during previous lives (not that he had lived that long, since a soul, after a body's death, may wait even thousands of years for a new body, according to Theosophic lore) through reincarnation and/or transmigration of souls. Also, he had passed through thirty-one separate and distinct reincarnations. The occasion of Krishnamurti's visit, ostensibly, was a convention at Chicago. He was accepted almost in triumph here, although cooler heads among the Christian clergy roundly denounced him and Mrs. Besant for the pretensions of Christly honors.

In Chicago crowds gathered about him in triumph, mostly Theosophists and curiosity seekers, and a newspaper story mentions that two boy scouts carried flowers before him. Krishnamurti spoke before a gathering of the Advertising Men's Post of the American Legion at Chicago, which post accepted him as "a regular fellow."

After this Chicago convention, Krishnamurti was supposed to have gone into retirement.

We next hear of him in this country again when he came on April 9, 1928, after teaching in Europe and Asia. His journey this time was devoid of the tremendous fanfare of publicity that attended his supposedly first arrival. As previously mentioned, the 1926 arrival here may have been his third, certainly no less than his second.

During his 1928 stay here, the ascetic Krishnamurti, in a more worldly outlook, was said to have told Beatrice Blackmar, in an interview about Katherine Mayo's *Mother India* published in the New York *World* on May 6, 1928, that "India hasn't too much sex. The poor devils haven't enough of it. It is the last thing in their lives."

In August, 1929, the Order of the Star in the East held another annual camp at Ommen, in Holland. During its progress, Krishnamurti threw a bombshell (*Times*, August 4, AP) into the ranks of his followers when he announced the dissolution of the Order of the Star in the East and (according to a later report) the return of all property and funds "donated" to the Order. Krishnamurti, in a story confused by the press, was said to have given as his reason, among others, *that truth could not be organized*. In the light of his later words, it is fair to guess that he may have been disgusted with the whole business and felt that he had been made an unwitting tool by Mrs. Besant to further her own aims.

He declared in his announcement of dissolution that "religious, philosophical and spiritual organizations are barriers to understanding of the truth. The truth needs no disciples.

It wants nothing from any man. Only a few will understand and they need no organization."

Krishnamurti explained that his Order had been preparing him for eighteen years to proclaim the truth, but said its members were not now willing to face the truth.

"What, then, is the use of this organization?" he asked the three thousand attending pilgrims and disciples.

On October 20, 1931, the New York *Herald Tribune* carried the story that upon Krishnamurti's arrival here the previous day he had told the reporters that he had renounced Theosophy and the representations made for him by Mrs. Besant. He declared that because of his early mystical nature Mrs. Besant had chosen him to become the vehicle of the world-teacher, through revelation. Then later, as his mental faculties matured, he had seen the error into which he had been led, possibly by emotional ardor. He said that gradually he drifted away from the beliefs held by Mrs. Besant, and in fact from Theosophy altogether.

"I learned that each of us must do his own thinking. The Deity—the better life—lies within each and all of us. You cannot organize a system of truth; neither can you nor I set a religious standard for another."

He sailed for India in November, and then nothing more was heard about him, at least in New York, until September 5, 1934, when the United Press carried a story with a date line from Ojai, California, where one of the Star's camps was formerly situated, and where Krishnamurti supposedly had a residence. The story, a short, was to the effect that Krishnamurti declared the world is heading for unbelievable catastrophe "unless men learn to think." The fact that the story came from one of Krishnamurti's camps may sound confusing, but although he repudiated Mrs. Besant and her teachings, Krishnamurti, in a New York *Times* short, dated March 5, 1930, when he was in New York, declared he had organized schools in India through which he and his followers are spreading his philosophy by instilling it in youth. The Ojai, California, camp may have been conducted under similar auspices.

In a March 12, 1935, story in the New York *Herald Tribune*, Krishnamurti lectured on March 11 at Town Hall on "Think for Yourself." His talk was in part against previous conceptions, particularly of religion, and against "leaders," particularly religious ones.

In a New York *Herald Tribune* story, dated May 31, 1936, Krishnamurti, on arriving here from Chicago the previous day, advised his followers to mistrust all Messiahs and religious leaders. Previously he had lectured in South America for seven months.

"It was just another cult, another ballyhoo, like any other church," he said of the Order of the Star of the East. When he dissolved the Order he returned property and funds which had been contributed by disciples all over the world.

"I couldn't tell people to beware of their exploiters and then exploit myself," he said. "They still ask me about truth, and God and immortality, but I tell them they must learn for themselves. You can't point out paths to any of the real things in life. And besides, the only thing I really know is myself." He spoke at Town Hall. He declared he had no message, no dogmas. The 1936 clipping is the last the *Times* or Associated Press has on him.

He is now in his early forties, living in Hollywood, a friend of the Aldous Huxleys and other intellectuals, respected and well liked, seldom appearing in public and never courting publicity. I believe he was, and possibly still is, a potentially great man.

I suspect that if the Lord Gautama Buddha, Moses, Mohammed, Confucius, Our Lord and Saviour Jesus Christ, had fallen into the hands of Annie Besant and Bishop Leadbeater, they also would have fallen down, gone boom, and ended their days in Hollywood.

3. PIERRE BERNARD (OOM THE OMNIPOTENT) first burst into the public eye in the East in 1910 when he was arrested by New York police on charges brought by two girls, Zella Hopp, 18, and Gertrude Leo, 19. The case was dropped after full investigation by the district attorney. The girls had refused to back up their accusations. They had apparently gone to the police through motives of jealousy. No indictment was then or ever has been brought against the man who later became famous in his peculiar field. Bernard, on arriving in New York late in 1909, had opened the New York Sanskrit College at 250 West 87th Street, but the venture was unsuccessful. Two or three years later he bobbed up in Leonia, New Jersey, where he met a Mlle De Vries, a professional dancer of exceptional ability. It was really this meeting, as events bear out, that started him on his road toward success. He married Mlle De Vries, taught her oriental dances, and not long afterward she gained the attention of various society women through her "health system of Tantrism." She is given credit for first enlisting the attention

354

of the then Mrs. Ogden L. Mills,[1] daughter of Mrs. W. K. Vanderbilt. De Vries became Bernard's "high priestess" at the Nyack mansion and estate, which he established in 1919, under the name of the Brae Burn Club.

In 1927, at Nyack, a ceremony was held to celebrate the tenth wedding anniversary of a Pittsburgh, Pennsylvania, couple, two of Bernard's devotees. This was the notorious "coffin ceremony." As related by an anonymous witness (in Hearst's Sunday *American*, magazine section, May 15, 1927):

For this ceremony, which was mystically a marriage as well as an anniversary, the "bride" and "groom" were dressed as at their first wedding. The girls and women of the cortege wore the robes and veils of nuns, covering brilliant and fantastic costumes beneath. The men wore the robes and cowls of monks, covering up equally gay and fantastic costumes in which they were to appear later.

All carried tall candles, like a procession in a cathedral.

Immediately behind the bride and groom were carried two coffins. These coffins were the symbol of the dead and the burying of the past.

Afterwards the coffins were covered with gay draperies and used as tables for an elaborate banquet, while the monks and nuns put off their sombre religious habits and reappeared as gay revelers.

In 1929, on September 8, a "society circus" was staged at Nyack. Featured was the "Dance of the Dead," in which Mlle De Vries, Bernard's wife, co-cultist and high priestess, arose from a coffin to do her dance. She wore a veil and exe-

---

[1] Margaret Rutherford was successively Mrs. Ogden L. Mills, Lady Dukes, and Princess Murat, and at one time the most fashionable member of the colony of Oom. Her latest husband is Frederick Leybourne Sprague, a portrait painter of Manasquan, N. J.

cuted a series of serpentine exercises featured by twistings and writhings of the body. Meanwhile she solemnly chanted:

> *That man has the whole world,*
> *He has me, he has you,*
> *He has all of us now,*
> *He has the whole world in his hands.*

Bernard then did an exotic solo all his own.

He also did a dancing specialty with a baby elephant. The animal was said to be a sacred elephant of India. The *American* reporter termed the dance "The Barbers' Itch."

To join the inner circle of the Secret Order of Tantriks, which wealthy people were invited to join, the man or woman must first have confessed to Bernard—as high priest—all sins, all secret desires, all inner thoughts; must then promise to abide by his decisions; must finally take the Tantrik vow.

In this inner circle, according to a woman who had lived in the Nyack colony, Oom was more than a high priest—he became, in the opinion of his followers, a sort of man-god. He is costumed as a high priest, and his devotees, garbed usually as his worshipers and followers, sing the Tantrik hymn:

> *Be to me a loving guru;* (teacher)
> *Be a loving Tantrik guru.*

Then the initiates kneel as in a church and sing, in a monotone: "Oom ma na padma oom."

It is sung repeatedly in a chanting monotone, like the beating of drums in a forest, and is supposed, if kept up long enough, to induce a state of ecstasy.

The secret of Bernard's powers, it has been stated, seems to be to give his followers a new conception of love. At the time he met Mlle De Vries at Leonia, New Jersey, she is supposed to have told him:

Half the domestic tragedies, three-fourths of the divorces, many of the nervous breakdowns and not a few suicides and murders in America are due to the inherent ignorance and stupidity of the average Anglo-Saxon man or woman on the subject of love. We will teach them—and maybe make our adventure a great success.

Winfield Nicholls, an adherent of Bernard's who subsequently married into the Vanderbilt clan, gave an interview to New York newspapers, in the course of which he said:

Under Dr. Bernard we tried to work out a sensible scheme of balanced living. We tried to face all the facts of nature and life and art with eyes open and unafraid. But we never overemphasized any of our functions or capabilities for happiness more than was its due. We admitted love, but all things else as well.

Bernard's principal aims are said to be "to teach men and women to love, and make women feel like queens."

In May of 1931 (*World-Telegram* of May 7, 1931) after a two-year study of Bernard, Dr. Charles Francis Potter, liberal New York City minister and founder of "Humanism," announced he was writing a serious biography of Bernard. Dr. Potter had made his residence in Nyack since 1929.

Bernard claimed that he was doing pioneer work in human body-building and character training. Potter "began to understand" why Bernard was called "Omnipotent Oom" after talking with many people "whom he had brought back to health and strength after they had decided life was not worth while."

His original methods of dealing with defeated personalities interested Potter, and he found Bernard "combined knowledge of age-old Indian methods of curing disease of mind and body with the best of Western methods, plus a refreshing amount of common sense."

Said Dr. Potter, "I was reminded again and again of the lives of the great religious leaders of the past whom I had studied for my book on 'The Story of Religion.' Dr. Bernard has all the ear-marks of genius."

Mrs. W. K. Vanderbilt is said to have contributed to Bernard's work. Her two daughters by a previous marriage, Barbara and Margaret Rutherford, became disciples of Bernard and his Nyack cult and married followers of the cult. Margaret had been previously divorced from Ogden L. Mills, and Barbara from Cyril Hatch.

Barbara became Mrs. Winfield Nicholls when she married the right-hand man of Bernard. Margaret, in turn, married Sir Paul Dukes, a well-known Britisher who during 1915-1918 was chief of the British intelligence service in Russia. He had joined Bernard's cult in Nyack in 1922.

Other of Bernard's disciples included Baron Droste von Knoblauch, Marshall Bartholomew, Mrs. Samuel N. Holliday, Mrs. Charles B. Alexander, Mrs. Chalmers Wood, Jr., Diana Hunt Wertheim, Dorothy Just, Christopher Hervey, Charles Wood, Jr. and Mrs. Wood, Edmund Trowbridge Dana, grandson of Henry Wadsworth Longfellow.

More recently (1939), Lou Nova, a heavyweight pugilist of considerable prominence, allegedly trained under the sponsorship of Bernard, Yoga methods and all. Pictures of Nova in "Yoga" postures appeared in the newspapers of New York. He was matched to fight Tony Galento. Galento knocked the disciple of Yoga cold in a Philadelphia ring.

Dr. Potter declares (*World-Telegram*) that he admires

Bernard's unusual qualities and completely disbelieves current stories about him. He plans in his book, he says, to "contrast the bizarre myth of 'Oom' as built up in newspaper accounts with the real facts of the man's life and character as I have come to know them."

Potter termed Bernard a "man both prophet and showman, who could lecture on religion with singular penetration and could with equal facility stage a big circus, manage a winning ball team or put on an exhibition of magic which rivaled Houdini. He knows the human body, anatomically and psychologically, in a way to amaze veteran surgeons and psychological experts. He delights to visit a seance incognito, and after the medium has done her best, he produces phenomena which makes her call in fright for the lights."

Reports that Bernard's club was a love cult and that mysterious orgies took place there from time to time, said Dr. Potter, "differed so greatly from my own impression of the place that I investigated further. I asked why Dr. Bernard had not contradicted the astounding stories about him and the club. The reply was that his policy was never to give interviews and never to correct false stories."

The club members were professional and business men and women of New York, Potter found, of an unusually healthy and happy sort.

The New York police, who used to visit the Nyack place occasionally, have never issued any such encomiums—but must be at least in pragmatic accord with Dr. Potter, since no action ever followed any of the visits.

5. MAGIC PENTAGRAMS AND CIRCLES occur for good and bad among all groups, from time immemorial, who

seek contact with the infinite—whether to use it as a harmful weapon (as do witches) or as a haven and sanctuary from kitchen and dining-room boredom, as do our ladies of the Eastern Star in Rhinebeck.

I should like it if they or my witch-friends could tell me why God, beauty, power, or a werewolf could be enticed or stopped or captured more quickly in a circle-shaped or star-shaped trap than in one shaped like the hat of my late aunt from Hawkinsville. All they have ever been able to explain is that, since God, power, werewolfs, have been enticed, stopped, or trapped in stars and circles drawn like these from the time of the early Egyptians—*these* must be the best traps.

They probably are—because they are the most tried and used, for good and bad—whether to entice gods or cozzen devils.

The British scolded A. C., and made him seem more monstrous by showing that the altar on which the wretched cat lost its life was a pentagram. Intrinsically, A. C.'s altar is as innocent as that of our ladies in Rhinebeck. It's never the shape of the altar that makes it good or bad. What sacrifices you offer and what you do around it make it good or bad. If Gertrude Stein had impaled pussycats on the thorns of her magic circle of roses, it could become as wicked as any magic circle Gilles de Retz stood in when he cut babies' throats.

Since, instead, Gertrude Stein has stood inside her magic circle only to tell the rest of us—who have mostly forgotten it—that a rose is a rose, I feel that the sweetest magic circle ever swirled was her rose circle. It looks lovely, and it doesn't tell us any more than we ever need to know.

Here are some to show you that they are all intrinsically similar:

360

A∴A∴   Publication in Class E

A. Crowley's pentagram and its surrounding symbols and the circle inside which the pussycat was slain—or was it?

O. T. O.

Issued by Order:

Symbols of Aleister Crowley's O.T.O.

Circle, visible, and pentagram concealed under their robes, in which
Drs. Dee and Kelley engaged in practices less respectable than the
slaughter of pussycats.

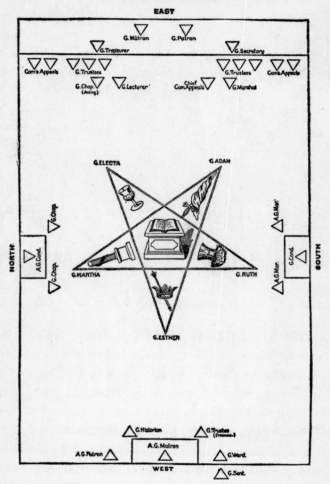

Altar of the Order of the Eastern Star in Rhinebeck. Please study it and note that the pentagram (star) shines with a pure, beautiful religious light.

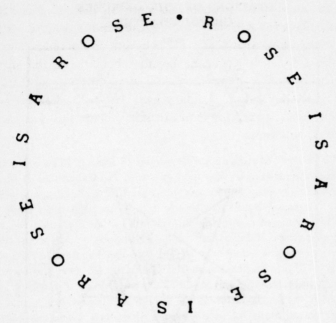

The sweetest magic circle ever swirled

6. NOSTRADAMUS IS AGAIN A BEST SELLER in Paris, according to the *New Yorker's* cable letter of October 29, 1939. He has never ceased to be a best seller in Arles and St. Rémy. When I went to St. Rémy in 1907, everybody in the workmen's restaurant told me there would be a world war within ten years "because Nostradamus had said so."

When I went back there in 1932, they were still reading their local prophet and told me there would be another world war within another ten years "because he had said so."

Maybe he had glimpses through the "slit in time." Maybe

he has merely had good breaks since his demise. His dates always have the advantage of vagueness in the original script, no matter how specifically his believers apply them, and if you're sufficiently vague or flexible about dates, the surest way to become a major prophet is to predict war as the ancestral voices did in Kubla Khan. It always comes, and here's what the *New Yorker* said about this particular prophet this time:

The author of the current best-seller in Paris is Michel Nostradamus, the astrologer who died in 1566. Nostradamus left about 5,000 lines of prophecy in a crabbed mixture of French and what New Yorkers would call "double talk"—each quatrain lends itself to dozens of conflicting interpretations. He has been the object of a tiny cult for a long time, but became an important publishers' item only when war began. You can buy small condensed versions of his prophecies on the bookstalls for two francs or a large annotated definitive edition by a Dr. de Fontbrune for thirty at the big bookstores; the Boulevard des Italiens branch of Flammarion alone has sold 3,000 copies of the expensive edition in the last month.

In one prophecy, Nostradamus speaks of the destruction of Paris by "birds from the East." Some Nostradamists hold that his forecast is for 2040, while others believe it was intended for 1937, in which case Nostradamus, like the German General Staff, has missed the boat. All adepts agree that the astrologer predicted an eventual overwhelming French victory. Nostradamus's "little epidemic," as the booksellers call it, represents one element in the Parisian mood of the moment. Few readers admit taking him seriously, and yet *c'est une guerre tellement bizarre.*

CHAPTER IV

2. BLANKING THE MIND, negative way, simply relaxing, as cats and animals do when at ease, is the first step in the direction which leads deeper when used by Mary Craig or my dervishes. It is a method of mental therapy which is beginning to receive deserved, renewed attention in our over-hurried modern world. A useful technique is described by Alan Devoe in *Coronet*, June, 1939, condensed October, 1939, in the *Reader's Digest*. Mr. Devoe says, in part:

To see how grievously ignorant we have become, it is only necessary to observe the pathetic behavior of men and women who have escaped from their jobs for a while and are earnestly trying to idle. Playing golf, tossing a medicine ball, driving an automobile, hiking, dancing—these furious pursuits are not proper ingredients for successful idleness. Nor is even the man who is raking autumn leaves or weeding his delphiniums or strolling with a friend practicing idleness. He is engaging, to be sure, in pleasant and agreeable occupations. But he is not idling.

The recipe for idleness is simple: it consists of the abeyance of physical strain and cessation of purposeful thinking. It requires that you allow yourself to become for a while as purposeless as a maple leaf or a stone, that you abandon those restless biddings and nagging energies with which civilization has infected you, and that you exchange the fatiguing habits of planned activity and planned thinking for a directionless and unguided drifting of the spirit. It requires, in a word, that you do nothing.

Look, sometime, at a relaxing tiger or fox; look at your cat. Those calm unseeing eyes are fixed on nothing; those muscles lie as quiet as stone; the usual preoccupations have been utterly stilled. The animal is idling. It is an experience as natural to him as eating or sleeping—but it is something which you will have to learn. And when you have learned it, a whole new world of sensation will be opened to you, a world of such peace and subtle awareness as you have never previously known, a realm which has unmatched powers for refreshing the weary human spirit.

Make your first try at idleness now. When you have finished the brief paragraphs that follow, put the magazine aside and consciously call a halt to all the little movements which you have absentmindedly been making . . . the foot-tapping, the nervous eye-winking, the drumming of fingers on your chair-arm. While you were reading, your breathing was quick and shallow, typical rhythm of our over-hurried days. Relax your lungs. Breathe deeply, slowly. A curiously pleasant feeling, isn't it?

If you wear glasses, remove them. That little pressure on the bridge of your nose is a distraction and vexation. And so is the binding tightness of your belt, and the constriction of your collar. Loosen them. Lie back now and be at rest. Do not attempt to follow any train of thought. Your thinking is going to be wholly purposeless now. Your spirit is going to drift and wander as it pleases.

Presently dim half-thoughts and recollections and awareness will stir in your newly freed consciousness. Because the tyranny of Thought and the tyranny of Action are alike in abeyance now, your spirit has a chance to be aware of, say, the fragrance of the flowers in that vase. The fragrance has been subtly in the room all day, but your spirit has not been free to savor it. Breathe that fragrance deep into your lungs, for to a drifting spirit it can be magically evocative. And now another awareness has come to you—the feel of that ray of sunlight on your hand. The world has somehow become not quite so bad, with the scent of flowers in your nostrils and the feel of sunlight on your flesh.

Drift on, and be at peace. How odd a music the buzzing of that fly. How breathtakingly blue that patch of sky. The feel of the chair against your relaxed muscles is a kind of benison, and the slow deep drawing of your breath has wrought a singular peace. Oblique and fragmentary recollections come to you . . . the smell of the sea that year in Maine, the look of the deer-tracks you once saw in a snowy woods, the remembered flash of pheasant-wings on a hazy October afternoon. You have wholly entered now, at last, into that lovely secret realm which is the habitation known only to masters of the art of idleness. To restore yourself to the quiet ways of life is an art worth learning.

By Mr. Devoe's technique you step through the first door leading into the antechamber of the secret realm which can only be penetrated further by the complete, difficult, and sometimes dangerous blanking of the mind as taught by Eastern mystics and practiced rarely in the Western world.

4. UPTON SINCLAIR'S MENTAL RADIO pictures include the following, reproduced with his permission. In each case the drawing at the left is the original, and what Craig wrote or drew is at its right. In two of the instances here shown—the fork and the star—she got it exactly. There were many such cases. But the ones which excited me most are those such as the subsequent instances, in which she seemed to see it partially but not exactly, and not completely.

5. BISHOP ARTHUR A. FORD OF THE SPIRITU-ALIST CHURCH first attracted general notice in the New York *Times*, October 10, 1927, during the course of a debate between him and the famous stage magician Howard Thurston, at Carnegie Hall. Several months later, on February 10, 1928 (*Times*, February 11), almost one and one-half years after Harry Houdini had died, Ford, in a spiritualist séance at his home—315 West 97th Street—declared that he had received a message from Houdini's mother containing the code word "forgive" which was to be evidence that there was a life after death. This word had supposedly been agreed upon between Houdini and his mother, who

July 13, 1428
See a table
fork. Nothing
else.

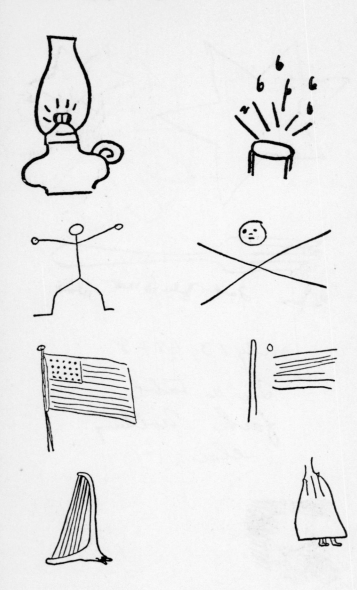

Bob drew watch, and
looked alternately at
his open face gold watch
+ at below picture

WATCH

JULY 9-1928

died in 1913, as the symbol of future life. However, after due investigation, it appeared that Houdini's wife had revealed in detail the "after-life" agreement between her husband and his mother in an interview in the Brooklyn *Eagle* dated March 13, 1927. Ford declared he knew nothing of the interview. On January 9, 1929, in a trance at Mrs. Houdini's home at 67 Payson Avenue, New York City, Ford, as minister of the First Spiritualist Church, declared he had received a message from Harry Houdini himself. Houdini's friends were not at all impressed. Joseph Rinn went so far as to offer Ford $10,000 if he were able to repeat the substance of a conversation Rinn had held with Houdini in 1926 at the New York Hippodrome. Also, Remigius Weiss of 954 North 5th Street, Philadelphia, declared Houdini had left with him a secret code, different from Mrs. Houdini's code. Incidentally, a $21,000 reward was up for the medium who would communicate successfully with Houdini. Ford's alleged message, which attracted great attention at the time, spelled, when deciphered, "Believe," the word arranged before Houdini's death as proof of life after death. Only his wife supposedly was aware of the word.

At the time, it was reported that Mrs. Houdini was convinced that Ford had indeed been in communication with her dead husband, but later she resented and repudiated the whole affair. She and her husband had an open mind regarding the possibility of life after death, as was evident in her attempts at communication. Mrs. Houdini was disappointed in her hopes, and Ford did not claim the $21,000 offered for "life-after-death" communication with Houdini.

On January 24, 1929, the spiritualist world was startled to hear that Ford was suspended from the Manhattan group of the United Spiritualist League because he had been guilty of "conduct unbecoming a Spiritualist minister" in the Houdini "séance" two weeks previously. The action was taken, according to the president of the group, on the basis of newspaper investigations of the message supposedly received by Ford from Houdini. But John Heis (Heiser?), president of the executive board of the league, declared that no evidence had been presented against Ford and had opposed the action on grounds that it violated bylaws of the group.

On February 24, one month later, Ford was cleared of the charges by the board of trustees of the First Spiritualist Church, headed by the John Heis mentioned previously, who was also head of the New York State group.

At his vindication hearing Ford announced that rumors had been circulated to the effect that he had been requested to leave England by prominent spiritualists. He offered a reward of $1,000 to anyone who could prove the truth of these rumors. On February 27, Ford went on a tour of the mid-Western United States and in the summer of that year was to go on a European tour with Sir Arthur Conan Doyle. A climax to the Houdini-Ford controversy was furnished on October 31, 1936, ten years after Houdini's death, when, after elaborate preparations had been made in Hollywood by Mrs. Houdini to communicate if possible with her departed husband's spirit, the "spirit" refused to communicate. On November 12, on her way East, Mrs. Houdini, at Little Rock, Arkansas, confided to the Associated Press that she was "firmly convinced that communication with the dead is a human impossibility and I challenge any medium who proclaims tangible proof." In 1938 a picture, *Religious Racketeer*, with Mrs. Houdini featured, was produced by an independent Hollywood woman producer, Fanchon Royer Gallagher. It treated of the attempt two years previously to communicate with Houdini's spirit, and exposed methods allegedly used by spiritualists.

On June 21, 1936, the Associated Press, from Buffalo, carried a story to the effect that spiritualists had begun a drive to eliminate racketeering in the movement. Substance of the report was that Ford, elected president of a new international group embracing "several hundred" churches in Canada, the United States, Mexico, and Cuba, as head of the General Assembly of Spiritualists in America (headquarters at Buffalo) aimed to "eliminate the racketeering element in spiritualism and protect not only ourselves but the public." Incidentally, this was supposed to be the fortieth annual convention of the group. Ford was now leader of a great part of the spiritualist movement in North America. He also stated that the new organization would co-operate with police in driving charlatans out of business. He declared that "a real medium will have papers from the assembly and always will be a member of a local church. An examining board will test applicants and educational standards will be high."

At an International General Assembly of Spiritualists meeting at Baltimore (AP, October 28, 1937), Ford, as president, declared that spiritualists would consider endowing a school for mediums and lecturers. The purpose, he declared, would be to "tighten up the restrictions on the profession and eliminate the fakes."

In a Brooklyn *Eagle* interview with John J. O'Neill on October 27, 1931, Ford had claimed to have been in communication with the spirit of Sir Arthur Conan Doyle, who through Ford corrected proofs of his biography then in the process of being published, written by the Rev. John Lamond, D.D., dean of the Scotch church. Ford also claimed that one year previously Doyle had communicated through him to Lady Doyle that the book was to be written by Lamond. This took place during Ford's 1931 European tour. In a *World-Telegram* interview with George Britt dated June 21, 1933, Ford's education was said to have been "orthodoxly theological." Britt also stated that Ford wrote short stories and articles under spiritual influence. Most of his stories were sold to the *Ghost Stories* type of magazine. Through his spirit connections, Britt said Ford had told him Ford had escaped financial loss in the 1929 Wall Street crash, and therefore had become a much-sought-after adviser of business men.

On the night of March 21-22, 1935, Ford arranged a séance in an airplane doing a flight over Newark airport. He had fourteen guests including representatives of the AP. He claimed that he had heard Doyle, Wilbur Wright, and Roald Amundsen, the explorer. An AP man remarked that Amundsen had forgotten his Norse accent during the séance.

During Ford's October 9, 1927, debate with Thurston at Carnegie Hall, Ford had explained his Spiritualist Church's teachings as follows:

Their central dogma was the immortality of the soul and praying for the infidels within the gate. Ford also declared that the study of psychic phenomena would solve the problem of the crowded insane asylums. He said, "A great many inmates of our asylums were committed for acts for which they were not responsible. By studying psychic laws and how to control obsessions we can return a great majority of the

insane to normal existence. In California I saw three persons
released from an asylum when they were released from the
control of the low spirits which possessed them. In Michigan
the number of inmates has been reduced by such studies. The
phenomena of modern spiritualism are no different from the
phenomena recorded by great religious leaders of the past.
Jesus demonstrated the same psychic powers which the
mediums of today demonstrated, but of course their powers
are of a much lower order."

Asked how he received the spirit messages, Ford has said,
"I hear them, but 'hear' is not the correct word to describe
their reception, because if I just heard them in the ordinary
way you would hear them at the same time I did. I don't
know where the impression is picked up, but the effect on my
mind is the same as if the sounds were picked up by my ear
and carried to my brain in the ordinary way."

After preaching a sermon at the Universalist Church of
the Divine Paternity, Central Park West and 76th Street
(*Times*, May 7, 1934), "the Rev. Arthur A. Ford, general
missionary of the General Assembly of the Spiritualist
Movement in America . . . gave a demonstration of spiritualism" on the steps leading to the chancel of the church.
He communicated messages which he said came from various
deceased relatives of the church's members. He called out
names and asked if they were recognized by anyone present.
When response was given—and in most cases it was given—
he said the spirit of the person named was standing near him
and had a message. In most cases the communication was that
the departed one was very happy and sent his or her love.
While speaking, Ford also included names of other members
of the families of which he was speaking and also some de-

tails about the age and appearance of the departed persons. His demonstration was received warmly.

Ford says about thirty million people throughout the world believe in spiritualism. "Our greatest enemy has been the church," Ford also declared. "We do not believe there ever were any miracles. They seemed miracles at the time because they were not understood. Every day we find things which we cannot understand, and they remain that way until some one comes along who can explain them to us. Spiritualism is a scientific fact which has conclusively proved that it is possible at certain times and under certain conditions to contact with the dead."

A feature of the Buffalo convention in 1936 was the demonstration of "mental mediumship—psychometry, clairaudience and clairvoyance." Psychometry was defined as "a spiritualist touching a body so as to take on its vibrations."

From all available data, Ford claims he is in touch with spirits of the dead, can transmit, to a certain extent, messages from them to others through his mediumship, and can foretell the future.

Any number of prominent people are followers of spiritualism. Wall Street men with well-known names and a State Supreme Court justice are among Ford's secret followers. If *anybody* could foretell the future on Wall Street, he could own Wall Street or wreck it. If *anybody* could foretell a jury's verdict, we'd have to invent something new to take the place of courts.

At the last Buffalo convention the following faithful were revealed as officials of Dr. Ford's assembly: Mrs. M. S. McGuire of Toronto, vice-president; F. W. Constantine of

Buffalo, secretary; Robert B. Collup of Akron, Ohio, treasurer; Dana McHenry, Los Angeles, second vice-president. Other names gleaned were: Dr. F. A. Wiggin of Boston; Dr. Alexander J. McIvor-Tyndall of London, orator of the movement, supposedly controlled by the spirit of Joseph Jefferson; a Dr. George A. Lingenbach of Pittsburgh or suburb. On conservative guess, there are close to a million believers in spiritualism in the United States.

CHAPTER VI

1. ONE SWAMI WHO KNOWS these implications is the Tibetan Abbot, Chao-kung, known in America as Timothy Lincoln, born originally in a Jewish Hungarian village where he was first known as Ignatius Trebitsch.

From his Tibetan monastery, with the help of the United Press and the cables, he hurled on December 19, 1939, an ultimatum to the world, from the Sax Rohmer masters of the world, which impressed the *Herald Tribune* sufficiently (whether ironically or not is their own business) to run it, with his picture, under the captions:

"WARNS EUROPEAN BELLIGERENTS OF TIBETAN ACTION."

"TREBITSCH LINCOLN CALLS WRATH OF BUDDHA ON WARRING NATIONS"

The subhead said:

"Former Pastor, British M.P. and Spy, Now in Asia as Abbot Chao-kung, Warns Powers (Except Finland) to Make Peace or Be Destroyed."

The dispatch follows:

SHANGHAI, Dec. 19 (UP).—The Abbot Chao-Kung, once known as Ignatius Timothy Trebitsch Lincoln, former pastor, member of the British House of Commons and international spy, announced to the world today that unless the governments of the chief European belligerent countries resigned at once so that a peace conference could be held, the Tibetan Buddhist "supreme masters" would eliminate them from the scene of action by unleashing forces against which there was no defense.

This, the Abbot said, was his final appeal for peace. He had made a preliminary one, in anticipation of the war, in the spring of 1939.

Emerging from the Buddhist retreat in which he has secluded himself for several years, the abbot demanded that the British, French, German and Russian governments resign simultaneously and immediately. He exempted Finland. New governments must be formed, the abbot said, and they must call a world-wide peace conference.

"Otherwise," he warned, "the Tibetan Buddhist supreme masters, without prejudice, pre-direction or favor, will unchain forces and powers whose very existence is unknown to you and against whose operations you are consequently helpless."

World leaders, Trebitsch Lincoln pointed out, were mere human beings, subject to all human limitations. The sole exceptions, he said, were the Buddhist "supreme masters, who, by their unlimited and unbounded knowledge of nature's secrets and their ability to use certain powers, have broken through those limitations."

The United States, he said, could have prevented the European war, but chose to follow the path of "open partiality, prejudice and downright injustice, cloaked in phrases which pretended to be all that is virtuous."

The British, French, Russian and German governments were all guilty of provoking the war, he said.

Discussing the Chinese-Japanese war, he said that regardless of its background, Japan was willing to discuss peace, but China continued its "insane scorched-earth policy."

Trebitsch Lincoln, born a Jew about fifty-eight years ago, left his native Hungarian village to seek his fortune in England. He entered the Church of England and became a curate, then entered politics and was elected to the House of Commons as a Liberal. He became wealthy in oil promotion ventures.

He was made a censor in the British post office at the outbreak of the World War, but after a period during which, the British alleged, he tried to act as a secret agent for Britain and Germany, he fled to the United States. Britain extradited him and kept him in prison until the war ended.

He was deported, went to Germany and played a big part in the Kapp putsch of 1921, when conspirators seized Berlin. Some years later he turned up in China to become a Buddhist monk.

Born Ignatius Trebitsch, he added the name Lincoln because Abraham Lincoln was his boyhood ideal.

Native Tibetan abbots, monks, adepts, and Western converts of theirs, have been suggesting for centuries that they could and can do these things. The chief basis of my skepticism is that they never have. I think the stuff is as shining bright if not as hot as lightning was on Franklin's kite string, but I keep wondering if there is any power in it, since up to now it has only given foxfire.

CHAPTER VII

4. DERVISH DANGLING'S EQUIVALENTS AMONG THE ESKIMOS are described in detail by Peter Freuchen on pages 129-137 of *Arctic Adventure* published by Farrar & Rinehart in 1935. The American Museum of Natural History has a number of prints illustrating these various ways in which the Eskimo mystics and wizards lie bound to induce

trance-states and excursions into the realm of the supernormal. Mr. Freuchen says:

> The old man, Sorqaq, who was also hunting in the district, announced that he would attempt a journey to the nether world. . . . He had met the devil and conquered him—perhaps he could do it again.
>
> At any rate, his preparations for descent proved his honesty. He fasted until his interior was completely cleaned out, examining his excrement until he was satisfied with his state. After three days he announced himself ready for the journey, and the time of departure was set for the following night. The old man meanwhile climbed high into the mountains seeking solitude to formulate his speech to the spirits and to train himself to swim through the rocks—which he would most certainly have to penetrate in order to meet the devil.
>
> A huge igloo was constructed by adding many blocks of snow to the largest house in the settlement. Several men worked at it, and the snowblocks were cut by the elders who realized the seriousness of the undertaking. After it was finished the inside was draped with a tapestry of old tent skins. Sorqaq inspected the stage which was to witness his marvels, said nothing, and departed for further meditation.
>
> Presently the natives were requested to gather and were led to their places by Krilerneq, Sorqaq's assistant. Krilerneq himself was an old man, but with the aid of a cane he was as strong and as spry as anyone. His eyes burned with his fervor, his gestures were quick, his walk nervous.
>
> Like a stage star making his appearance in an ancient vehicle, Sorqaq was the last man to enter the house, and he was announced three times before he finally arrived. He greeted us all by saying that we were a pack of fools to have come: what he proposed to do was nothing, and furthermore he could not even do it.
>
> * * *
>
> He peeled off his clothes, which were taken by Krilerneq, and sat stark naked. Krilerneq then took up several sealskin lines and

382

bound him tight, tying his arms beside his body and binding his legs together, the thongs cutting deep into his muscles. The old man held himself rigid during this process. Occasionally a deep sigh escaped him.

When there were no more lines at hand, Krilerneq placed his drum and a large section of dried sealskin beside him on the ledge. The lights were extinguished and the only illumination came from one tiny flame. We could barely make out each other's faces; we could see nothing distinctly.

Then Krilerneq took his place among us to make sure that no one approached the angakok, for it would mean death.

After a few minutes of utter silence we heard Sorqaq's voice in song. It was weak and quavery, but slowly grew stronger and seemed to emanate from different parts of the igloo. After a moment we heard the voice of the drum, as if beaten by a padded stick, and slowly its sound, too, grew in volume, until the house was filled with the song, the crashing of the drum and the rattling of the dry skin, now over our heads, now beneath our feet!

The noise was almost unbearable, and I took hold of Krilerneq's arm, pretending fright. Actually I wanted to ascertain whether or not he was contributing to the noise. Obviously he was not.

How long the din lasted I am unable to tell. I remember that when it finally calmed I felt as if I had been dreaming. By now all of us had joined in Sorqaq's song, but slowly it seemed that the voice of the angakok was fading away. At last I definitely felt that it reached us through the walls of the igloo, perhaps from above or below. And then suddenly we could hear him no more.

None of us realized what had happened or when it had happened, but when Krilerneq turned up the flame so that it was possible to see a little clearer—there was no Sorqaq on the ledge.

The drum was there and the skin was there, but that was all. I was intoxicated by the heat and the odor of bodies and the song, and perhaps I did not examine the igloo carefully enough.

But I did look at the tapestry to see if he could be hidden behind it, and he was not.

All of us sat there singing as we had before. Ecstasy was upon the face of every man and woman. Their cheeks were swollen, their eyes bright and shining. Their mouths hung open, and their bodies were naked from the waist up in order to endure the heat. They swayed back and forth to the rhythm of the song, and their heads marked the double beats. No one seemed to see anything, but merely to use his eyes as beacon lights. In the middle of the floor was Krilerneq writhing and twisting like a dancer.

Beside me sat a young girl, Ivaloo. Her naked body was pressed against mine, and her strong young scent swept over me. I tried to speak to her, but she did not hear. Instead, her eyes followed Krilerneq directly in front of us. Her long hair sprayed loose from the knot on her head, and swung from side to side as she sang. The rhythmic swish of her hair made me as senseless as the rest of them. . . .

When I looked into the faces of these people I could scarcely recognize them as the calm, quiet friends who came down to Thule to trade with us. Whence has come this leaning toward mysticism? No one knows the origin of the Eskimo, but it is not difficult to trace them to a moderate climate; many of their traditions derive from the worship of trees, snakes and frogs. Perhaps they were Asiatics originally and have drawn from the Far East their reliance upon the supernatural. Here I saw them caught up by a spirit which they could not possibly understand, the prey to emotions and passions which in everyday life would puzzle them.

* * *

The song continued and I fell completely under the power of the spirit. No longer was I able to observe dispassionately what occurred. Ivaloo lay naked across me, and I could feel someone else chewing my hair, clawing my face. The noise, the odor of the bodies and the mystery of the moment caught me completely unprepared.

Then suddenly all was changed. Krilerneq, who had been the

leader of the madness, announced that Sorqaq was trying to return.

He beseeched us all to take our original positions and told us to sit up and sing. No thoughts should concern us but those of the angakok who was at this moment fighting his way up through the granite beneath the igloo. We were as yet unable to hear him, but Krilerneq, who had himself made the pilgrimage a number of times, said that he could feel his imminent arrival, and complained over the suffering he was undergoing. Krilerneq, being the assistant, shared the travail of his friend who had to swim through the rocks as if they were water. . . .

"Quiet! Quiet! The shadow is ripened. The shadow is ripened." . . .

We all listened, and as from afar off we could hear Sorqaq's voice. Krilerneq extinguished the light completely, since no one must look upon the angakok "muscle naked"—he has been forced to leave his skin when descending into the ground—lest he die. . . .

But magically we knew at last that he had returned—from the sky or from the depths his "shadow" had "ripened." The igloo reverberated with the noise of his drum and the rattle of the crackling sealskin sometimes over our heads, sometimes under our feet. I raised my hand to try to grasp the skin and received such a blow on my arm that the bone was almost shattered. Hell itself had suddenly come to earth.

And then it all stopped. Krilerneq murmured a long rigmarole, and the igloo was quiet save for the crying of the children. They may have been crying the whole time, but no one had known it. Krilerneq's droning voice prayed to the supposedly present angakok to learn what secrets he had learned concerning the cause of the accidents.

Sorqaq's voice answered: "Three deaths are still to come. The Great Nature is embarrassed by the white men who have come to live with us, and refuses to betray the real reason for its anger. But no great disaster will come to us if the women of the tribe refrain from eating meat of the female walrus until the sun sets again in the fall."

The angakok had done his duty and the performance was over. I have no idea how long it had lasted. Someone brought fire from the next igloo and lighted the lamps.

There was Sorqaq sitting on the ledge still wrapped in his many strands of sealskin. I did not have the opportunity of examining him to see whether he had been free and bound again. He was extremely weak, covered with sweat, and spittle ran down his chest. Krilerneq warned me not to touch Sorqaq as the fire from the earth was still in him, and would be until he moved again.

He sat quiet until Krilerneq removed the lines, then fell back and lay in a coma. At last he opened his eyes. His voice was weak and his mouth dry. He tried to smile as he saw me.

"Just lies and bunk, the whole thing!" he said. "Do not believe in anything. I am no angakok. I speak nothing but lies. The wisdom of the forefathers is not in me!"

He fell back again, and we all assured each other that we had indeed witnessed an amazing thing and been in the presence of truth itself.

Next day I tried to talk with the natives about yesterday's performance, but they were mute. Ivaloo and my hostess, Inuaho, said it made them realize I was a white man—an Eskimo would not want to discuss things which were never mentioned, only done.

Freuchen also recounts a poignant tragedy which occurred one day when some Eskimo children, playing at a form of dervish dangling, let it get out of hand. The children as well as the grownups incline to mysticism, and one of the tricks by which they pass into unconsciousness and trance is to hang themselves by their hoods. Says Mr. Freuchen:

When the hoods tighten about their necks blood is kept from their heads and they eventually lose consciousness. The other chil-

386

dren in the house take them down as soon as their faces turn purple.

The state of unconsciousness is so delightful, the children say, that they play this game at every opportunity, over and over again. They played it on the day Angudluk and his wife were away.

Angudluk's son was the largest child in the group. One after another he hung the smaller children up and lifted them down when they were purple, and laid them on the ledge to recover. When all of them had had their turn he helped them to hang him up. Eventually he grew purple in the face and kicked his legs as the signal to be taken down. The children tried to lift him off the hook, but he was too heavy. They made every effort and still could not lift him, and, as he soon stopped kicking and threshing about, the children forgot about him and ran out-of-doors to play, leaving him hanging in front of the window over the door.

When the sledges came home the mother cared for the dogs and Angudluk, cold from sitting all day, hurried inside. He crawled through the tunneled entrance and saw the feet of his son hanging down over the doorhole. . . .

We saw the sad little funeral procession. Only the best skins were used as a coffin. The father drove the dogs up into the hills, and some of them turned stubborn and bolted. Everyone had to stop and punish the dogs, whose howling added to the dolefulness of the occasion. The poor family, whose privations were stringent enough already, left many gifts for the boy, especially a little gun he had wanted, a big knife, and the pipes and tobacco belonging to the whole family—he would be there a long time and need all these things. All the mittens which had been used in constructing his stony grave were left also.